Acclaim for *Blessed Among All Women*
Winner of three Catholic Press Awards*

This book should be on every Christian school shelf and church library, as well as used often in the liturgies and services where people gather to embody the Christian narrative. — *Sojourners*

Ellsberg's crisp, inspiring, and insightful writing enhances this excellent illustration of the use of the literary genre of biography in the Christian tradition.... *Blessed Among All Women* is excellent spiritual reading for a daily/weekly routine or for a retreat experience. Moreover, it would be of intellectual interest as a more inclusive source of our Christian history and spirituality. — *New Theology Review*

The diversity of women represented here is extraordinary. Ellsberg has identified holy women in various centuries practicing their faith amid cruel or ordinary circumstances. — *America*

This easily readable anthology makes female saints more understandable and makes sainthood seem more attainable for the rest of us. I recommend it for ordinary Catholics and for religious.
— *St. Anthony Messenger Online*

Does your faith in humanity need a boost? Looking for a shot of girl power? Either way, you'll get your fix in *Blessed Among All Women*.... Ellsberg arranges the stories according to the Beatitudes. In doing so, he introduces real women who struggled with their own flaws and foibles but nonetheless lived lives of action, conviction, and holiness.
— *US Catholic*

Ellsberg has a special place in his heart for laywomen who have tried to practice their faith in the realms of work, family, community, and the ordinary business of life. — *Spirituality & Health Magazine*

---

*Popular presentation of the Catholic faith (first place); Spirituality (Hardcover) (second place); Gender issues (first place)

Finally we have here in Robert Ellsberg's *Blessed Among All Women* a collection of women saints whose lives and spiritual gifts are recounted with respect and with depth. As a history of the strengths routinely modeled by women, it is essential not only for the spiritual life of women but most of all, perhaps, for the development of the spiritual sensitivity of men. The introduction alone, in fact, is worth the price of the book because it expands the notion of the so-called "female" virtues to include the broadest scope of human qualities. This book makes a serious contribution to the newly emerging consciousness of the full equality of women, spiritual as well as professional. It is necessary spiritual reading for us all.

–JOAN CHITTISTER, OSB, author of *Called to Question* and *The Rule of Benedict*

This is a book that, in honoring women, honors humanity in its longing to become free and lovely children of the God who made us male and female, and "saw that it was good." Robert Ellsberg casts his authorial net very wide; he tells us of Bible women, canonized saints, women of other religions, famous women, women known only to God (like the Mothers of Argentina). There are poets here, an artist, a photographer, a murderer, millionaires and beggars: all are shown in their inspiring courage, and the quotations are breathtakingly beautiful. They brought tears to my eyes.

–SISTER WENDY BECKETT, author of *Sister Wendy's Story of Painting*

Those who have complained about the absence of women in the calendar of saints have found their answer at last. These stories inform and surprise us, combining holy women we know with many from other cultures and religions we don't, and introducing us to a few who have lived among us. It's delightful to read. Put it next to his *All Saints* for frequent reference.   –SALLY CUNNEEN, author of *In Search of Mary*

What a gathering of saints Robert Ellsberg has convened. From Mary to the present, here they are — the excommunicated, the heretics, saints of the church and saints of the people, the prostitute, a tough union organizer called "Mother," one executed by the state of Texas, little children, women we have heard of and women rescued from anonymity. Robert Ellsberg has brought them to our table, Christian and non-Christian alike, speaking truth to power whether that power be state or church. What an honest gathering of saints this is — women whose lives, beliefs, and accomplishments are simply breathtaking. I urge you, read from this collection to your young children. Begin or end each day yourself with one selection, the story of one saint, until you have read them all. Then think of their lives and the pathways of service they open to us. As I read, I kept thinking of all these remarkable women sitting around a table and exchanging their ideas, thoughts, and beliefs. What a gathering of saints that would be. What a joy it would be to draw up a chair and listen. —SISTER DIANNA ORTIZ, author of *The Blindfold's Eye*

Human lives are more compelling than concepts. Holy lives are more persuasive than narrative. Women's lives are too often untold. Robert Ellsberg does it all again — and with magnificence!
—RICHARD ROHR, O.F.M., author of *Everything Belongs*

Robert Ellsberg has given us a rare and eloquent gift. Spanning centuries and continents, recounting the lives of missionaries and martyrs, activists and authors, *Blessed Among All Women* provides intimate portraits of women who changed the world. Together, these portray a panoramic landscape of feminine courage and strength. This inspiring classic should be on the shelf of anyone serious about faith and its transforming power. —JOYCE HOLLYDAY, author of *On the Heels of Freedom*

Blessed Among All Women not only retells familiar stories of popular saints with the author's trademark spirit and style, but also restores unjustly forgotten women heroes to their proper place in our spiritual consciousness. Simply put, stories in Ellsberg's comprehensive new volume are utterly fascinating, consistently well written, and always inspiring. This is a stunning achievement.
—JAMES MARTIN, S.J., author of *My Life with the Saints*

Also by Robert Ellsberg

*All Saints: Daily Reflections on Saints, Prophets,
and Witnesses for Our Time*

The Saints' Guide to Happiness

BLESSED AMONG ALL WOMEN

Women Saints, Prophets, and Witnesses for Our Time

ROBERT ELLSBERG

A Crossroad Book
The Crossroad Publishing Company
New York

The Crossroad Publishing Company
16 Penn Plaza, 481 Eighth Avenue
New York, NY 10001

Printed in the United States of America.

This text of this book is set in 10/13.25 Palatino.
The display face is Galliard Italic.

Library of Congress Cataloging-in-Publication Data

Ellsberg, Robert, 1955-
    Blessed among all women : women saints, prophets, and witnesses
for our time / Robert Ellsberg.
       p. cm.
    Includes bibliographical references and index.
    ISBN 0-8245-2251-6; 0-8245-2439-X (pbk.)
    1. Christian women saints – Biography. 2. Religious biography.
3. Women – Biography. I. Title.
BX4656.E45 2005
270′.092′2 – dc22
[B]
                                                2005011363

1   2   3   4   5   6   7   8   9   10   12   11   10   09   08   07

To Catherine and Christina

That is why I must try to live
a good and faithful life to my last breath;
so that those who come after me
do not have to start all over again.

—ETTY HILLESUM

Contents

Introduction 1

BLESSED ARE THE POOR IN SPIRIT

Mary: *Mother of Jesus (first century)* 8

Anna: *Prophetess (first century)* 9

Sts. Martha and Mary of Bethany: *Friends of Jesus (first century)* 10

St. Mary Magdalene: *Apostle to the Apostles (first century)* 12

St. Marcella: *Widow (325–410)* 14

St. Clare of Assisi: *Founder of the Poor Clares (1193–1253)* 15

St. Elizabeth of Hungary: *Franciscan Queen (1207–1231)* 18

St. Agnes of Bohemia: *Princess and Abbess (1203–1280)* 20

St. Angela Merici: *Founder of the Ursulines (1474–1540)* 22

St. Jeanne de Chantal: *Co-Founder of the Order of the Visitation (1572–1641)* 24

St. Elizabeth Feodorovna: *Martyr (1864–1918)* 25

St. Josephine Bakhita: *Ex-Slave and Nun (1869–1947)* 27

St. Katherine Drexel: *Founder of the Sisters of the Blessed Sacrament (1858–1955)* 29

Madeleine Delbrêl: *Missionary and Activist (1904–1964)* 31

Little Sister Magdeleine of Jesus: *Founder of the Little Sisters of Jesus (1898–1989)* 33

Mev Puleo: *Witness of Solidarity (1963–1996)* 36

Ade Bethune: *Catholic Worker Artist (1914–2002)* 38

BLESSED ARE THOSE WHO MOURN

Hagar the Egyptian: *Slave Woman*   42

The Samaritan Woman: *Evangelist (first century)*   43

The Anointer of Bethany *(first century)*   44

St. Monica: *Widow (332–387)*   45

Heloise: *Abbess of the Convent of the Paraclete (1100–1164)*   47

Bd. Angela of Foligno: *Franciscan Mystic (1248–1309)*   49

Bd. Lydwina of Schiedam: *Patron of Sufferers (1380–1433)*   51

Margery Kempe: *Mystic and Pilgrim (1373–1438?)*   52

St. Catherine of Genoa: *Mystic (1447–1510)*   55

St. Xenia of St. Petersburg: *Holy Fool (late eighteenth century)*   57

Cornelia Connelly: *Founder of the Society of the Holy Child Jesus (1809–1879)*   59

Maude Dominica Petre: *Catholic Modernist (1863–1942)*   61

St. Edith Stein: *Carmelite Martyr (1891–1942)*   64

Adrienne von Speyr: *Mystic (1902–1967)*   67

Mothers of the Disappeared: *Argentina (1977–1983)*   69

Martyrs of El Mozote: *El Salvador (d. 1981)*   71

Jessica Powers: *Carmelite Poet (1905–1988)*   73

Karla Faye Tucker: *Penitent (1959–1998)*   75

BLESSED ARE THE MEEK

The Syrophoenician Woman: *Faithful Witness (first century)*   80

The Woman with a Flow of Blood *(first century)*   81

St. Lydia: *"Worshiper of God" (first century)*   82

St. Scholastica: *Nun (d. 543)*   83

St. Dymphna: *Martyr (d. 650?)*   84

Mechthild of Magdeburg: *Beguine Mystic (1210?–1282?)* 85

Bd. Margaret Ebner: *Mystic (1291–1351)* 87

Bd. Julian of Norwich: *Mystic (1342–1416)* 89

Emily Dickinson: *Poet (1830–1886)* 92

St. Therese of Lisieux: *Doctor of the Church (1873–1897)* 94

Mary Slessor: *Missionary (1848–1915)* 97

Evelyn Underhill: *Spiritual Guide (1875–1941)* 99

Edel Quinn: *Missionary of the Legion of Mary (1907–1944)* 101

Anne Frank: *Witness of the Holocaust (1929–1945)* 103

Gabrielle Bossis: *Mystic (1874–1950)* 105

Martyrs of Birmingham *(d. 1963)* 107

Gladys Aylward: *Missionary (1902–1970)* 108

Sister Thea Bowman: *African American Franciscan (1937–1990)* 111

BLESSED ARE THOSE
WHO HUNGER AND THIRST FOR RIGHTEOUSNESS

Rahab: *Faithful Prostitute* 116

Mary and Elizabeth: *Prophetic Mothers (first century)* 117

Lady Godiva of Coventry: *Defender of the Poor (eleventh century)* 118

St. Birgitta of Sweden: *Mystic and Prophet (1303–1373)* 119

St. Joan of Arc: *Maid of Orleans (1412?–1431)* 122

St. Teresa of Avila: *Mystic, Doctor of the Church (1515–1582)* 124

Anne Hutchinson: *Puritan Prophet (1591–1643)* 126

Sor Juana Inés de la Cruz: *Poet and Scholar (1651–1694)* 129

Margaret Fell: *Quaker (1614–1702)* 131

Sarah Grimké *(1792–1873)* **and Angelina Grimké** *(1805–1879):*
Abolitionists and Feminists 134

Lucretia Mott: *Abolitionist and Feminist (1793–1880)* 137

Contents xi

Sojourner Truth: *Abolitionist Preacher (1797–1883)*   139

Pandita Ramabai: *Indian Christian and Reformer (1858–1922)*   142

Mother Jones: *Labor Agitator (1830–1930)*   144

Simone Weil: *Philosopher and Mystic (1909–1943)*   146

Viola Liuzzo: *Martyr for Civil Rights (1925–1965)*   149

Fannie Lou Hamer: *Prophet of Freedom (1917–1977)*   152

Catherine de Hueck Doherty: *Founder of Madonna House (1896–1985)*   154

BLESSED ARE THE MERCIFUL

St. Brigid of Ireland: *Abbess of Kildare (c. 450–525)*   158

St. Mechtild of Hackeborn: *Nun and Mystic (1241–1298)*   159

St. Louise de Marillac: *Co-Founder of the Daughters of Charity (1591–1660)*   160

St. Joan Delanou: *Founder of the Sisters of St. Anne of the Providence of Saumur (1666–1736)*   162

Nano Nagle: *Founder of the Presentation Sisters (1718–1784)*   164

St. Elizabeth Ann Seton: *Founder of the Daughters of Charity of St. Joseph (1774–1821)*   165

Elizabeth Fry: *Quaker Reformer (1780–1845)*   167

Bd. Anne-Marie Javouhey: *Founder, Sisters of St. Joseph of Cluny (1779–1851)*   169

Bd. Jeanne Jugan: *Founder of the Little Sisters of the Poor (1792–1879)*   171

Florence Nightingale: *Healer (1820–1910)*   173

Harriet Tubman: *Abolitionist (1820?–1913)*   176

St. Frances Xavier Cabrini: *Founder, Missionary Sisters of the Sacred Heart (1850–1917)*   178

Rose Hawthorne: *Founder of the Servants of Relief for Incurable Cancer (1851–1926)*   180

St. Maria Skobtsova: *Orthodox Nun and Martyr (1891–1945)*   182

Caryll Houselander: *Mystic (1901–1954)*   184

Satoko Kitahara: *"The Mary of Ants Town" (1929–1958)*   187

Maura O'Halloran: *Christian Zen Monk (1955–1982)*   190

Corrie Ten Boom: *Rescuer and Witness (1892–1983)*   192

Bd. (Mother) Teresa of Calcutta: *Founder of the Missionaries
of Charity (1910–1997)*   195

BLESSED ARE THE PURE OF HEART

St. Thecla of Iconium: *Evangelist (first century)*   200

St. Agnes: *Virgin and Martyr (d. 304?)*   202

St. Catherine of Alexandria: *Martyr (date unknown)*   203

St. Hilda of Whitby: *Abbess (610–680)*   205

St. Christina of Markyate: *Maiden of Christ (1097–1161)*   206

St. Hildegard of Bingen: *Abbess and Visionary (1098–1179)*   208

Beatrice of Nazareth: *Mystic (1200–1268)*   211

Hadewijch of Brabant: *Beguine Mystic (thirteenth century)*   212

St. Gertrude the Great: *Mystic (1253–1302)*   214

Bd. Kateri Tekakwitha: *"Lily of the Mohawks" (1656–1680)*   216

Mother Ann Lee: *Shaker (1736–1784)*   217

St. Bernadette Soubirous: *Visionary of Lourdes (1844–1879)*   219

St. Maria Goretti: *Martyr (1890–1902)*   222

Etty Hillesum: *Mystic of the Holocaust (1914–1943)*   223

Mollie Rogers: *Founder of the Maryknoll Sisters (1882–1955)*   226

Raïssa Maritain: *Poet and Contemplative (1883–1960)*   228

Flannery O'Connor: *Novelist (1925–1964)*   230

Cassie Bernall: *Witness of Columbine (1981–1999)*   233

Daria Donnelly: *Laywoman (1959–2004)*   235

BLESSED ARE THE PEACEMAKERS

St. Catherine of Siena: *Doctor of the Church (1347–1380)*   240

St. Elizabeth of Portugal: *Queen (1271–1336)*   242

Ida B. Wells: *Reformer (1862–1931)*   243

Jane Addams: *Social Reformer and Nobel Laureate (1860–1935)*   245

Sophie Scholl and Companions: *Martyrs of the White Rose (d. 1943)*   246

Käthe Kollwitz: *Artist (1867–1945)*   248

Muriel Lester: *"Ambassador of Reconciliation" (1884–1968)*   250

Dorothy Day: *Co-Founder of the Catholic Worker (1897–1980)*   252

Peace Pilgrim *(?–1981)*   255

Mirabehn: *Servant of Peace (1892–1982)*   257

Penny Lernoux: *Journalist (1940–1989)*   260

Eileen Egan: *Peacemaker (1912–2000)*   262

Dorothee Soelle: *Theologian (1929–2003)*   265

BLESSED ARE THOSE WHO ARE PERSECUTED FOR RIGHTEOUSNESS' SAKE

St. Blandina and Companions: *Martyrs of Lyons (177)*   270

Sts. Perpetua and Felicity: *Martyrs (d. 203)*   271

St. Crispina: *Martyr (d. 304)*   274

Marguerite Porete: *Beguine Martyr (d. 1310)*   276

Anne Askew: *Protestant Martyr (1521–1546)*   277

St. Margaret Clitherow: *English Martyr (d. 1586)*   279

Mary Dyer: *Quaker Martyr (d. 1660)*   280

Mary Ward: *Founder of the Institute of the Blessed Virgin Mary (1586–1645)*   283

Rebecca Nurse and Companions: *"Witches" of Salem (1692)*   285

St. (Mother) Theodore Guerin: *Founder of the Sisters of Providence of St. Mary of the Woods (1798–1856)* 288

Bd. Mary McKillop: *Founder of the Sisters of St. Joseph of the Sacred Heart (1842–1909)* 290

Agneta Chang: *Maryknoll Sister and Martyr (d. 1950)* 293

Alicia Domon: *Martyr (d. 1977)* 294

Maura Clarke and Companions: *Martyrs of El Salvador (d. 1980)* 296

Introduction

From its earliest days the church has venerated those men and women who, by their heroic faith and love, exemplified the gospel challenge. These "saints" made the gospel concrete. They walked the path prepared by Christ, reminding us of the goal to which all are called.

Thousands of saints have been officially recognized or "canonized" by the church, with more added every year. The list includes many notable women, beginning with Mary, the mother of Jesus, whose consent to God's mysterious plan set in motion the subsequent history of salvation. First among the company of saints, she is addressed in prayer with the words originally spoken by her kinswoman Elizabeth: "Blessed are you among women, and blessed is the fruit of your womb."

Among the women who followed her, many are widely celebrated: Monica, Brigid of Ireland, Clare of Assisi, Joan of Arc, Teresa of Avila, and, closer to our own time, Mother Teresa of Calcutta. And yet any consideration of women saints must begin with an unavoidable fact — that among the wide company of official saints women are vastly underrepresented.

One can speculate about the reasons for this. Many holy women in history tended to spend their lives in the relative seclusion of the cloister. Perhaps they did not leave writings or generate biographies that extended their reputation to a wider circle. Other reasons might be cited as well. But lurking behind them all there lies a deeper fact: that the process of canonization, like the general exercise of authority in the church, has been entirely controlled by men. This has affected not only the selection of saints for canonization, but the interpretation of their lives.

Traditional accounts of women saints — almost always written by men — have tended to emphasize "feminine virtues" of purity, humble service, obedience, or patient endurance. Seldom have women been recognized for questioning authority; for defying restrictive codes and models of behavior; for audacity and wit in surmounting the obstacles placed in their paths. Even the labels attached to women saints reflect a narrow range of categories. Apart from the martyrs, women

1

are generally remembered as "foundresses" of religious orders, "virgins" (a category that applies not only to the so-called "virgin martyrs" but to all women in consecrated religious life), widows, or occasionally "matrons." Such labels elide the range of functions such women may have performed, whether as theologians, prophets, healers, visionaries, or trailblazers in the spiritual life.

Of course the tendency to shape the lives of holy people to match a stereotypical image of sanctity is not confined to women. All too often the process of officially naming saints has involved measuring them against preconceived standards of holiness. The saints who emerge from this process are depicted as "perfect people," free of faults, rough edges, or idiosyncrasies. The resulting impression is that someone is either "born a saint" or becomes one by suppressing his or her individual personality. Thus, living people are transformed into plaster statues.

The truth is that perfect people — if any exist — have little to teach us. But from the real saints we have much to learn. We learn that what we call holiness was a quality expressed in the way they lived; in the choices they made; in their struggles to be faithful, even in the face of doubts and disappointments; in their everyday victories over pride and selfishness; in their daily efforts to be more truthful, loving, and brave.

There are as many types of saints as there are people. Each one offers a unique glimpse of the face of God; each enlarges our moral imagination; each offers new insights into the meaning and possibilities of human life. To the extent that women's names have been forgotten, their stories untold, their dreams, vision, and wisdom marginalized, those possibilities remain unknown and unfulfilled.

Nevertheless, the history of Christianity is marked by the stories of countless holy women who struggled hard to assert their full humanity and to follow where God was calling them, even when this challenged the prevailing options of the time. For some, this meant claiming the freedom to remain unmarried; for others, to escape the restrictive enclosure of a convent, to engage in active apostolic work among the poor, or to travel across the world to proclaim the gospel. Some claimed the authority to write their own community rules, to interpret scripture in new ways, or simply to describe their own experience of God. Others found in Christ a mandate to oppose slavery, war, and social injustice. Later, in light of their achievements and the space they created for new models of discipleship, such women might be honored as "faithful daughters of the church." But while they lived they often endured extraordinary opposition or even persecution.

An ironic motif is the number of women saints who were at some point excommunicated (see, for example, Bd. Mary McKillop, Bd. Anne-Marie Javouhey, or St. Theodore Guerin). But in the struggle to pursue their vocations — especially if this involved any form of innovation — holy women have typically contended with male authorities who were only too eager to inform them that their visions or desires contradicted the will of God. Some — like the Beguines — were suppressed and effectively written out of history. Others prevailed. But more than a few could share the motto applied to St. Angela Merici, founder of the Ursuline order: "A Woman Faced with Two Alternatives. She Saw and Chose the Third."

This book draws heavily on the list of official saints, but I have reached much further, recalling the lives of women throughout history whose manner of faithfulness speaks to the needs of our time. Some, like Rose Hawthorne, Cornelia Connelly, or Dorothy Day, might well be candidates for canonization. Others surely not — if for no other reason, than that they were not Catholics or, in some cases, even Christians.

It would be presumptuous for the church to canonize women outside its communion, especially those who might be offended by the very suggestion. And yet the gospel message is written in many lives — marked by love, hope, and a passion for life — and we may read them as we like. Such lives may never qualify for canonization, yet they stand under the far wider blessing Jesus himself applied to every act of genuine mercy: "Blessed of my Father, inherit the kingdom prepared for you from the foundation of the world; for I was hungry and you gave me food, I was thirsty and you gave me drink, I was a stranger and you welcomed me, I was naked and you clothed me, I was sick and you visited me, I was in prison and you came to me.... Truly, I say to you, as you did it to one of the least of these you did it to me."

The stories recounted here include women from the Gospels, many of them anonymous, whose faith and devotion set a standard of true discipleship. There are women like Lydia, Thecla, and Marcella, evangelists and pioneers in building the early church; martyrs like Perpetua and Felicity, who bore witness to the promise of the resurrection, and so strengthened the faith of their fellow Christians; ascetics, contemplatives, mystics, and prophets who held kings and popes alike accountable to the word of God. There are founders of religious communities, apostolic movements, and new schools of spirituality. Some of these women played dramatic roles on the stage of history, while others remained closer in spirit to what Madeleine Delbrêl called "the ordinary people of the street."

Among the women from modern times I have included mystics, martyrs, and missionaries; reformers, artists, and scholars; peacemakers, champions of justice (including the rights of women), and others who dreamed of a "new heaven and a new earth." Some of them reflect a more traditional path of holiness. Others may be more surprising: a Christian-Zen monk, revered by many as a modern Bodhisattva; a convicted murderer, executed by the state of Texas; a young girl from Colorado, killed in a shooting in her high school; a group of Latin American mothers, united by shared grief for their missing children, who became the conscience of a nation.

Among these women of modern times I have been struck by the number who rejected a conventional "religious" vocation, choosing instead to find God in the realm of work, family, community, and the ordinary business of life. These laywomen represent a type of religious vocation largely ignored in the traditional canon of saints. Such women, including several whose memory is more personal, indicate the typical, if anonymous, face of holiness in our age. I hope they will serve, for the reader, as a reminder of all those women who have inspired us and guided our paths, generally without reward or official recognition.

These stories could be arranged in many ways. I have chosen to group them according to the Beatitudes, the litany of virtues and attitudes by which Jesus summarized the spirit of discipleship: "Blessed are the poor in spirit.... Blessed are the meek.... Blessed are the pure of heart...." It is good to recall that these blessings are not directed to abstract qualities (poverty of spirit, meekness, purity of heart) but to the people who embody them. They do not describe the traditional criteria for canonization. But by standing in the presence of such people, or by reading their stories, we may feel a renewed sense of what it means to be a human being.

The story of each holy person is also a story about God. In each of these stories there is an invitation — not simply to imitate the good deeds of these women, but to enter into the larger universe that they inhabited. What happens next is the beginning of our own story.

•

This book builds on a previous work, *All Saints*, in which I told the stories of 365 "saints, prophets, and witnesses for our time." Soon after that book's publication I was pleased to receive an invitation from a small contemplative community of Maryknoll Sisters. While they appreciated my nontraditional approach to saints, they noted with some passion that I had maintained the traditional imbalance of women and men (about one out of four). Reinforcing their point, they plied me with several lists of possible candidates for a future volume. The Sisters' criticism was soon echoed by many other readers, some of whom were kind enough to send me biographies of their favorite overlooked saints. Thus chastened as well as inspired, I was receptive to the invitation from Gwendolin Herder, publisher of Crossroad Publishing Company, to compile this volume dedicated entirely to women.

Many friends and family members have provided invaluable support and encouragement with this project. I am especially grateful to Jim Martin, Rachelle Linner, the Bruderhof community, Bill McNichols, Ann Ball, Jana Kiely, Catherine Morrissey, Shirley Harriott, Ellen Calmus, Jim Forest, Michael Plekon, and my son, Nicholas. John Jones of Crossroad has rendered exceptionally insightful assistance; it has been a pleasure working with him, along with John Eagleson and all the Crossroad staff. I am grateful as always to my wife, Peggy, my finest editor and best friend.

This book is dedicated to my daughters, Catherine Day and Christina Therese, in hope that the stories recounted here will help them find their own way.

See: *Butler's Lives of the Saints*, 12 vols. (Collegeville, Minn.: Liturgical Press, 1995–2000); Elisabeth Stuart, *Spitting at Dragons: Towards a Feminist Theology of Sainthood* (New York: Mowbray, 1996); Mary T. Malone, *Women and Christianity*, 3 vols. (Maryknoll, N.Y.: Orbis Books, 2000, 2001, 2003); Kathleen Jones, *Women Saints: Lives of Faith and Courage* (Maryknoll, N.Y.: Orbis Books, 1998); Elizabeth A. Johnson, *Friends of God and Prophets: A Feminist Theological Reading of the Communion of Saints* (New York: Continuum, 1998); Joan Chittister, *A Passion for Life: Fragments of the Face of God* (Maryknoll, N.Y.: Orbis Books, 1996).

BLESSED ARE
THE POOR IN SPIRIT

The Mother of Jesus • a Franciscan princess • an emancipated slave • an heiress • a modern mystic • an artist • a witness to solidarity

In St. Luke's version of the Beatitudes this opening verse is somewhat different — simply, "Blessed are the poor...." That is consistent with Luke's overall emphasis on Christ's preferential option for the poor and marginalized. Matthew's Beatitudes, in contrast, address the qualities of true discipleship. The spiritual poverty cited here is not measured by the lack of property. It implies, instead, a spirit of emptiness and availability for whatever gifts, plans, or mission God may send us. As the Virgin Mary replied to the Angel Gabriel, "Behold the handmaiden of the Lord."

Such a spirit is inconsistent with the avarice and ambition that drive our culture. To be spiritually poor is to stand apart from the criteria by which the world measures success, status, and achievement. For that reason, the lives of most saints are marked by a certain "downward mobility."

Above all, those who are poor in spirit have an acute sense of their own limitations and of their reliance on grace. As one translation puts it, "Blessed are those who know their need of God."

"The Kingdom of Heaven is theirs."

Mary
Mother of Jesus (first century)

"Behold the handmaid of the Lord."

Mary, a young Galilean woman of Nazareth, was betrothed to a carpenter named Joseph. One day, according to the Gospel of Luke, she was visited by the angel Gabriel, who greeted her with the words, "Hail, O favored one, the Lord is with you!" After calming her fears he announced that she would conceive and bear a son named Jesus, who would be called "the Son of the Most High."

Mary was troubled by this news, for she was as yet unmarried. If she were charged with adultery she could be stoned to death. But the angel told her that she would conceive by the power of the Holy Spirit. "With God nothing will be impossible," he assured her. And so Mary responded in faith: "Let it be done to me according to your word."

It was in the space created by Mary's faith — and not simply in her womb — that the Word became flesh. For this reason she has been called not only the Mother of Jesus but the Mother of the Church. In the past it was common to emphasize the ways in which Mary was set apart from and above all other women and the ordinary conditions of humanity. Today there is a new emphasis on her status as a woman of the people and her solidarity with the rest of humanity. A "Mariology from above" emphasized God's initiative in selecting Mary for her part in the divine mystery of redemption. In contrast, a "Mariology from below" begins with the poor woman, Mary of Nazareth, who was rooted in the faith and struggles of her people, subject to the cruelties of the world, and heir to the ancient hope for deliverance and salvation. In this light, Mary is honored not so much for her special nature as for her exceptional faith.

Two stories in the Gospels highlight this point. One time Jesus was told that his "mother and brothers" were looking for him. Gazing at those who were seated around him he answered, "Who are my mother and my brothers? These are my mother and my brothers. Whoever does the will of God is brother and sister and mother to me" (Mark 3:33–35). Another time someone called out from a crowd, "Blessed is the womb that bore you and the breasts that nursed you!" To this Jesus responded, "Rather, blessed are they who hear the word of God and keep it" (Luke 11:27–28).

Neither of these stories reflects a disregard on the part of Jesus toward his mother. But they do show that he rejected the claims of blood or natural kinship in favor of discipleship. In this perspective Mary's preeminence is due to her having exemplified the spirit of true discipleship: attention, reverence, and obedience to the word and will of God.

The Gospel of John places Mary at the foot of the cross beside "the beloved disciple." According to Luke, she was among the disciples who gathered in the upper room in Jerusalem after Jesus' ascension. She was in effect the first and paradigmatic disciple. She is thus the first to be honored among the saints. In the darkness of faith, she offered her consent to the mysterious plan of God. In the light of grace she responded with her extraordinary song of praise and thanksgiving:

> My soul magnifies the Lord,
> and my spirit rejoices in God my Savior,
> for he has regarded the lowliness of his handmaiden.
> For behold, henceforth all generations will call me blessed;
> for he who is mighty has done great things for me,
> and holy is his name....

See: Elizabeth A. Johnson, "Saints and Mary," in *Systematic Theology: Roman Catholic Perspectives*, vol. 2, ed. Francis Schüssler Fiorenza and John P. Galvin (Minneapolis: Fortress, 1991).

Anna
Prophetess (first century)

"And there was a prophetess, Anna, the daughter of Panuel of the tribe of Asher; she was of a great age, having lived with her husband seven years from her virginity, and as a widow till she was eighty-four. She did not depart from the temple, worshiping with fasting and prayer night and day. And coming up at that very hour she gave thanks to God, and spoke of him to all who were looking for the redemption of Israel."

—Luke 2:36–38

This short text is all that is recorded of the prophetess Anna, an old woman who haunted the temple of Jerusalem awaiting some sign of Israel's Redeemer. Her long years of patient vigil were rewarded one day when Mary and Joseph brought their infant son to the temple for his ritual presentation to the Lord. Anna's story follows the longer account of Simeon, an old man who had been assured by the Holy Spirit that he would not die before he had seen the Messiah. When he saw the child Jesus accompanied by his parents, he blessed God and said, "Lord, now lettest thou thy servant depart in peace, according to thy word; for mine eyes have seen thy salvation, which thou hast prepared in the presence of all peoples."

Although no words are attributed to Anna, there is a similar sense of fulfillment in her story. Beyond Jesus' immediate family, she is the first woman to be granted such insight into the divine mystery concealed in these humble beginnings. And she is the first to proclaim this good news to those like herself — poor and of no account — who lived by faith and waited in hope.

Sts. Martha and Mary of Bethany
Friends of Jesus (first century)

"If you had been here, my brother would not have died. But I know that whatever you ask from God, God will give you."   —John 11:21–22

Sts. Martha and Mary make significant appearances in the Gospels of both Luke and John. These two sisters and their brother Lazarus evidently enjoyed a special relationship with the Lord, who was a frequent guest in their home in Bethany. It is a fact, as John puts it, "that Jesus loved Martha and her sister and Lazarus."

Martha and Mary are best remembered for one occasion when Jesus was visiting their home. While Mary sat at the Master's feet and "listened to his teaching," Martha was left to wait on their guest. When she pointedly suggested to Jesus that he instruct Mary to lend her a hand, he answered her, "Martha, Martha, you are anxious and troubled about many things; one thing is necessary. Mary has chosen the good portion, which shall not be taken away from her."

This passage in the Gospel of Luke has drawn enormous attention. In the history of Christian spirituality the story of Martha and Mary has often been interpreted to represent the contrast between two types of living: the active or apostolic way (Martha, busy in the kitchen) and the contemplative way (Mary, silently taking in the word of the Lord). Naturally, those who followed the contemplative path found particular justification in this passage. The fourteenth-century English mystical classic *The Cloud of Unknowing* devotes several chapters to this story. It is Mary, who "gazed with all the love of her heart" and who focused her attention on "the supreme wisdom of his Godhead shrouded by the words of his humanity," who is the evident hero of the story. It is she who has chosen "the better part."

But the implications of this story for women in general have been ambiguous. On the one hand, this passage has been used to set the contemplative life of cloistered nuns on a higher, ideal level, above the ordinary life of women bustling in the world. Women through the centuries who have "merely" occupied themselves with the necessary work of cooking, cleaning, and maintaining life have surely felt the sting of Jesus' retort. At the same time, however, the story shows Jesus challenging the kind of gender stereotypes that would restrict women to domestic work. Breaking with custom, he recognizes Mary's right to assume the role of a religious disciple, to sit at the Master's feet and study his teachings. Was his statement really a rebuke to Martha, or was it not also a powerful sign directed at the other disciples who recorded his words?

The Gospel of John has Martha engaging Jesus in a theological exchange. When he arrives — too late, it seems — after the burial of her brother Lazarus, it is Martha (the "active one") who rushes out to him, crying, "Lord, if you had been here, my brother would not have died." This time Jesus does not trivialize her concerns but draws her into a conversation about deeper mysteries. "I am the resurrection and the life," he tells her; "he who believes in me, though he die, yet shall he live, and whoever lives and believes in me shall never die."

Does she believe him? Here it is Martha who responds with the great words of faith, otherwise attributed only to his closest disciples: "Yes, Lord; I believe that you are the Christ, the Son of God, he who is coming into the world." Her faith is justified when Jesus raises Lazarus from the dead.

John describes a final encounter that occurs soon after. Only days before his Passion, Jesus is once again enjoying the hospitality of his friends Martha and Mary, their ardor for their guest doubtless magnified by his miraculous gift of their brother's life. Once again, "Martha served," though this time without complaint. Mary makes a gesture otherwise attributed in the Gospels to another unnamed woman in Bethany: She takes a pound of costly ointment and proceeds to anoint

Jesus' feet and to wipe them with her hair. Once again her attitude toward Jesus is criticized by the bystanders — not, this time, by her sister, but by the false disciple, Judas, who notes that this oil could have been sold and the money given to the poor. But once again Jesus affirms the value of Mary's deed, at once deeply intimate and mysteriously christological in its import: "Leave her alone, let her keep it for the day of my burial. The poor you always have with you, but you do not always have me."

Both Martha and Mary, in their different ways, had found the "one thing necessary" — to respond with love, in whatever appropriate fashion, to the Christ in their midst.

St. Mary Magdalene
Apostle to the Apostles (first century)

"I have seen the Lord."
—John 20:18

Mary Magdalene was one of the original Galilean disciples of Jesus and the most eminent among the many women who followed in his itinerant ministry. Little can be said about her origins; she is characterized simply as "a woman from whom seven demons had gone out," a statement subject to various interpretations. It was St. Gregory the Great who identified Mary with the woman, "a sinner," who sought Jesus out in the home of a Pharisee to wash his feet with her tears and dry them with her hair. This gesture, which scandalized the other dinner guests, prompted Jesus to say, "Her sins, which are many, are forgiven, for she loved much." From this conflation, now rejected by scholars as well as the church, there came about the popular representation of Mary Magdalene as a penitent sinner or prostitute.

This image of "the Magdalene" has appealed to artists and dramatists throughout history, and it has doubtless been a comfort to many. But in attaching such a stereotypically female image to Mary Magdalene the Western fathers also helped to efface the memory of the leadership and prominence of women in the early Jesus movement. This amnesia was already well under way by the time the Gospels were written in the late first century. One of the most distinctive features of Jesus' movement was the presence of women among his intimate disciples.

And yet the story and even identity of many of these women was left on the margins.

It is all the more significant when women such as Mary of Bethany, her sister Martha, or Mary Magdalene *are* named. It is a sign of just how vital a place they still occupied in the church's living memory. Mary Magdalene, in particular, was firmly associated with two vital facts: that she was a witness to the crucifixion and that she was the first witness of the Risen Lord.

All four Gospels name Mary among the women who followed Jesus to Golgotha and there witnessed his passion and death. While all the male disciples fled, it was these women who remained faithful to the end. It was also they, including Mary Magdalene, who went to his tomb on the day after the sabbath hoping to anoint his body.

Instead they found an empty tomb, guarded by an angel who revealed the astonishing news that Jesus was risen. The women were charged to tell the disciples to meet the Lord back in Galilee. In the Gospels of John and Matthew Mary Magdalene actually sees the Risen Lord. John provides a particularly poignant account, reflecting most clearly the special relationship that evidently existed between Mary and Jesus.

Here, after summoning Peter and the "beloved disciple" to see the empty tomb for themselves, "Mary stood weeping outside the tomb." Suddenly she sees Jesus, but does not recognize him. Taking him to be the gardener she says, "Sir, if you have carried him away, tell me where you have laid him, and I will take him away." Jesus answers her with a single word — "Mary" — which is enough to identify him. "Rabboni!" she cries, "Teacher." He instructs her not to hold him, "but go to my brethren and say to them, I am ascending to my Father and your Father, to my God and your God." And so Mary goes out to the disciples and says, "I have seen the Lord."

Nothing else is known of Mary Magdalene. Her deeds are not reported in the Acts of the Apostles, nor does she figure in the writings of Paul. (In listing the appearances of the Risen Lord he begins with the appearance to Peter.) But the name of Mary Magdalene deserves special honor, particularly at a time when women are struggling to be heard in the church and society. It was she, the faithful disciple, who first proclaimed the good news to the Twelve. Thus she has often been called the "Apostle to the Apostles."

St. Marcella
Widow (325–410)

"By heaven's grace, captivity has found me a poor woman, not made me one. Now I shall go in want of daily bread, but I shall not feel hunger since I am full of Christ."

All that we know of Marcella is contained in the many letters that she received from her friend St. Jerome and especially from an eloquent memorial, in which he called her "the glory of all the saints and particularly of the city of Rome."

Marcella was born to a wealthy and noble family of Rome. After the death of her father she was urged to marry and did so. Her husband was also a wealthy man, but his death left her a widow after only seven months of marriage. Henceforth she resisted all invitations to remarry, happily dedicating herself to a life of chastity. When a ranking — and elderly — consul proposed to leave her all his money if she would marry him, she answered, "If I wished to marry...I should in any case look for a husband, not an inheritance."

After this Marcella's life was occupied by prayer, study of scripture, and frequent visits to the shrines of the martyrs. She gave away all her fortune, "preferring to store her money in the stomachs of the needy rather than hide it in a purse." At this time she came across an account of the life of St. Antony and was inspired, as much as her circumstances would allow, to emulate his monastic life. Thus she began to gather a community of like-spirited women, both widows and unmarried maidens, who shared her appetite for holiness. Most were of similar social background, though they conformed to Marcella's voluntary poverty. They followed no formal rule. Nevertheless, this was perhaps one of the earliest such communities of Christian women.

When Jerome arrived in Rome, he was introduced to Marcella's circle of holy women, and he was induced, somewhat reluctantly, to serve as their spiritual director. So impressed was he by their learning and piety that he compared them to the holy women who surrounded Jesus. Marcella, he claimed, was another Mary Magdalene. A number of these women became his lifelong friends. So frequent a visitor to this community was Jerome that, in "a slander-loving place...where the triumph of vice was to disparage virtue and to defile all that is pure and clean," his enemies found ample material for gossip. Such an atmosphere contributed to his decision to flee Rome for the Holy Land.

Nevertheless, he maintained his close correspondence with Marcella until her death.

She continued her holy life until the sack of Rome in 410. The spectacle of this violence and the ensuing famine made an impact on the entire classical world. As Jerome wrote, "The city which had taken the whole world was itself taken." At one point the invading hordes broke into the home of Marcella, then eighty-five, and beat her savagely in order to discover her hidden treasures. In vain she protested that she owned nothing but the robe she wore, and she had fears lest they would take even that from her. Nevertheless her brave composure arrested the assault, and eventually the shame-faced attackers escorted her to the refuge of a nearby church.

Marcella died within a few months of this assault. Though her sisters wept, Jerome writes, "she smiled, conscious of having lived a good life and hoping for a reward hereafter."

See: St. Jerome, "Letter CXXVII: To Principia," in *Select Letters of St. Jerome,* trans. F. A. Wright (New York: G. P. Putnam's Sons, 1932).

St. Clare of Assisi
Founder of the Poor Clares (1193–1253)

"Place your mind before the mirror of eternity!
Place your soul in the brilliance of glory!
Place your heart in the figure of the divine substance!
And transform your whole being into the image
of the Godhead Itself through contemplation!"

The story of St. Clare of Assisi is inevitably linked with St. Francis, the one she called her Father, Planter, and Helper in the Service of Christ. It was Francis who gave her a vision and enabled her to define a way of life apart from the options offered by her society. But her goal in life was not to be a reflection of Francis but to be, like him, a reflection of Christ. "Christ is the way," she said, "and Francis showed it to me."

Like Francis Clare belonged to one of the wealthy families of Assisi. Like everyone else in the town, she was aware of the remarkable spectacle that Francis had made in abandoning his respectable family and assuming the poverty of a beggar. Doubtless there were those in Assisi who respected Francis as a faithful Christian, just as there were others who believed he was a misguided fool. It was bad enough that a man

of his background was tramping about the countryside, repairing abandoned churches with his bare hands and ministering to the poor and
sick. But within a few years he had begun attracting some of the most
distinguished young men of the town to follow him in his brotherhood.

What Clare's family thought of all this is not known. But we know
what impact it had on Clare. She heard Francis deliver a series of Lenten
sermons in 1212, when she was eighteen. She arranged in stealth to
meet with Francis and asked his help that she too might live "after the
manner of the holy gospel." On the evening of Palm Sunday, while her
family and all the town slept, she crept out a back door, slipped through
the gates of Assisi, and made her way through the dark fields and olive
groves to a rendezvous with Francis and his brothers at the chapel of
St. Mary of the Angels. Before the altar she put off her fine clothes and
assumed a penitential habit, while Francis sheared off her long hair as
a sign of her espousal to Christ.

It is tempting to read into this episode the romance of a spiritual
elopement. To understand Clare, however, we must realize that it was
not Francis whom she rushed to meet in the night. He provided the
meeting place. But her assignation was with Christ.

Yet after Clare had taken the plunge of rejecting her family and her
social station, it was not clear what the next step should be. Apparently
neither Clare nor Francis had considered that far ahead. Although she
wished to identify with Francis's community, it was not seemly that
she should live with the brothers. Francis arranged for her to spend the
night in a nearby Benedictine convent. There her family and a company
of angry suitors tracked her down some days later in Holy Week. When
pleading proved fruitless, they laid hands on her and tried to drag her
out by force. She finally stopped them short by tearing off her veil and
revealing her shorn head. They were too late. She was already "one of
them."

Francis had long intended that a community of women, corresponding to his fraternity, should be established. In Clare he had found the
partner he was seeking. She was easily persuaded to found a women's
community, which was established at San Damiano. It required con-
siderably more effort by Francis to persuade her to serve as abbess.
Nevertheless, Clare quickly attracted other women. Over time these
included a number of her personal relatives, including her sister Catherine and even her widowed mother. Within her lifetime additional
communities were established elsewhere in Italy, France, and Germany.

Unlike the Friars, the Poor Ladies, as they were originally known, lived within an enclosure. But Clare shared Francis's passionate commitment to "Lady Poverty." For her this meant literal poverty and insecurity — not the luxurious "spiritual poverty" enjoyed by so many other convents, richly supported by gifts and endowments. To defend this "privilege of poverty" Clare waged a continuous struggle against solicitous prelates who tried to mitigate her austerity. This was the centerpiece of the rule she devised for her community. When the pope offered to absolve her from her rigorous vow of poverty, she answered, "Absolve me from my sins, Holy Father, but not from my wish to follow Christ." Two days before her death, in 1253, she enjoyed the grace of receiving from Rome a copy of her rule embellished with the approving seal of Pope Innocent IV. A notation on the original document notes that Clare, in tearful joy, covered the parchment with kisses.

It has been said that of all the followers of Francis, Clare was the most faithful. Many stories reflect the loving bonds of friendship between them and the trust that Francis placed in her wisdom and counsel. According to one story, Francis put the question to Clare whether he should preach or devote himself to prayer. It was Clare who urged him to go into the world: "God did not call you for yourself alone, but also for the salvation of others." During a period of dejection, Francis camped out in a hut outside the convent at San Damiano. It was there that he composed his exultant hymn to the universe, "The Canticle of Brother Sun." Later, when Francis received the stigmata, Clare thoughtfully made him soft slippers to cover his wounded feet.

Finally, as Francis felt the approach of Sister Death, Clare too became seriously ill. She suffered terribly at the thought that they would not meet again in this life. Francis sent word that she should put aside all grief, for she *would* surely see him again before her death. And so the promise was fulfilled, though not as she had wished. After Francis's death, the brothers carried his body to San Damiano for the Sisters' viewing. Francis's early biographer, Thomas of Celano, records that at the sight of his poor and lifeless body Clare was "filled with grief and wept aloud."

Francis was canonized a mere two years later. Clare lived on for another twenty-seven years. In her own final "Testament," written near the end of her life, Clare makes only a discrete reference to the pain of their separation and what it meant to her: "We take note . . . of the frailty which we feared in ourselves after the death of our holy Father

Francis. He who was our pillar of strength and, after God, our one consolation and support. Thus time and again, we bound ourselves to our Lady, most Holy Poverty."

See: Francis and Clare: The Complete Works, trans. Regis Armstrong, O.F.M.Cap., and Ignatius Brady, O.F.M., Classics of Western Spirituality (New York: Paulist, 1982).

St. Elizabeth of Hungary
Franciscan Queen (1207–1231)

"We must give God what we have, gladly and with joy."

St. Elizabeth was the daughter of Hungarian royalty. At the age of four, in a politically arranged match, she was betrothed to the future landgrave (prince) of Thuringia in southern Germany. So she was sent away from her family to live in the castle of her future husband, Ludwig, at the time a boy of nine. It may be supposed that such matches seldom tended to genuine romance. In this case, however, it appears that the two children developed an intimate friendship that eventually blossomed into loving devotion. This endured the growing disapprobation of Ludwig's family as Elizabeth's piety steadily transgressed the boundaries of what was considered good taste. The young princess dressed too simply, it was said; she was inordinate in her prayer and profligate in her almsgiving. Ludwig, however, rejected any suggestion of returning her to Hungary; he declared that he would sooner part with a mountain of gold than be parted from the woman he affectionately called his "dear sister."

In due time they were married amid much ceremony. Elizabeth gave birth to three children in quick succession, and she rejoiced that as landgravine of Thuringia, she now had much greater scope for her charitable activities. She established several hospitals for the indigent and aroused scandal by nursing the sick and even lepers with her own hands. Her instinctive spiritual poverty was only magnified with the arrival of the first Franciscan missionaries in Germany. She was captivated by the story of Clare and Francis (from whom she received the gift of his cloak), and she eventually embraced the rule of a Franciscan tertiary.

In all her piety and service to the poor, Elizabeth received the loyal support of her husband. When famine struck the kingdom while Ludwig was away, Elizabeth took it upon herself to open the royal granaries to the poor. Many lives were spared through her generosity. Nevertheless, upon his return Ludwig was shocked to discover that his wife had become an object of scorn among the rich and elite members of the court. Aside from her charity, they were offended by a personal discipline she had imposed on herself never to eat any food that might be the fruit of injustice or exploitation.

In 1227 Ludwig revealed that he had accepted command of a force of Crusaders bound for the Holy Land. Elizabeth, who was pregnant, felt a terrible premonition that they would not meet again, and their parting was a scene of heartbreak. Some months later the news returned that Ludwig had died of plague on his journey. In a paroxysm of grief, Elizabeth cried, "The world is dead to me, and all that was joyous in the world."

Shocking developments followed. Without Ludwig to shield her from the resentment of her in-laws, Elizabeth was banished from the castle. She left in a winter night, leaving her few belongings and carrying nothing but her newborn child. She who had embraced the spirit of poverty now found herself happy to accept shelter in a pig-shed, for no reputable home would take her in. Eventually the scandal of her impoverishment was too much for her relatives to bear, and she was provided with a simple cottage in Marburg. Aside from her virtue, Elizabeth was equally admired for her "dark beauty." Her fall from grace did not prevent Emperor Frederick II, whose wife had recently died, from making inquiries regarding her marriageability. But she was determined to remain a widow and devote herself to prayer and service of the poor.

Meanwhile, behind these public sufferings, Elizabeth had another cross to bear. Before her husband's death, she had accepted from Pope Honorius III the services of a spiritual director, Conrad of Marburg, who exacted from Elizabeth a vow of unquestioning obedience. This priest's most recent service had been as an Inquisitor of heretics, an experience he applied to his new undertaking. Ostensibly his aim was to advance Elizabeth's sanctification by weaning her of any vestige of attachment to the world. Thus, he cruelly upbraided her and even beat her with a stick for any infraction of his rules. He forced her to part with her two closest friends, the ladies-in-waiting who had accompanied her from Hungary as a child, and he replaced them with two "harsh females" who spied and reported on her activities. Escaping their attentions was one of the benefits of her exile from the court. Despite such treatment she maintained her gentleness of spirit and even responded to these cruelties with subversive humor, evidence, if any were needed, of how little encouragement her sanctity required.

In the meantime Elizabeth's reputation for holiness began to take root. The spectacle of this princess working at a spinning wheel or nursing the sick in their homes or in the hospices she had endowed inspired the grudging respect of those who had persecuted her, as well as the devoted affection of the poor and common folk. When not at prayer or engaged in other service, she liked to go fishing in nearby streams, selling her catch to provide alms.

In 1231 she fell ill and announced calmly that she would not recover. She died on November 17, at the age of twenty-four. Her confessor, Master Conrad, worked energetically (and with ill-concealed self-interest) to promote her cause. It was easy to assemble a dossier of reputed miracles and other documentation of her sanctity. His efforts were rewarded with her canonization a mere three years after her death — an event, however, which he did not live to witness. For many years the remains of Elizabeth, buried in the church in Marburg, were the object of pilgrimage until, during the Protestant Reformation, a future landgrave of Thuringia had her body removed to an unknown location.

See: Nesta de Robek, *Saint Elizabeth of Hungary: A Story of Twenty-Four Years* (Milwaukee: Bruce, 1954).

St. Agnes of Bohemia
Princess and Abbess (1203–1280)

"Though you, more than others, could have enjoyed the magnificence and honor and dignity of the world, and could have been married to the illustrious Caesar with splendor befitting you and his excellency, you have rejected all these things and have chosen with your whole heart and soul a life of holy poverty and destitution. Thus you took a spouse of a more noble lineage." —St. Clare of Assisi to Agnes of Bohemia

Although she died in 1280, St. Agnes of Bohemia was canonized only in 1989. But throughout the intervening seven centuries she remained the subject of a devoted following, a symbol of integrity and virtue, even during the years when a repressive communist government in

Czechoslovakia, sustained by what Vaclev Havel called "the culture of lies," tried hard to erase the religious memory of the people. Among the faithful it was widely believed that the day of Agnes's eventual canonization would signal a rebirth for the Czech people.

Agnes was born in 1203 in Prague. She was a princess, the daughter of King Ottokar of Bohemia and Queen Constance of Hungary. Despite the luxury and privileges of her station, she enjoyed no freedom to decide her own destiny. In keeping with the role assigned to young noble women, she was simply a commodity to be invested wherever she might bring the highest return for her family and its dynastic interests. Repeatedly, starting at the age of three, she was shipped to various kingdoms and betrothed to strangers she had never met, only to be returned to sender when some impediment arose. Her first betrothal — to Boleslaus, son of the duke of Silesia — came to naught when her future husband died at the age of six. Her next engagement, to the son of the emperor Frederick II, ended when the prospective groom ended up marrying a different princess. Henry III of England sought her hand. So did the emperor Frederick himself. This at last was the ultimate match and her brother, King Wenceslaus, insisted that she cooperate.

But at this point Agnes dared to claim her own way. She wrote to Pope Gregory IX, asking him to prevent the marriage on the grounds that she had not consented and that her wish was instead to consecrate herself to Christ. Her brother put the awkward matter to the emperor, who — to everyone's surprise — responded by respecting Agnes's desire. "If she had left me for a mortal man, I should have made my vengeance felt," he said, "but I cannot take offense if she prefers the King of Heaven to me."

What led the princess to exercise this bold option? Agnes may have drawn inspiration from the example of her cousin, St. Elizabeth of Hungary, who, upon the death of her husband, had caused a scandal by abandoning the privileges of her royal station to become a Franciscan tertiary. Certainly Agnes was deeply affected by the arrival in Prague of the first Franciscan friars. She later initiated a correspondence with St. Clare, who responded by sending five of her Sisters to Prague. In 1236, her royal life behind her, Agnes formally joined them.

St. Clare's letters to Agnes, among her very few surviving writings, are a precious window on the early Franciscan movement. With warmth and obvious affection, Clare addressed Agnes as "the half of her soul and the special shrine of her heart's deepest love." Speaking as a "mother" to "her favorite daughter," she commended Agnes for the poverty she had chosen. In rejecting the false riches of the world, she had claimed a prize of greater worth. In declining false honors she had secured a place on "the path of prudent happiness." "Place your mind before the mirror of eternity!" she counseled her. "Place your soul in the brilliance of glory! Place your heart in the figure of the divine substance! And transform your whole being into the image of the Godhead Itself through contemplation."

Agnes spent forty-four years as a Poor Clare. Her decision to renounce her royal title, wealth, and comfort for the poverty of a religious cell sent ripples far beyond her native land. In Bohemia alone, one hundred young girls accompanied her into the Poor Clares, while all across Europe other high-ranking ladies followed her example. Some believe her influence extended even further. Following only a week after her canonization by Pope John Paul II in 1989, the "Velvet Revolution" in Prague swept aside four decades of communist rule without the firing of a single shot.

See: Francis and Clare: The Complete Works, trans. Regis Armstrong, O.F.M.Cap., and Ignatius C. Brady, O.F.M., Classics of Western Spirituality (New York: Paulist, 1982).

St. Angela Merici
Founder of the Ursulines (1474–1540)

"Each member of the Company should strive to despoil herself of everything and set all her good, her love, her delight, not in robes, nor in food nor in relatives, but in God alone and in his benign and ineffable Providence."

It is easy to take for granted the scores of religious congregations dedicated to the works of mercy and other apostolates. As their numbers decline, it becomes harder to recall a time when a vast system of schools, orphanages, and hospitals was run by legions of Sisters, each wearing the distinctive habit of her congregation. It is harder still to recall that there was a time before such communities existed when it fell to certain visionaries and their devoted pioneers to imagine a new way of living out the gospel in response to the needs at hand. Many of them consciously sought a new way for women to live a Christian life in the world — apart from the alternatives of marriage or the enclosure of the convent. One of these visionaries was Angela Merici (sometimes called Angela of Brescia).

Angela was born in the town of Desenzano in northern Italy. She was orphaned at an early age and soon thereafter lost a beloved sister. In her grief she was consoled by a vision — the first of many in her life — which offered assurance of her sister's salvation. In thanksgiving she became a Franciscan tertiary and ever after adopted a life of prayerful simplicity. She devoted many years to continuous pilgrimage, visiting the shrines of Italy. Eventually she took up the irresistible challenge for all pilgrims of her day, a trip to the Holy Land. Before arriving, however, she was mysteriously struck blind and consequently saw nothing of the holy shrines. On her return, her eyesight just as miraculously returned.

The motif of sight or vision appears elsewhere in her biography. She had one remarkable vision in which she saw a company of angels and maidens descending from a ladder in the heavens. A voice revealed that she would one day found a new community of women whose members would be as numerous as those maidens thus revealed to her.

In her youth Angela had been moved by the poverty and ignorance of her neighbors and had undertaken to provide simple religious instruction to their children. Over the years, when not traveling, she had made this her regular occupation. Gradually other women were attracted to join her. In 1533, when she was fifty and had settled in Brescia, she set about to formalize a community of these women. Two years later she had a group of twenty-eight women ready to consecrate themselves with her to the service of God. They chose as their patron St. Ursula, a legendary fourth-century martyr who was popularly venerated as a protector of women.

Although she devised a simple rule for her community of Ursulines, Angela did not conceive of them as a religious order. They did not wear habits; they took no vows; they continued to live with their families rather than behind an enclosure. The idea of such an association of religious women was unheard of at the time and it aroused concerns. But the work of Angela and her companions, which centered on the education of poor girls, was widely admired.

Angela was elected the association's first superior general, in which position she devoted herself primarily to spiritual formation. By this time she was revered as a living saint of Brescia. Crowds of people would follow her to church, attracted in part by her reputed ability to levitate several inches off the ground while gazing on the Eucharist.

She died on January 27, 1540, after a long illness. Four years later Rome approved a constitution for her religious community, which would in time come to number many tens of thousands of women. She was canonized in 1807.

See: Philip Caraman, *Saint Angela* (New York: Farrar, Straus, 1963).

St. Jeanne de Chantal
Co-Founder of the Order of the Visitation
(1572–1641)

"Sometimes put yourself very simply before God, certain of his presence everywhere, and without any effort, whisper very softly to his sacred heart whatever your own heart prompts you to say."

Jeanne de Chantal was born into a wealthy family in Dijon, France. At the age of twenty she married a baron, Christophe de Rabutin. It was a happy marriage, despite the fact that three of their seven children died in infancy. In 1600, however, after eight years of marriage, her husband was killed in a hunting accident. In the following years, as she struggled with her children's upbringing, dependent on her in-laws for support, her heart increasingly turned to the attractions of religious life. She vowed that she would never again marry.

In 1604 she heard a sermon preached by the bishop of Geneva, Francis de Sales. This was a turning point in her life, the beginning of a deep spiritual friendship and partnership that would advance them both along their respective paths to sanctity. Francis was already renowned as a preacher and spiritual director. Rather than present the spiritual life as something fit only for monks and nuns, he tried to present a spirituality accessible to everyone and capable of being lived out in the world. Jeanne immediately responded to his message and asked him to become her spiritual director.

After several years, in 1610, the two of them founded the Order of the Visitation of Mary, a congregation dedicated to prayer and works of charity. Their original intention was that the order would be adapted for widows and other women who, for reasons of health or age, could not endure the rigors of enclosed life. But the plan met with such carping disapproval from ecclesiastical authorities that in the end Jeanne consented to accept enclosure. Jeanne's daughters were married by this time, but her fifteen-year-old son, Celse-Benigne, resisted his mother's plan to enter religious life. He was the occasion of a melodramatic test, for which Jeanne is especially remembered. Laying his body across the threshold of their home, he implored her not to leave. Without hesitation she stepped over him and proceeded on her way.

Jeanne proved a gifted superior, combining superb administrative skills with a profound instinct for the spiritual life. "No matter what happens," she wrote, "be gentle with yourself." In her lifetime the order grew to include eighty communities in several countries. Along the way she encountered persistent criticism from church authorities as well as internal tensions within the congregation. The order attracted many women from an aristocratic background who found it difficult to adapt themselves to the spirit of poverty and obedience. Jeanne weathered these and greater trials, including the death of her son in war and, later, in 1622, the passing of her beloved friend, St. Francis.

She lived on for almost twenty years, dying in 1641 at the age of sixty-nine. Another holy friend, St. Vincent de Paul, was moved to observe: "She was full of faith, and yet all her life long had been tormented by thoughts against it.... But for all that suffering her face never lost its serenity, nor did she once relax in the fidelity God asked of her. And so I regard her as one of the holiest souls I have ever met on this earth."

See: Francis de Sales, Jane de Chantal: Letters of Spiritual Direction, ed. Wendy Wright and Joseph F. Powers, Classics of Western Spirituality (New York: Paulist, 1988).

St. Elizabeth Feodorovna
Martyr (1864–1918)

"I am leaving the brilliant world where I occupied a high position, and now . . . I am about to ascend into a much greater world, the world of the poor."

St. Elizabeth was born for a life of opulence and luxury. A German princess and the granddaughter of England's Queen Victoria, she was married at the age of twenty to Grand Duke Sergei Alexandrovich, younger brother of Tsar Alexander III of Russia. As the Grand Duchess Elizabeth Feodorovna she embraced her new homeland with enthusiasm, immersing herself in its language, religion, and culture. In 1891 she formally converted to the Orthodox faith — a decision apparently based on genuine conviction, not just family obligation.

When her husband became the governor of Moscow, Elizabeth assumed many social duties. But to a degree rare among her peers, she was sensitive to the desperate condition of the poor, and she used her influence to respond to their needs. In addition to her extensive charitable contributions, she devoted much of her personal time to visiting hospitals, prisons, and orphanages.

In 1894 her sister Alexandra married the new Tsar Nicholas II. This put Elizabeth at the center of Russian royal society. This also happened to be the center of social forces in Russia that were rapidly approaching a violent crisis. In 1905, in a foreshadowing of things to come, her husband was killed by a bomb-throwing assassin in front of the Kremlin. Elizabeth was close enough to hear the explosion and, rushing to the scene, to see the mangled remains of her husband. Later, she would secretly visit the assassin in his prison cell, offering him forgiveness and interceding on his behalf with her brother-in-law. A memorial cross she erected at the site of Sergei's death bears the inscription, "Father, forgive them, for they know not what they do."

With the death of her husband, Elizabeth immediately altered her life. Withdrawing from the palace, she devoted herself to hospital work, personally nursing men who had been wounded in the Russo-Japanese war. With the proceeds from the sale of her jewelry she bought a piece of property on the outskirts of Moscow and established a women's religious community, occupied with serving the poor. The community was dedicated to Saints Martha and Mary, the sisters of Lazarus, in whose home Christ enjoyed frequent hospitality. The dedication of the community was significant, for its members sought to combine the virtues of each of these saints: with Mary, listening to the words of Christ, and with Martha, entering into service of the least of his brethren. Their rule was based on the words of scripture: "I was hungry and you fed me..." (Matt. 25:35ff). In 1909 they became a formal monastic community, the Sisters of Love and Mercy, with Elizabeth as their abbess.

This was not a monastery removed from the cares of the world. The Sisters combined their discipline of daily prayer with active care for the poor and others in need. They nursed the sick, fed the hungry, cared for abandoned children, and otherwise performed the works of mercy. With the outbreak of World War I they made provision to care for wounded soldiers, who returned from the front in terrible numbers.

As revolutionary strife began to emerge in Russia, there were threats against Elizabeth's life — due not only to her royal station, but also to

St. Elizabeth Feodorovna

her German blood. Friends and diplomats urged her to leave the country. She was determined, however, to share in the fate of the Russian people. Eventually the Tsar abdicated his throne. He and his family were deported to the countryside and held under guard. In April 1918 Mother Elizabeth was also arrested. On the way to prison she wrote a letter of farewell to her community: "The Lord has found that it is time for us to bear His Cross. Let us try to be worthy of it."

On July 17, 1918, the Tsar and his family were murdered. The next day Mother Elizabeth and other members of the royal family were bound and delivered to an abandoned mine shaft. Even after being hurled into the pit, their voices could still be heard singing hymns from the Holy Liturgy. Their executioners tossed hand grenades in after them, and then the voices were stilled.

The bodies of Elizabeth and her companions were recovered the next year. The remains of Mother Elizabeth were eventually interred in a Russian chapel in Jerusalem. In 1991 she was canonized by the Russian Orthodox Church.

See: Lily Emilia Clerkx, "St. Elizabeth: From Riches to Martyrdom," *In Communion* (Journal of the Orthodox Peace Fellowship), January 1998.

St. Josephine Bakhita
Ex-Slave and Nun (1869–1947)

"Seeing the sun, the moon, and the stars, I said to myself: Who could be the Master of these beautiful things? And I felt a great desire to see him, to know him, and to pay him homage."

Among the distinctive features of the pontificate of John Paul II was his keen interest in enlarging the field of canonized saints. In his first eighteen years as pope he canonized and beatified nearly a thousand saints — more than were canonized in the several previous centuries since the Council of Trent. Apart from his belief in the teaching value of holy lives, he was particularly interested in recognizing "local saints" — persons whose lives bear a special meaning for the churches he made a point of visiting around the world. Typical of these new saints was Sister Josephine Bakhita of Sudan, beatified on May 17, 1992.

Bakhita ("the fortunate one") was born in a village in the southern Sudan in 1869. When she was nine she was kidnapped and sold into slavery. Transferred from one master to another over a period of years, she experienced brutality in many forms. A turning point came in 1883 when she was sold to an Italian family who treated her with relative kindness and brought her back to Italy to work as a maid and nursemaid to their baby, Mimmina. Bakhita became devoted to the child. When Mimmina was old enough to be sent to a boarding school in Venice Bakhita accompanied her. The school was run by the Daughters of Charity, or "Canossian Sisters." It was there that Bakhita first heard the gospel and divined that it was God's will that she be free.

When, after nine months, Bakhita's mistress announced that they were returning to the Sudan, Bakhita expressed her intention to remain. The Signora professed to be hurt. Hadn't they always treated her as a member of the family? How could she now be so ungrateful? As difficult as it was to resist these entreaties, Bakhita remained firm in her resolution: "I am sure the Lord gave me strength at that moment," she later wrote, "because he wanted me for himself alone."

When pleading did not work the Signora tried another tack: she sued in court for the return of her "property." But the superior of the Canossian Sisters and the cardinal of Venice intervened and came to her defense. It was only thus that Bakhita discovered what no one had bothered to inform her of, namely, that slavery was illegal in Italy. She had been free all along.

And so Bakhita remained in Italy. On January 9, 1890, she was baptized, taking the name Josephine Bakhita. By this time she heard "more and more clearly the gentle voice of the Lord from the bottom of my heart, urging me to consecrate myself to God." She was accepted into the novitiate of the congregation that had sheltered her. Finally, in 1896 she made her religious vows.

Sister Josephine lived to the age of seventy-eight. She spent her life in simple tasks, cooking, sewing, serving as sacristan and doorkeeper. No work was unimportant when performed for "the Master" — her favorite word for God. She became famous for her quiet faith and the care she brought to assignments big and small. It was said that she had a gift for making the ordinary extraordinary. To those Sisters who were schoolteachers she said, "You teach catechism; I will stay in the chapel to pray for you that you may teach well."

She lived on through World War I and then World War II. By this time her reputation for holiness was so widespread in the town of Schio, where she lived, that she was invoked as a protection against falling bombs. She had assured the people that no bomb would damage the town, a promise that was fulfilled.

In her last years she became ill and could not leave her wheelchair. When a visiting bishop asked her what she did all day in her wheelchair, she replied, "What do I do? Exactly what you are doing — the will of God." Sister Josephine Bakhita died on February 8, 1947. She was canonized in 2000, the first native of the Sudan to be so recognized.

See: Alicia von Stamwitz, "Blessed Josephine Bakhita: Woman of Faith and Forgiveness," *Liguorian* (February 1993).

St. Katherine Drexel
Founder of the Sisters of the Blessed Sacrament
(1858–1955)

"Resolve: Generously and with no half-hearted, timorous dread of the opinions of Church and men to manifest my mission.... You have no time to occupy your thoughts with that complacency or consideration of what others will think. Your business is simply, 'What will my Father in heaven think?'"

Katherine Drexel came from one of the wealthiest families in America. Her father was an extremely successful banker, a Catholic of Austrian descent. Katherine did not know her mother, who died five weeks after her birth. But a year later her father remarried another eminent Catholic, Emma Bouvier, who exerted a strong influence on Katherine and her two sisters. When Francis Drexel died he established a trust for his three daughters of fourteen million dollars. Inspired by their Catholic faith, they all three regarded this fortune as an opportunity to glorify God through the service of others.

This was the great era of Catholic immigration, as American cities stretched to accommodate new arrivals from Europe. The church responded with an extraordinary system of schools, hospitals, orphanages, and other charitable institutions, proving to the world that Catholics knew how to "look after their own." There were certainly plenty of claims on the generosity of a young Catholic heiress. But Katherine Drexel's concern extended to those outside the church, indeed to those all but excluded from American society — namely, Indians and blacks. She began by endowing scores of schools on Indian reservations across the country. In 1878 during a private audience with Pope Leo XIII she begged the pope to send priests to serve the Indians. He responded, "Why not become a missionary yourself?"

At this point Katherine realized that it was not enough to share her wealth. God was calling her to give everything. Consequently she embarked on a long search to find a religious order corresponding to her own sense of mission. But when none could be found, she received the support of her bishop to establish her own religious congregation. In 1891 she was professed as the first member of the Sisters of the Blessed Sacrament for Indians and Colored People. Within the year ten other women had joined her order.

Though Katherine embraced a vow of personal poverty, she continued to administer the income from her trust — the enormous sum of $400,000 a year. She might well have spent the money to endow the establishments of her own congregation, but she insisted that her own Sisters rely on alms. The money would continue to be used to support other projects of service to Indians and blacks. Among her gifts, over time, were a total of a million dollars to the Bureau of Catholic Indian Missions and $100,000 a year to the support of mission schools on the reservations. In the 1920s she contributed $750,000 toward the founding of Xavier University in New Orleans, the first Catholic college established for blacks. All told she was personally responsible for establishing 145 Catholic missions and 12 schools for Indians, and 50 schools for black students.

Mother Drexel died on March 3, 1955, at the age of ninety-six, her life having spanned the era of slavery and the Indian wars to the dawn of the modern civil rights movement. It was a period in which blacks and Indians, the communities to which Mother Drexel devoted her life, were far from the consciousness of most American Catholics. Her charitable works did little directly to challenge the structures of racism and discrimination. But in the era of rigidly enforced racial segregation her work had a profound "witness value." The exceptional character of her commitment is reflected in a letter from her contemporary, Father Augustus Tolton, at that time the sole black priest in America:

> In the whole history of the Church in America we cannot find one person that has sworn to give her treasure for the sole benefit of the Colored and Indians. As I stand alone as the first Negro priest of America, so you, Mother Katherine, stand alone as the first one to make such a sacrifice for the cause of a downtrodden race.

Katherine Drexel was canonized by Pope John Paul II in 2000.

See: Sister Consuela Marie Duffy, S.B.S., *Katherine Drexel: A Biography* (Cornwell Heights, Pa.: Sisters of the Blessed Sacrament, 1966); Kenneth L. Woodward, *Making Saints* (New York: Simon & Schuster, 1990).

St. Katherine Drexel

Madeleine Delbrêl
Missionary and Activist (1904–1964)

"Lord, let the thick skin that covers me not be a hindrance to you. Pass through it. My eyes, my hands, my mouth are yours. This sad lady in front of me: here is my mouth for you to smile at her.... This smug young man, so dull, so hard: here is my heart, that thou may love him, more strongly than he has ever been loved before."

Madeleine Delbrêl was born on October 24, 1904, in southern France. Her father was a railroad worker. Slight (only four and a half feet tall) and nimble, she exuded an energy and passion for life that enlivened her every surrounding. Above all she had a passion for the absolute. Though she spent her youth as a confirmed atheist, when, at the age of twenty-four, she became convinced of God's existence, she saw no alternative but to dedicate her life to his service. Her conversion was an overwhelming, "bedazzling" experience that marked her forever.

Delbrêl briefly considered becoming a nun, but she ultimately discerned that her vocation was in the world. God might call some people to stand apart, she decided, but "there are those he leaves among the crowds.... These are the people who have an ordinary job, an ordinary household, or an ordinary celibacy. People with ordinary sicknesses, and ordinary times of grieving.... These are the people of ordinary life, the people we might meet on any street." Casting her lot with this anonymous crowd, she declared, "We, the ordinary people of the streets, believe with all our might that this street, this world, where God has placed us, is our place of holiness."

With several friends she conceived the idea of a small lay community dedicated to leading a contemplative Christian life in the midst of the world. For the sake of this vocation she prepared herself for three years with ardent discipline, quietly praying, studying scripture, and taking courses in social work. Finally, in 1933, with the blessing of her spiritual director, she and her companions set forth for Ivry, a working-class city near Paris and a stronghold of the French Communist Party.

From the start, the local pastor had trouble comprehending what these women were up to. Having expected that they would occupy themselves with parish duties, he was perplexed when they seemed more interested in spending time with their communist neighbors. Delbrêl and her companions were themselves struggling to find their way. In their engagement with the workers, who had been long estranged from the church, they felt they were undertaking a new kind of missionary work. They called themselves "missionaries without a boat" — not traveling overseas, but crossing the borders of faith to bear witness to the gospel in friendship and solidarity.

Over time they won their neighbors' trust. With the outbreak of World War II the city government even asked Delbrêl to oversee services for refugees flooding the town. She organized soup kitchens, clothing drives, and emergency shelters. In recognition of this service, the communist government wanted to give her a medal after the war, but she declined the honor.

In the meantime, wartime sufferings had broken down many of the historic barriers between the church and the working class, while revealing how much work remained to be done. Cardinal Suhard of Paris endorsed the view that historically Catholic France was now a "mission territory." Calling for a *Mission de France,* he established a seminary to train priests to work in factories alongside the poor. Delbrêl was invited to serve as a lay advisor. It was the beginning of what became the Worker Priest movement.

Delbrêl threw herself into this movement with all her vitality and enthusiasm. But the movement was short-lived. Conservative sectors of the church in France and Rome opposed this "compromise" with the secular world — particularly the strongly Marxist atmosphere of the trade unions. The experiment was eventually suppressed by the Vatican.

Delbrêl remained as committed as ever to her essential missionary project, building a bridge between the church and the secular world. Apart from any other accomplishment, such contact with unbelievers strengthened her own faith, forcing her, as she said, to be more authentic, to think critically, to avoid pious clichés. When asked how she prayed, she described her "Prayer of the Agenda." It was simply a heightened awareness of the presence of God in all the ordinary activities of life — whether meeting people, answering the phone, or running errands. In these ordinary circumstances, she insisted, a person could experience the deepest spiritual dimensions of life.

At last, with the arrival of Pope John XXIII ("a tiny miracle of God," as she called him) she lived to see the beginnings of a new season in the church. In many ways Delbrêl's spirit was embraced by the Second Vatican Council, especially in its affirmation of the special vocation of the laity. As Delbrêl put it, "We are called to be the visible body of Christ in the midst of the human body of society." In turn, she certainly would have embraced the opening words of *Gaudium et Spes,* the final document of the council, which she did not live to see: "The joy and hope, the grief and anguish, of the people of our time, especially of those who are poor or afflicted in any way, are the joy and hope, the grief and anguish of the followers of Christ as well."

But Delbrêl did not place her hopes in grand and historic events. The most significant events in the universe, she believed, were often small and seemingly *ordinary:*

Each tiny act is an extraordinary event, in which heaven is given to us, in which we are able to give heaven to others. It makes no difference what we do, whether we take in hand a broom or a pen. Whether we speak or keep silent. Whether we are sewing or holding a meeting, caring for a sick person or tapping away at the typewriter. Whatever it is, it's just the outer shell of an amazing inner reality: the soul's encounter, renewed at each moment in which the soul grows in grace and becomes ever more beautiful for her God. Is the doorbell ringing? Quick, open the door! It's God coming to love us. Is someone asking us to do something? Here you are! It's God coming to love us. Is it time to sit down for lunch? Let's go — it's God coming to love us. Let's let him.

The end came for Madeline Delbrêl as she worked at her desk. She died on October 13, 1964, two weeks before her sixtieth birthday.

See: Madeleine Delbrêl, *We, the Ordinary People of the Streets* (Grand Rapids, Mich.: William B. Eerdmans, 2000); Charles Mann, *Madeleine Delbrêl: A Life beyond Boundaries* (San Francisco: New World Press, 2000).

Little Sister Magdeleine of Jesus
Founder of the Little Sisters of Jesus (1898–1989)

"As you work, as you come and go, as you pass among the crowds, to be a contemplative will mean simply that you try to turn to Jesus within you and enter into conversation with him, as with the one you love most in the world."

While growing up in France, Madeleine Hutin felt a powerful devotion to Jesus, but she could find no religious congregation that reflected her sense of vocation. Then, in her twenties, she happened upon a biography of Charles de Foucauld, the French explorer, priest, and finally desert father who died in North Africa in 1916.

Foucauld had envisioned a new kind of contemplative life, rooted in the world of the poor and based on the "hidden years" that Jesus spent as a carpenter in Nazareth. In his hermitage in the Sahara, he had conceived of a "fraternity" of men and women who would live among their Muslim neighbors as brothers and sisters, embracing poverty, manual labor, and a spirit of prayer. Thus, they would proclaim the gospel, not with their words, "but with their lives." For many years Foucauld had patiently prepared the way for followers who never came. In the end he died alone, his message bequeathed to the appreciation of a later generation. Decades later, it was discovered by Madeleine Hutin, among others. Upon reading his biography she determined immediately to adopt Foucauld as her spiritual guide and to make his vision her own.

Because of poor health and family obligations, Hutin was not able to make a beginning until 1936, when, at the age of thirty-eight, she finally set sail for Algiers. She embarked with few if any plans, determined to trust herself entirely to providence. Soon she was introduced to Father René Voillaume, who had been converted by the same biography of Foucauld and whose Little Brothers of Jesus had been living in the desert since 1933. When she confided to him her sense of vocation, he responded with encouragement as well as invaluable assistance in obtaining the support of local church authorities. In 1939 the new congregation, the Little Sisters of Jesus, was finally established under the leadership of Little Sister Magdeleine, as she was henceforth known.

The word "Little" had special meaning for Magdeleine. During the early years of her vocation she had experienced a number of intense visions inspired by her meditations on the Infant Jesus. The humility, weakness, and vulnerability of a baby were the disguises under which the world's savior first appeared. And it seemed appropriate to her that this baby should also be the inspiration and model for those who wished to bear witness to divine love among the poorest and most powerless of the world.

It was years before the congregation was fully recognized by Rome. Along the way it was necessary to overcome many doubts and criticisms arising from the originality of Magdeleine's vision. Her Little Sisters were neither enclosed contemplatives nor were they engaged in traditional apostolic activities. They lived in small "fraternities," some consisting of no more than a couple of Sisters. While maintaining an intense commitment to contemplative prayer, they endeavored to enter fully into the life and culture of their poor neighbors. Among other things this meant supporting themselves by common labor. Instead of a traditional habit, they wore a simple denim habit adorned with a cross. What was essential to the Little Sisters was that wherever they lived they should find themselves among the very poor. As for misunderstandings, she noted that "the world looks for efficiency more than for the unobtrusiveness of the hidden life." Thus, "Bethlehem and Nazareth will always remain a mystery to it."

In the beginning, basing her vision on the literal model of Brother Charles, Magdeleine had conceived of the mission of the Little Sisters exclusively in relation to the Muslims of North Africa. It was there that the congregation took root and flourished. But gradually Magdeleine enlarged her vision to conceive of a universal mission. Hence the fraternities spread throughout the world, attracting women of all races and nationalities. By the time of her death there were 280 fraternities with 1,400 Little Sisters from 64 different countries. These included Little Sisters who traveled with gypsy caravans in Europe, who lived with nomadic circus troupes, and who even volunteered to be incarcerated as prisoners. There were communities among the pygmies of Cameroon, in remote Eskimo villages in Alaska, among boat people in Southeast Asia, and in the slums of London, Beirut, and Washington, D.C. In her later life Magdeleine felt a special call to bear witness in the communist countries of the Eastern bloc. Driving in a converted minivan, she made dozens of trips throughout Eastern Europe, including eighteen trips to Russia. Quietly she was able to establish fraternities in a number of these countries. Whatever the setting, the aim of the Little Sisters was not to evangelize in a formal sense but to serve modestly as a kind of leaven in the midst of the world, thereby imparting a spirit of love.

In 1949 Little Sister Magdeleine formally relinquished leadership of the congregation. She preferred to play an informal role as mother to her Sisters, traveling constantly around the globe rather than confining herself to the administration of a growing congregation. Although she had been sickly in her youth, she remained remarkably robust into her old age, continuing to do manual labor well into her eighties and undertaking her final exhausting trip to the Soviet Union at the age of ninety-one. She died later that year on November 6, 1989.

See: Kathryn Spink, *The Call of the Desert: A Biography of Little Sister Magdeleine of Jesus* (London: Darton, Longman and Todd, 1993).

Mev Puleo
Witness of Solidarity (1963–1996)

"When I was in my early teens, a thought took hold of me: Jesus didn't die to save us from suffering — he died to teach us how to suffer. . . . Sometimes I actually mean it. I'd rather die young, having lived a life crammed with meaning, than to die old, even in security, but without meaning."

So wrote Mev Puleo as a college student at St. Louis University. Years later, her words were remembered by a former professor and close friend, Father John Kavanaugh, who presided over her funeral in 1996. He added the comment, "Such are the dangers of our high and holy desires." Her friends understood the obvious: She had indeed died young after having lived a life "crammed with meaning." Under the tutelage of Jesus and the poor she had even learned to suffer. And she had left many others, only remotely touched by her loving spirit, an enduring challenge to recognize and treasure the preciousness of life.

From a young age Mev felt a strong sense of "religious wonder" in the presence of nature and other people. From her parents, devout Catholics, she also learned that the practice of Christian faith should involve service to others. But a turning point in Mev's life came at the age of fourteen when she accompanied her parents on a trip to Brazil. She was riding on a bus up a steep hill to view the famous statue of Christ the Redeemer that overlooks the city of Rio de Janeiro. On one side of the hill she could see the opulent homes, posh hotels, and immaculate beaches enjoyed by the rich. The view on the other side told a different story, of "ramshackle homes, children in rags, young and old begging for our coins."

Certain questions were inevitable: "What does it mean to be a Christian — a follower of the way of Jesus — in a world of contradictions and conflicts? What does it mean to be on the way to Jesus when I view the world of poverty from an air-conditioned tour bus?" Such questions make an impact on the conscience of a sensitive young person. But in Mev's case they laid the foundation for her later vocation. Over time she felt the call to create a bridge between the different worlds she had viewed from that bus.

While a college student she worked at the St. Louis Catholic Worker house. She went on to earn graduate degrees in theology. But her studies only confirmed her belief in the need for a new language of faith, a language addressed not only to the head but to the heart. As she said,

"I believe less in theology and more in God, because I believe that in theology there's only so much you can say about God."

Early in her life Mev had discovered a great talent for photography. In trips to Brazil, El Salvador, Haiti, and elsewhere in the Third World, her photographs documented the life, struggles, and humanity of the poor. Her aim was "to revere the human spirit and bridge the distance between persons." She gave much thought to the spiritual aspects of her art. "The camera lens," she wrote, "is the eye of my soul, through which I touch the world and the world touches me." But she also acknowledged the ethical ambiguities of photography. Often, she admitted to having asked herself, " 'Dare I invade their lives, steal this moment?' Yet how can I *not* share these children with the world, bringing them back with me to hearts who might receive them, voices who might speak for them?"

Mev was not simply touched by the suffering of the poor. She also identified with their struggle for justice and liberation. In her travels throughout the Third World she was exposed to a new model of the church arising from the faith of the poor. She conducted scores of interviews with grassroots activists, prophetic bishops, and liberation theologians. She was fully committed to their vision of a church and a world renewed in the light of God's reign. Some of this work was reflected in her book on the church in Brazil, *The Struggle Is One*, but she also carried the message through photo exhibits, lectures, and a video completed in the last months of her life. Her photographs were published widely in the religious press, and they won her several awards.

No summary of these achievements adequately reflects Mev's extraordinary personality — her enthusiasm for life, her capacity for joy. Her photography expressed a profound ability to connect with other people. She had a contemplative eye, a knack for penetrating to the spiritual essence of things and especially people, in whom she saw reflections of the face of God. In 1992 she married Mark Chmiel, a fellow theology student. It was a marriage filled with love and promise.

But in 1994 Mev was found to have a malignant brain tumor. The initial prognosis, after surgery, was that she had six months to live. She was determined to remain fully alive for each day that remained, and her final months were filled with many accomplishments. She published her book, completed her video, and gave numerous lectures. In 1995 she received the U.S. Catholic Award for furthering the cause of women in the Catholic Church.

But ultimately she left her friends a deeper gift in the example of her own faith, courage, and hope as she completed her earthly journey. As Father Kavanaugh noted, "She had wanted to give the poor a face, a voice. She always wanted to be identified with them. And so it came to pass: by the time of her last days, you could see them all in her face — the poor of Bosnia, the hungry of Haiti, the powerless of Brazil. She who gave them voice, lost hers. She who helped us see their faces, could finally see no more.... She became the poor she loved."

Mev Puleo died on January 12, 1996, at the age of thirty-two.

See: Mev Puleo, *The Struggle Is One: Voices and Visions of Liberation* (Albany, N.Y.: SUNY Press, 1994); John F. Kavanaugh, with photographs by Mev Puleo, *Faces of Poverty, Faces of Christ* (Maryknoll, N.Y.: Orbis Books, 1991).

Ade Bethune
Catholic Worker Artist (1914–2002)

"The saints are Christ. In their heroic deeds shines Christ's example, reflected and multiplied through time and space. Their death is his death; their love is his love, pure and selfless. Their works are his work of mercy and forgiveness. Whether in death or in work, in word or silence, theirs is the Spirit of Christ. Their fruits are love, peace, joy."

Adelaide de Bethune owed her professional name to a typographical error. She had sent a selection of drawings to the *Catholic Worker* in its early days, signing her name "A. de Bethune." When this was rendered "Ade," she liked the sound of it, as well as the opportunity to shed her aristocratic heritage. And so *Ade* she became. But she owed more than a name to the Catholic Worker. Through her association with the movement she found her vocation and mission in life — indeed, as she put it, her "salvation."

This turning point came when she was a nineteen-year-old art student in New York, "dreaming of color and light in stained glass." She had emigrated with her family from Belgium in 1928. They were once prosperous, but their fortunes had been greatly reduced by World War I, and now the family lived in virtual poverty. Ade's interests were centered entirely on arts and crafts. Nevertheless, she was intrigued when some friends told her about a new movement called the Catholic Worker that sought to relate the gospel to social issues. They had a newspaper, and they lived by their convictions — feeding the hungry, harboring the homeless, and otherwise practicing the "works of mercy."

When she saw a copy of the paper she was attracted by its message, though she found it visually drab. On her own initiative Ade produced a series of illustrations that captured the spirit of the movement. One of these was a picture of Joseph and Mary being evicted from the inn in Bethlehem by an irate innkeeper. The others depicted saints in modern clothes, going about their everyday business. A few days after mailing these off, she decided to visit the Worker headquarters on East 15th Street, bringing along two shopping bags of clothes to donate. As she stood bashfully at the doorway, "a tall, bony older woman with straight, graying hair" strode toward her. It was Dorothy Day, then in her mid-thirties. After glancing sympathetically at Ade's bulging shopping bags, Day said, "I'm terribly sorry, we have no more room. But we will try to find another place for you." At last Ade managed to stammer: "I'm the girl who sent the pictures." "Oh, you are?" the tall woman replied. Immediately she took out a prayer book and began discussing the saints whose feast days fell in the next month — St. Catherine of Siena and John Bosco. Could she make pictures of them as well? Immediately, Ade saw a great program open up before her. "In the lives of two actual holy people of the fourteenth and nineteenth centuries, this energetic woman had sketched a lifetime plan for me."

For Dorothy Day, Ade's arrival was likewise auspicious. She had been longing for an artist who could communicate in images the ideas that she and her mentor, Peter Maurin, were striving to convey in words: the dignity of work, the social implications of the Incarnation, the radical spirit of the works of mercy. With their stark simplicity Ade's images perfectly captured the Worker's message. Ade even took it upon herself to redesign the masthead of the paper. In the middle of the new masthead there was a figure of Christ standing before the cross, his arms embracing two workers — one black and one white — their hands joined in solidarity. (For the fiftieth anniversary of the paper in 1983, she updated the image, substituting a female farmworker for one of the male figures.)

In the years to come Ade would redefine the character of modern religious art. Apart from her *Catholic Worker* illustrations she worked in virtually every medium — sculptures, stained-glass windows, liturgical vestments, bronze medallions, and mosaics. But whatever her medium, her vocation as an artist always served her religious vision.

This vision had roots in her early life. She described a moment of deep conversion that occurred on Holy Thursday in 1934, soon after her encounter with Dorothy Day. She was wandering through the Lower East Side around sunset. The streets were crowded with pushcarts. From one of them a little man was selling tiny tangerines. "My heart opened to love the man who was selling them. Somehow a light bathed these people in my mind. I could see that God loved them, so I had to love them too. A great spirit of love for humankind, for people, came upon me."

Ade later built up a studio in Newport, Rhode Island, where she took in apprentices. She taught not only art and design but basic crafts and household arts as well. As Day put it, "To Ade...the holy man was the whole man, the man of integrity, who not only tried to change the world, but to live in it as it was." (Day sent her own teenage daughter, Tamar, to live and study with Ade for a year.) Peter Maurin had spoken of the need for a "philosophy of work." To Ade this meant simply "the love of work." Everything she did reflected this spirit. Day called it "a sense of the sacramentality of life, the goodness of things." It was a lesson Ade had learned from the saints she depicted.

At first, she said, she had tried to concentrate on "worker saints." But then she realized that all saints were workers; all of them engaged not only in the chores and business of daily life, but also in the works of mercy. They showed us that there is a road to holiness in everything we do, provided we do it with love:

> When I am hungry and I eat a good meal for the glory of God, it is a work of mercy.... It is all the more a work of mercy when I grow, reap, peel, cook, or serve a square meal for my family or wash the dishes afterwards, or sweep the kitchen, or take out the garbage. It is all the more a work of mercy when I do it for strangers, and still more so when I do it for my enemies.

Ade worked until the day she died on May 1, 2002, the feast of St. Joseph the Worker. She was eighty-eight. She was buried in a coffin she had designed and built for herself, and kept always in her bedroom. The lid bore an inscription in her fine hand: "Unto thy faithful, Lord, life is changed, not taken away; and the abode of this earthly sojourn being dissolved, an eternal dwelling is prepared in heaven."

See: Judith Stoughton, *Proud Donkey of Schaerbeek: Ade Bethune, Catholic Worker Artist* (St. Cloud, Minn.: North Star Press, 1988); Dorothy Day, *The Long Loneliness* (New York: Harper & Row, 1952).

Ade Bethune

BLESSED ARE
THOSE WHO MOURN

A devoted disciple • a victim soul • a "holy fool" • a lovelorn abbess •
a philosopher and martyr • an unhappily married nun • a mystic with a
"gift of tears" • the mothers of the "disappeared" • a penitent murderer

Of all the Beatitudes this is in some ways the most mysterious. Mourning may be a natural response to suffering and loss, but it is not generally regarded as a virtue. After a point, we are usually advised to "get help," to do whatever it takes to cope and move on. As a priest remarked to the medieval mystic Margery Kempe, when told that her weeping was prompted by the sufferings of Christ: "Woman, Jesus is long since dead."

But if there is a time for rejoicing and a time for moving on, there is also a time when mourning is the only sane and appropriate attitude. Under those circumstances, when the world advises us to "get over it," to smile and "be happy," that is a true invitation to despair. Jesus' blessing is not an endorsement of chronic depression. Addressing the spirit of discipleship, it warns us against becoming jaded or making an easy peace with the miseries of the world.

Many saints were especially attuned to the pain around them. This was their gift as well as their cross. Jesus did not urge such mourners to put their sorrows behind them, to exchange their hearts of flesh for hearts of stone. But he did make them a promise: "They shall be comforted."

41

Hagar the Egyptian
Slave Woman

"Thou art a God of seeing."

In the biblical narrative in Genesis, Hagar was an Egyptian slave who belonged to Sarah, the wife of Abraham. When Sarah was unable to provide Abraham with a child, she proposed that her husband beget a child with her slave. It was a solution permitted under the law. Presumably Hagar had no choice in the matter. So she served as a surrogate mother for her mistress. But by the time she was pregnant Sarah apparently regretted the arrangement. Sarah treated her so harshly that she tried to flee. But an angel of Yahweh appeared to her and urged her to return and bear her child. She was promised, like Abraham, descendants so numerous that "they cannot be numbered for multitude." And she was told that she should name her child Ishmael, which means "God hears." Hagar in wonder named the source of this annunciation: "Thou art a God of seeing.... Have I really seen God and remained alive after seeing him?"

Ishmael, the son of Hagar and Abraham, was duly born. But after many years another child of God's promise was born to Sarah and Abraham. Sarah was now displeased at the thought that her son, Isaac, should be an equal heir with the son of her bondswoman. At her insistence Abraham sent Hagar and her son alone into the wilderness — a shocking deed, even if mitigated, in the text, by God's assurance that no harm would come to them.

Hagar and Ishmael wandered in the desert heat until their water supply was finished. Then Hagar put the boy under a bush and wandered off alone, unable to bear the sight of her child's death. But God heard the tears of Ishmael and comforted Hagar, assuring her that her son would be the father of a great nation. "Then God opened her eyes, and she saw a well of water; and she went and filled the skin with water, and gave the lad a drink."

Though Hagar is not the main protagonist in the story of Abraham and Sarah, she plays an important role in the characterization of God. Though she is an outsider, a foreigner, a woman of no account, a discarded slave in the wilderness, it is yet she who "sees" God and names him in turn as the God who sees. Her experience discloses furthermore that Yahweh is a God of life and liberation who hears the voice of the oppressed. Thus, her deliverance in the desert prefigures the later deliverance of Abraham's descendants from slavery in Egypt. Hagar is a witness to the power of God who "makes a way out of no way."

See: Genesis 16:1–15, 21:1–21; Delores S. Williams, *Sisters in the Wilderness: The Challenge of Womanist God-Talk* (Maryknoll, N.Y.: Orbis Books, 1993).

The Samaritan Woman
Evangelist (first century)

"Give me this water, that I may never be thirsty."

As Jesus passed through the land of the Samaritans, he stopped by a village well (see John 4:1–42). It was midday and he was "weary from his journey." When a Samaritan woman came to draw water from the well, Jesus asked her for a drink. At first she was astonished by his attention. As a woman and a Samaritan — a people despised by the Jews for their unorthodox religious practice — she expected only scorn. After she had voiced her astonishment, he responded in a puzzling way: "If you knew the gift of God and who it is that is saying to you, 'Give me a drink,' you would have asked him and he would have given you living water."

At first she was confused by this symbolic language. But then Jesus took their conversation to a different level. "Everyone who drinks of this water will thirst again," he said, "but whoever drinks of the water that I shall give him will never thirst; the water that I shall give him will become in him a spring of water welling up to eternal life."

With surprising suddenness a conversation begun with Jesus' thirst had turned to the woman's own existential thirst for a deeper, more meaningful life. "Sir," she said, "give me this water, that I may not thirst."

In response Jesus reached out to touch her most guarded secret. He asked her to call her husband. "I have no husband," she replied. "You are right in saying, 'I have no husband,'" Jesus told her, "for you have had five husbands, and he whom you now have is not your husband; this you said truly."

We can only imagine the mysterious significance of this brief statement. But for the Samaritan woman it seemed to sum up the whole story of her life, a life that had evidently left her thirsting for something more.

She dared to interview him about religious matters — the differences between Jews and Samaritans regarding styles and modes of worship — but he brushed these questions aside, challenging her to attend to the truth unfolding before her eyes.

"I know that the Messiah is coming; when he comes, he will show us all things," she said. That moment had arrived: "I who speak to you am he," he answered.

It took no more than a minute or two, this encounter between passing strangers in the heat of the day. Suddenly an ordinary well had become holy ground. A woman, burdened by shame, who drew her water alone after all the other village women had left, was suddenly raised up — a different person, washed clean by a new kind of living water.

Immediately she went to tell everyone what had happened: "Come see a man who told me all that I ever did. Can this be the Christ?"

This woman was one of the first recorded evangelists in the Gospels. As John records, "Many Samaritans from that city believed in him because of the woman's testimony, 'He told me all that I ever did.'"

The Anointer of Bethany
(first century)

"Truly, I say to you, wherever the gospel is preached in the whole world, what she has done will be told in memory of her." —Mark 14:9

One of the great women of the Gospels is remembered by her deed alone; her name is totally lost. St. Mark relates that as Jesus sat at table in Bethany an anonymous woman proceeded to anoint his head with precious oil. As a gesture of hospitality, the deed itself provokes no comment. What gives rise to grumbling is the extraordinary value of the oil expended — virtually the equivalent of a year's wages. Could not the money have been spent on the poor?

But Jesus stills the complainers and accepts the woman's gesture. In fact he does more. He underscores the prophetic timeliness of her deed and so names it as one of the exceptional and defining moments of the gospel. A similar moment occurred with Peter's famous confession: "You are the Christ [the Messiah/Anointed One]." In that episode and elsewhere, however, Jesus had shown a determination to correct the disciples' understanding of what it means to be God's Anointed One: he will have to suffer and die. The pattern of this interaction is repeated

The Anointer of Bethany

several times. Jesus is acclaimed as the Messiah; this is misunderstood by his disciples in terms of simple power and glory; Jesus redefines his identity in terms of suffering and death.

As he approaches Jerusalem the way is strewn with portents of his messianic authority: the waiting colt, the entry into the royal city with its overtones of the coronation of Solomon. Now in the climax of his ministry he is anointed with oil. The extravagance of the gesture points to its prophetic-symbolic significance. Once again the exchange between master and disciples echoes previous controversies: Jesus the Anointed is anointed; the disciples do not comprehend the action, or comprehend it falsely (a waste of precious oil); Jesus accepts the form of this symbolic acclamation, but uses the situation once again to reinterpret the meaning of his Messiahship — his mission — in terms of suffering and death. "She has done what she could; she has anointed my body beforehand for my burial."

Thus, Jesus accepts the import of the woman's "christological" gesture in a way that he could not, without qualification, accept the naive confession of Peter. In her wordless act of compassion she has recognized in Jesus, the Poor Man par excellence, the Christ who is about to die. She alone has responded appropriately. Though her name would be forgotten, Jesus holds her forth as the faithful disciple whose deed should be remembered wherever the gospel is preached.

See: Mark 14:3–9; Elisabeth Schüssler Fiorenza, *In Memory of Her* (New York: Crossroad, 1983).

St. Monica
Widow (332–387)

"Nothing is far from God."

It would be nice to suppose that behind every great saint there is a saintly mother. If so, few have been so ably memorialized by their children as St. Monica, the mother of St. Augustine. In his *Confessions* he gives her special credit for his conversion, noting that "in the flesh she brought me to birth in this world: in her heart she brought me to birth in your eternal life."

Monica, like her son, was an African, born near Carthage of Christian parents. Though she was devout in her faith, her parents arranged her marriage to a non-Christian, Patricius. It seems their relationship was marked more by mutual respect than warmth. Nevertheless, before his death, Patricius followed Monica's pious example and was received into the church. They had three children, of whom Augustine was the eldest. Augustine's account suggests that from the moment of his birth in 354 until her death thirty-three years later, Monica's relationship with her brilliant and sometimes prodigal son was the center of her life.

She had great hopes for Augustine and encouraged his academic ambitions. But her hopes extended beyond his worldly success, and she suffered greatly from the fact that he did not share her faith. Her sufferings were compounded by his amoral conduct and later by his immersion in the Manichean cult. She was consoled, however, by a prophetic vision in which an angel assured her, "Your son is with you." When she repeated this to Augustine, he replied flippantly that this might just as well foretell her own apostasy. No, she corrected, "He did not say that I was with you: he said that you were with me."

She did not cease to suffer on his behalf, praying constantly for his conversion and weeping over his sins. Finally, a sympathetic bishop reassured her: "Go now, I beg of you: it is not possible that the son of so many tears should perish."

When Augustine left for Rome to study rhetoric, Monica was determined to travel with him. Though Augustine tricked her and left without saying goodbye, Monica went in pursuit. She found him finally in Milan, where he confronted her with the joyous news that he wished to become a Christian. They both received spiritual direction from the holy bishop of Milan, St. Ambrose. Augustine's baptism came in 387.

Soon thereafter they traveled to Ostia, awaiting a ship for their return to North Africa. Augustine describes a conversation there that lasted most of a day concerning the mysteries of faith and the joys of heaven. The beauty of the moment was such that "for one fleeting instant" they seemed to touch the eternal Wisdom for which they both longed. Monica sensed that her life was drawing to a close. She confided to her son that she found no further pleasure in this life. "There was one reason, and one alone, why I wished to remain a little longer in this life, and that was to see you a Catholic Christian before I died. God has granted my wish.... What is left for me to do in this world?" In fact, within days she fell mortally ill. When asked whether she did not fear dying so far from home, she replied, "Nothing is far from God."

Her death at the age of fifty-five left Augustine bereft. After describing her passing, he adds a poignant reflection on his futile effort to restrain his tears. As a Christian, he felt on one level that such an outpouring of grief was an ill reflection on his faith. But at the thought of his mother, and all she had suffered on his behalf, he could not hold back any longer: "This was the mother, now dead and hidden awhile from my sight, who had wept over me for many years so that I might live in your sight." If any reader might charge him with sin, he begs, "let him not mock at me, but weep himself, if his charity is great. Let him weep for my sins to you, the Father of all the brothers of your Christ."

See: Augustine, *Confessions*, trans. R. S. Pine-Coffin (Baltimore: Penguin, 1961).

Heloise
Abbess of the Convent of the Paraclete (1100–1164)

"You know, beloved, as the whole world knows,
how much I have lost in you."

The story of Heloise, inseparable from that of her beloved Abelard, is one of the most memorable episodes in medieval literature. Though it has been frequently recounted, the story retains its poignant mystery.

Heloise, a beautiful and exceptionally intelligent girl, was raised by her uncle Fulbert, a canon of the cathedral in Paris. Such was her brilliance that Fulbert hired the most famous scholar in France, the renowned Peter Abelard, to be her tutor. Heloise was about seventeen, while Abelard, then at the peak of his powers, was in his mid-thirties. In his later account of their affair, Abelard blamed himself for seducing Heloise. Nevertheless, however ignoble his initial intentions, the two were soon passionate lovers. Their lack of discretion led to tragic consequences.

Heloise became pregnant and bore a son. Fulbert was enraged, and he was not appeased by the couple's secret marriage. Hoping to resolve the conflict, Abelard sent Heloise to a convent. In the meantime, however, Fulbert's men broke into Abelard's chamber one night and violently castrated him. In agony and shame Abelard retired quickly to a monastery, intending never again to see his wife or the son she had borne.

Years passed. Abelard had suffered much, both from his public humiliation and a series of bruising theological controversies. But as a monk he had gradually regained a good deal of his former renown. He had even had some indirect contact with Heloise. Having learned that her religious community was without a home, he established them in the Oratory of the Paraclete, which he had founded. There remained, however, much unresolved business between them.

In 1132 Abelard wrote a letter to a fellow monk, a "History of My Misfortunes," in which he recounted in intimate detail the story of his relationship with Heloise and its tragic denouement. The text found its way to Heloise, now abbess of the convent in which she had so long lived. It was many years since she had taken her final vows as a nun, but the wounds of her abandonment by Abelard had never healed. In his self-centered "History" she was shocked to find another betrayal of their relationship, and so at long last she was moved to break her silence.

In a long letter she addressed him with blunt irony: "To her master, or rather her father, husband, or rather brother; his handmaid, or rather his daughter, wife, or rather sister; to Abelard, Heloise." She described her emotions upon reading his letter — pity for all his sufferings, mixed, however, with a certain resentment. What of *her* sufferings?

> Why, after our entry into religion, which was your decision alone, have I been so neglected and forgotten by you? ... It was not any sense of vocation which brought me as a young girl to accept the austerities of the cloister, but your bidding alone, and if I deserve no gratitude from you, you may judge for yourself how my labors are in vain. I can expect no reward for this from God, for it is certain that I have done nothing as yet for love of him.

In responding Abelard tried to turn her bitter thoughts to some spiritual resolution. Their love could not be. She should try to love him in Christ. Heloise in turn accused herself of hypocrisy. The world thought her devout and chaste when all the while her body burned with the memory of their illicit union. It was for love of him that she had taken the veil: "Look at the unhappy life I lead, pitiable beyond any other, if in this world I must endure so much in vain, with no hope of future reward." Abelard urged her still to accept their condition as a fact, and to seek in suffering the path to sanctification.

At this point Heloise abruptly changed course. She gave up her personal appeals and asked him instead to give her a rule and instruction for her monastic community. Obviously relieved, Abelard responded with several long treatises. They never again referred to their common history.

Abelard died in 1142 in the midst of a theological dispute that brought him close to official condemnation. His abbot arranged for him to be buried in the abbey church of Heloise's community. She lived on for another twenty-one years and died on May 16, 1164. Her body was placed beside her husband's.

Over the centuries Heloise and Abelard have attracted their respective champions. Certainly Heloise was one of the great women intellectuals and writers of the Middle Ages. Was she also, as some have suggested, a kind of saint? The answer depends to some extent on whether one accepts, at face value, her own assessment of her condition. Did she ever achieve the peace of mind to which Abelard had urged her? Is that the best criterion of holiness?

Under her administration the Paraclete became one of the great religious communities of Europe, and Heloise was widely revered as a wise and holy abbess. Is it possible, as Etienne Gilson has said, that "Heloise did not know everything about her own situation"? Because she would not renounce her human love for the love of God, she believed herself a hypocrite. But who can say whether God desired such renunciation? Perhaps it was her insistence on the integrity of her love — even at the cost of great suffering — that was her own path to sanctification. In any case it was sufficient to sustain her through a lifetime of prayer and service.

In returning Abelard's body to the Paraclete, Peter the Venerable offered a touching acknowledgment of Heloise's claims, both in this world and in the light of eternity: "Christ cherishes him in your place, indeed as a second you, and he will restore him to you of his grace on the day that the Lord shall come down from heaven. "

See: *The Letters of Abelard and Heloise* (New York: Penguin, 1974); Elizabeth Hamilton, *Heloise* (Garden City, N.Y.: Doubleday, 1967); Etienne Gilson, *Heloise and Abelard* (Ann Arbor: University of Michigan Press, 1960).

Bd. Angela of Foligno
Franciscan Mystic (1248–1309)

" 'Lord,' I cried, 'tell me what thou dost want of me; I am all thine.' But there was no answer, and I prayed from Matins till Terce — and then I saw and heard."

One of the great legacies of St. Francis was the foundation of his Third Order, a movement of lay followers of the Franciscan rule who chose to remain in the world rather than adopt an enclosed religious life. Its members were attracted from all walks of life — even queens like Elizabeth of Hungary and Elizabeth of Portugal. With their spirit of poverty and their zeal for the apostolic life these Franciscan tertiaries had an enormous influence on the religious and social life of the Middle Ages. Angela of Foligno, mystic and theologian, was one of the remarkable members of this spiritual family.

Angela came from a wealthy background. Her early life was given over to worldly frivolity and pleasure-seeking. She married a rich man and had three sons. But it was an existence without higher purpose. By the time she was thirty-seven she found her life such a burden that she prayed to St. Francis for some relief. The next day she went to church and heard an unfamiliar preacher, a Franciscan friar named Brother Arnold, whose sermon made a tremendous impression. She felt impelled to make her confession to him, after which she decided to transform her life.

Before long, the opportunity for a radical change came about through tragic circumstances — the loss of her entire family during an outbreak of plague. Through her loss Angela discerned the hand of God leading her to a life of penance and prayer. While standing before a crucifix she was moved, in a gesture reminiscent of Francis, to strip off all her fine clothing and to offer her life to Christ's service. During a subsequent pilgrimage to Assisi she was overwhelmed by an experience of the love of God. She gave away all her property, joined the Third Order of St. Francis, and resolved to live on alms.

Brother Arnold, who remained her confessor, was initially suspicious of her dramatic conversion and of the extravagant mystical experiences that followed. At some point, however, he became convinced of the divine origin of her wisdom and revelations, and their roles were reversed. Ultimately he became her devoted scribe and disciple. In the verbatim accounts of her discourse, Angela recounts the progress of her spiritual journey, submitting her motivations to careful scrutiny, and describing the constant temptations that assail her on her path. But she also describes in vivid detail a series of experiences in which she witnesses the power, the humility, the justice, and the love of God. Most of all she describes her own sense of having experienced a deep communion with God in the private "cell" of her soul, an experience of such intimacy that it exists beyond the realm of joy and suffering.

And yet Angela's communion with God did not absent her from concern for others. "The world," she said, "is great with God." In time

Bd. Angela of Foligno

she gathered around herself a family of Franciscan tertiaries, both men and women, for whom she served as spiritual mother. In the spirit of Francis, she maintained a standard of strict poverty. This was a form of identification with Christ, but it was also a constant reminder to remain sensitive to the needs of others.

One Holy Thursday she exhorted her companions, "Let us go and look for Christ our Lord. We will go to the hospital and perhaps among the sick and suffering we shall find Him." She had them beg for food, which they brought to the hospital: "And so we offered food to these poor sick people and then we washed the feet of the women and the men's hands, as they lay lonely and forsaken on their wretched pallets." Thus, she concluded, they had successfully fulfilled their quest to find Christ on that Holy Thursday.

Angela eventually died peacefully, surrounded by her spiritual children, on January 4, 1309.

See: Paul Lachance, ed., *Angela of Foligno: Complete Works*, Classics of Western Spirituality (New York: Paulist, 1993).

Bd. Lydwina of Schiedam
Patron of Sufferers (1380–1433)

"Meditation on the Passion and reception of the Eucharist became, as it were, the two arms with which Lydwina embraced her Beloved."
— John Brugman, Lydwina's first biographer

There is hardly any saint whose life was unmarked by suffering. In this, they shared in the human condition. But in their sufferings, as many of them recognized, they also shared most intimately in the experience of Christ. In the light of the cross their suffering was endowed with a deeper purpose and meaning. It might become a potent force, benefiting others and bearing untold fruit in the wider spiritual order. Inspired by such reasoning, certain saints have even prayed for affliction, or imposed it on themselves through rigorous self-punishment. But for others, like Lydwina of Schiedam, it came unbidden. Her sanctity was expressed in her response to circumstances beyond her control.

One of nine children, Lydwina was born in 1380 to a poor family in the small Dutch town of Schiedam. On a winter's day when she was fifteen she had an accident while skating on the frozen canal. At first she seemed to have suffered only a few broken ribs — no cause for great alarm. But her condition rapidly deteriorated, inaugurating an illness that would leave her an invalid for the next forty years. Though she received the best medical care available, nothing brought any relief; in fact, her symptoms only grew more alarming and even repulsive.

In time, at the urging of her parish priest, Lydwina began to meditate on the sufferings of Christ, striving to unite her own sufferings with his. Through this reflection she gradually perceived a wider meaning in her suffering. This was her vocation: to bear her sufferings with courage and faith as a loving sacrifice for the sins of others.

Before long, word of Lydwina's suffering and faith spread widely. Pilgrims came from great distances to witness someone so intimately united with the passion of Christ. Doctors too came to study her mysterious symptoms, though none could recommend anything that would reduce her pain. For her part, Lydwina experienced visions in which she visited the Holy Land and held conversations with Christ and his Mother. She was credited with healing miracles and gifts of prophecy.

And yet she also had her detractors. One parish priest thought she was a fraud. He accused her of diabolical delusions and refused to give her Holy Communion. Eventually, however, a church inquiry upheld her good faith and restored her access to the Eucharist. In fact, as many would attest, the Eucharist constituted virtually her entire food for the last nineteen years of her life — one of the many extraordinary signs that accompanied her witness.

At last Lydwina's sufferings came to an end. She died on April 14, 1433. She was beatified over four hundred years later in 1890, at which time she was named the patron of all those who suffer for the sins of others.

Margery Kempe
Mystic and Pilgrim (1373–1438?)

"And this creature wept and sobbed as plenteously as though she had seen our Lord with her bodily eyes suffering His Passion at that time."

Margery Kempe was born in 1373 to a well-to-do family in King's Lynn, Norfolk. When she was twenty she married John Kempe and within a year bore the first of her fourteen children. This birth precipitated a grave spiritual crisis, approaching madness, which lasted more than six months. She emerged only after experiencing a visitation by Christ, who spoke to her these comforting words: "Daughter, why have you forsaken me, and I never forsook you?"

Afterward Margery recovered her wits, but her heart remained fixed in the world. She dressed in finery, boasted of her social standing, and went in for the business of brewing beer. Evidently her failure in this venture convinced her that God had other plans for her. One night soon after, as she lay in bed with her husband, she seemed to hear a sweet music and immediately jumped up, saying, "Alas that ever I sinned! It is full merry in heaven." It was at this moment that she experienced a dramatic conversion, dedicating herself to a life of prayer, penance, and service of God. She also committed herself to celibacy. Unfortunately, her husband did not immediately share this commitment, a source of ongoing marital discord that lasted throughout many years and the birth of many more children.

Meanwhile Margery began adopting a rigorous penitential discipline. She also began to experience frequent conversations with Christ, his Father, his Mother Mary, and many of the saints. Through these "dalliances," reported in her autobiography in the same matter-of-fact way she uses to describe encounters with her contemporaries, she received assurance of her vocation as a penitent, as well as the extraordinary assurance of her own salvation.

While all this was going on within, externally Margery was most conspicuous for her "gift" of tears. She wept loudly throughout much of the day, especially when she came near a church or happened upon any scene that reminded her of the love of God and the sufferings of Christ. Under certain circumstances, Margery's "gift" inspired wonder and admiration. But by and large it attracted ridicule and contempt.

Margery wandered widely in England, seeking interviews with religious authorities and spiritual guides. Some, like Dame Julian, the holy anchoress of Norwich, approved her spiritual vocation. Others were plainly at a loss to make sense of her.

England at the time was in the throes of religious turmoil, stirred up by the Lollard heretics. These followers of the reformer John Wycliffe championed a simplified biblical faith in place of all priestly religion. Margery, with her frequent recourse to confession and weekly communion, was clearly not a Lollard. Nevertheless, the epithet was regularly hurled at her by clerics and other citizens scandalized by her unregulated enthusiasm. It was a dangerous charge, which could lead to imprisonment or death at the stake. Fortunately, Margery was always able to demonstrate her orthodoxy. But this did not prevent certain clerics from wishing she would "go to sea in a bottomless boat."

Actually, the clergy of her acquaintance differed widely in their estimation of Margery. There were certainly some, especially those whose sermons she interrupted with her uncontrollable weeping and screams, who considered her a holy nuisance. But many others became convinced of the genuineness of her vocation. Among these she eventually found willing scribes to whom she dictated her autobiography, *The Book of Margery Kempe.*

When she was about forty she finally won her husband's consent to accept a mutual vow of chastity. At about the same time she widened the scope of her pilgrimage, beginning with a trip to the Holy Land. Her fellow pilgrims quickly tired of her incessant weeping and became openly rude in their efforts to keep her at bay and even to lose her along the way. Nevertheless, she completed the journey, and among the holy shrines she found an even more vivid reference for her constant meditations on the life and passion of the Lord. Her weeping was now punctuated by unbidden "cries," which if anything only added to her strangeness. As Margery notes, "The crying was so loud and so amazing that it astounded people."

Along with the usual curses and rude accusations, Margery's behavior won a certain respect, and many were impressed with the edifying power of her public contrition. When once a priest said to her, "Woman, Jesus is long since dead," she replied: "Sir, his death is as fresh to me as if he had died this same day, and so, I think, it ought to be to you and to all Christian people. We ought always to remember his kindness, and always think of the doleful death that he died for us."

From her autobiography, the single manuscript of which was discovered only in the twentieth century, Margery Kempe emerges as one of the most vivid personalities of the Middle Ages. Scholars, like her contemporaries, have been divided in their opinion of her. There is no doubt as to her eccentricity; even she refers to herself as a "singular lover of God." But what stands out is Margery's bold determination to live out a unique spiritual vocation, in full public view, even in the face of ridicule and persecution. It is clear that the purpose of her public spectacle was not to draw attention to herself or to inspire imitators of her extreme spirituality. Rather, she hoped to inspire others to share just a small portion of her contrition for their sins and a small measure of her emotion at the thought of Christ's sufferings. In one of her mystical colloquies, the Lord told her: "I have ordained you to be a mirror amongst [your fellow Christians], to have great sorrow, so that they should take example from you to have some little sorrow in their hearts for their sins, so that they might through that be saved."

See: *The Book of Margery Kempe*, trans. B. A. Windeatt (New York: Penguin, 1985); Clarissa W. Atkinson, *Mystic and Pilgrim: The Book and the World of Margery Kempe* (Ithaca, N.Y.: Cornell University Press, 1983).

St. Catherine of Genoa
Mystic (1447–1510)

"All goodness is a participation in God and His love for his creatures."

Catherine of Genoa was a mystic and the author of several spiritual classics. She spent much of her days and nights in ardent prayer, in which, it is said, she experienced the burning flame of God's presence in her heart. What is more remarkable, however, is that this contemplative life was not spent in a convent. Catherine remained a laywoman, immersed in hands-on nursing care for the sick and dying poor. She helped to found and maintain the first hospital in Genoa, at various times performing every type of work from the most menial to the office of director. It is this extraordinary combination of action and contemplation that has made her one of the most compelling figures in the history of Christian spirituality. But this exquisite spiritual balance was not achieved at once. It was the fruit of a long and costly struggle.

Catherine was born into one of the great aristocratic families of Genoa. Her desire from a young age was to enter a religious order. But at the age of fifteen, before she could realize her dream, she was married to a young man, Julian Adorno. He came from a rival family, and the marriage was evidently arranged by the two families as an act of reconciliation. Unfortunately the matchmakers gave little heed to the obvious fact that Catherine and her husband were singularly unsuited for one another. While she aspired to religious life, Julian, as her biographer notes, was "entirely the opposite of herself in his mode of life." It appears that Julian lived his own quite separate and notorious life and that Catherine quickly sank into a state of chronic depression. This lasted for five years. For another five years she tried to engage in the frivolous diversions of society life. But this only left her all the more empty and melancholy.

At the age of twenty-five she uttered a desperate prayer for some relief from the torment of her existence, even praying that some illness might send her to bed "for three months." Instead, on March 22, 1473, while kneeling for confession, she was suddenly overcome with an infusion of divine love which impressed her simultaneously with the immensity of her sins and with the goodness of God. "No more world," she was heard to utter, "no more sins." The well-justified resentments and the petty bitterness that had steadily cramped her spirit were discarded, and from that moment she began to live a new life.

With newfound faith she also found new purpose for her existence. Immediately she threw herself into hospital work — hardly the normal profession for a woman of her social standing. Forcing herself to overcome her fastidious nature, she deliberately took on the most filthy and even repulsive cases. The miracle was that as she grew in the practice of love so also she found herself growing in her capacity for happiness.

Coincidentally, it was also at about this time that Julian's extravagant tastes finally reduced the couple to bankruptcy. They gave up their grand house and moved into a simple cottage, much more to Catherine's tastes. Eventually — perhaps through her example — Julian himself underwent a conversion and became a Franciscan tertiary. They then moved into the hospital, where, after many years of work, Catherine eventually assumed the job of director.

In running the hospital, it is said that Catherine was able to account for every farthing. But she was particularly renowned for her devoted care of the sick. During the plague of 1493, which killed four-fifths of those who remained in the city, Catherine stayed at her post. She herself became ill and nearly died after kissing a dying woman. She recovered. But that same year she had occasion to nurse Julian during a fatal illness. He had caused her much suffering over the years, but before he died, she confided, "My sweet Love [that is, Christ] assured me of his salvation."

In her later years Catherine drew a devoted circle of disciples, attracted not only by the opportunity to work beside her in her charitable work, but by the chance to benefit from her spiritual wisdom. Her most famous work is her mystical treatise on purgatory, based on her own experience of divine love. Rather than stressing the misery and suffering of souls in purgatory, Catherine describes this state as a kind of antechamber to paradise, the state in which the soul is stripped and purified so as to be able to bear the light of divine love. While we are still attached to our sins the flame of love burns us. But the pain is endurable because, unlike the pains of hell, it has a limit, and each moment brings the soul nearer to union with the Beloved.

> There is no joy save that in paradise to be compared to the joy of the souls in purgatory. This joy increases day by day because of the way in which the love of God corresponds to that of the soul, since the impediment to that love is worn away daily. This impediment is the rust of sin. As it is consumed, the soul is more and more open to God's love.... The more rust of sin is consumed by fire, the more the soul responds to that love, and its joy increases.

In her final years Catherine often experienced mystical ecstasies. It was said that she conversed with angels. And yet this profound "other-worldliness" was combined with fastidious attention to practical detail and constant availability to the needs of others. In 1510 she became very ill. After much physical suffering she died on September 15. She was canonized in 1733.

See: Catherine of Genoa, *Purgation and Purgatory, The Spiritual Dialogue,* Classics of Western Spirituality (New York: Paulist, 1979).

St. Xenia of St. Petersburg
Holy Fool (late eighteenth century)

"Having renounced the vanity of the earthly world, thou didst take up the cross of a homeless life of wandering; thou didst not fear grief, privation, nor the mockery of men, and didst know the love of Christ."
— Prayer to St. Xenia

There has always been an honored place in the Russian tradition for those called Holy Fools. These wandering ascetics, subsisting on the margins of society, bore witness to a spiritual wisdom that was often folly in the world's eyes.

For the essential facts of St. Xenia, a "holy fool" of St. Petersburg, there is little to add to the inscription that appears on her tombstone: "In the name of the Father, Son, and Holy Spirit. Here rests the body of the Servant of God, Xenia Grigorievna, wife of the imperial chorister, Colonel Andrei Theodorovich Petrov. Widowed at the age of twenty-six, a pilgrim for forty-five years, she lived a total of seventy-one years. She was known by the name Andrei Theodorovich. *May whoever knew me, say a prayer for my soul that his own may be saved. Amen."*

In her early married life, as her epitaph suggests, St. Xenia enjoyed a comfortable existence. Her husband's position as "imperial chorister" implies a position in the lesser nobility. But her fortunes took a drastic turn one night when her husband dropped dead after a night of drinking. Confronted by the vanity of her life, Xenia abruptly put aside all earthly pleasures and disposed of her property. Her relatives were horrified and sought to have her declared insane. But a judge ruled otherwise, determining that she was perfectly sane and entitled to do whatever she liked with her possessions.

For some years Xenia disappeared from view and from the historical record, perhaps adopting the life of a solitary pilgrim. When she returned to St. Petersburg, penniless and clothed in one of her husband's old uniforms, she would answer only to his name: Andrei Theodorovich. It was as if Xenia, and not her husband, had died. The one who remained lived only for Christ.

At first Xenia's odd appearance and strange behavior attracted ridicule and abuse. She had no home, sleeping outdoors in the cemetery. By day she wandered the streets of the poorer quarters, constantly repeating the name of God and urging passersby to remember their sins. But gradually the people of St. Petersburg came to respect and honor this eccentric witness to Christ. Her presence became a blessing, and townsfolk were delighted when she held their children or agreed to accept a meal in their home.

It was believed that Xenia had prophetic gifts, and people learned to take her odd pronouncements seriously. In one case she came upon a woman sitting in her home. "Here you are sitting and sewing buttons," she said, "and you don't know that God has given you a son! Go at once to the Smolensk Cemetery!" The woman did what she was told. At the cemetery she found that a pregnant woman, knocked down by a carriage, had gone into labor and died on the spot after delivering a baby boy. When the police could find no relatives for the dead mother, this woman adopted the baby and raised him as her own.

St. Xenia died sometime toward the end of the eighteenth century. No record was kept of the date, though her grave became a popular pilgrimage site. Her memory endured and spread — a small candle tended throughout the succeeding centuries, even during the dark night of the Soviet era. In 1988 she was formally canonized by the Russian Orthodox Church.

See: Jim Forest, *Praying with Icons* (Maryknoll, N.Y.: Orbis Books, 1997).

St. Xenia of St. Petersburg

Cornelia Connelly
Founder of the Society of the
Holy Child Jesus (1809–1879)

"Is not our faith a sword of strength? I feel it so, my Lord."

Through much of her life Cornelia Connelly struggled hard to discern her vocation amid the claims and demands which others made on her. But when she was certain she had heard God's voice she stood firm, despite the terrible sacrifices this entailed.

She was born in 1809 to a wealthy Philadelphia family. In 1831 she married an Episcopal priest named Pierce Connelly. When his studies convinced him that Catholicism was the true religion, he renounced his Anglican orders and entered the Catholic Church. Cornelia joined him. Although in her conversion, as in many subsequent decisions, Cornelia was to some extent carried along by the tide of her husband's strong will, she too felt a call to holiness. She hoped to discover this in the setting of family life; circumstances dictated that it should come instead through suffering and sacrifice.

In 1839 Cornelia and Pierce, with their three children, were living in rural Louisiana, where they both taught in Catholic schools. A fourth child, Mary Magdalene, died after only seven weeks. Five months later, while this wound was still fresh, their two-year-old, John Henry, was pushed by a dog into a vat of boiling sugar cane juice. He died forty-three hours later. During that time, as all the while she held his scalded body, Cornelia experienced a deep identification with the sorrows of Mary. When the child died on February 2, the feast of the Presentation, Cornelia wrote in her diary, "He was taken into the Temple of the Lord."

Later that year Pierce confided that he wished to seek ordination as a Catholic priest. Cornelia was stricken. It would mean the breakup of the family and, for her, a lifelong commitment to celibacy. To her spiritual advisor she asked, "Is it necessary for Pierce to make this sacrifice and *sacrifice me*? I love my husband; I love my darling children; why must I give them up?" Still the dutiful wife, she tried to believe in the coincidence between her husband's wishes and the will of God. So she agreed to cooperate with her husband's plan. She accepted the trial of the celibate life and remained behind, pregnant with her fifth child, Adeline, while Pierce went off to Rome to explore the possibilities for his vocation.

Eventually Pierce summoned the family to join him. He had secured an audience with Pope Gregory XVI, who accepted his vocation and cleared the way to his ordination, provided Cornelia would make a vow of chastity. While Pierce pursued his studies, Cornelia lived with her children in the Sacred Heart convent on Trinità de Monte. Though Pierce visited once a week she was, for all practical purposes, quite alone. Prayer offered little consolation. She wrote, "Incapable of listening or understanding or thinking...I forced my will to rejoice in the greatness of God."

In 1845 Cornelia made the requisite vow and Pierce was ordained. It was not clear what she was now supposed to do. She supposed she would return to America. At this point, however, several bishops and priests urged her to go to England. There the struggling Catholic Church, emerging from long suppression, was undergoing a period of expansion and renewal. It was suggested to Cornelia that her true calling was to establish a religious congregation in England for the education of girls. Cornelia accepted the challenge, provided she could keep her children with her. And so in 1846 she arrived in England to take over a newly built convent school in Derby.

There were numerous twists and turns in the foundation of this school and the community that attended it. But within a few years Cornelia had achieved some eminence within the English Catholic Church. In 1847 she took religious vows, and Bishop Wiseman formally installed her as superior of her congregation, the Society of the Holy Child Jesus. The name reflected her profound devotion to the Incarnation, specifically to the "humbled God" who had revealed himself in the form of a helpless infant. In this spirit she instructed her Sisters, "As you step through the muddy streets, love God with your feet; and when your hands toil, love Him with your hands; and when you teach the little children, love Him in His little ones." Her toil at this point was only beginning.

After only three years of her new life a new round of trials began. By this time Pierce had grown restless and dissatisfied with the priesthood. At first he tried to interfere with and take over Cornelia's congregation. After she asked him please to stay away from her convent, he announced that he was leaving the priesthood and wished her to resume her marital duties. Once again Cornelia was appalled. Though her husband's will had led her to the religious habit, now that she wore it, it was her own, and she would no longer accept his word as the word of God. When she refused his demand he brought a suit against her in a high ecclesiastical (Anglican) court. Now a professional anti-Catholic, Pierce painted a lurid picture of his wife being held captive by agents of Rome. Nevertheless, the court decided in Cornelia's favor. Enraged, Pierce retaliated by kidnapping her children and taking them out of the country. She was never to see them again.

Cornelia remained the superior of her congregation for over thirty years. During those years she saw new schools established in England, America, and France. Her congregation did much to promote the advancement and education of young women, especially the poor. Nevertheless, Mother Cornelia always bore the weight of her many sorrows. Toward the end of her life she suffered from an excruciating case of eczema that gave her the appearance of a leper — as though, it was said, "she had been scalded from head to foot." It seemed she was revisiting in her illness the experience of her greatest sorrow as well as her deepest identification with the Holy Child. Now it was she who was to be offered in the Temple. On the day before she died, on April 18, 1879, she turned to the nursing Sister and exclaimed, "In this flesh I shall see my God!"

See: Mary Andrew Armour, *Cornelia* (Society of the Holy Child Jesus, 1979); Juliana Wadham, *The Case of Cornelia Connelly* (New York: Pantheon, 1957).

Maude Dominica Petre
Catholic Modernist (1863–1942)

"The church has lighted my way. Instead of struggling through a wilderness I have had a road — a road to virtue and truth. Only a road — the road to an end, not the end itself — the road to truth, not the fullness of truth itself.... In one word, she has taught me how to seek God."

Throughout the nineteenth century a number of Catholic intellectuals sought a way to reconcile the church with the positive features of modernity. By and large their efforts were scorned. By the turn of the century, faced with the rising tide of liberal and secular modes of thought, the church had come to define itself against the dominant social and political values of the age. With a state-of-siege mentality, many church leaders felt compelled to define their mission largely in terms of condemning error and asserting their authority.

The Modernist movement at the turn of the century was the most serious challenge to this mentality. To speak of a "movement" is a somewhat misleading reference to a handful of formally unrelated scholars working in various European countries. In general they sought to interpret and present the faith in terms of modern historical consciousness, critical biblical study, and an apologetic method rooted in philosophy's "turn to the subject." The seriousness of their challenge evoked an unusually severe response from the Vatican — a condemnation so vehement that it was many decades before any Catholic scholar could safely refer to their work without evincing horror.

Among this group the English writer Maude Petre was the lone woman. She outlived the other protagonists of the affair by many years. But she is otherwise distinguished, alone among them all, for having remained a loyal member of the church while also proudly and without repentance owning the epithet of Modernist.

Maude Petre grew up in a Catholic household. Although she belonged for some years to a community of vowed religious, she felt her contribution to the church would be in the intellectual realm. She pursued theological studies in Rome, and so became one of the first Catholic women theologians in modern times.

A great event in her life came in 1900 when she became acquainted with George Tyrrell (1861–1909), a charismatic Jesuit theologian, who was to figure as a principal actor in the Modernist drama. A deep intellectual and spiritual bond quickly developed between Petre and Father Tyrrell, and she devoted herself wholeheartedly to his cause and his struggles. Tyrrell's work challenged the extrinsic and rationalistic mode of Catholic teaching. Instead of the appeal to dogmatic authority, he emphasized the affective and mystical dimension of Christianity and its appeal to human experience. In her own books Petre did not so much address such theological matters as defend the principle of freedom within the church to raise the kinds of questions posed by Tyrrell and his friends. She later compared her efforts with the famous motivation for World War I: to make the world — in this case the church — safe for democracy.

The response of the Vatican was swift and furious. In 1907 Pope Pius X issued the encyclical *Pascendi* condemning the errors of "Modernism" in sweeping terms. The Modernists were depicted as archenemies of the faith to be combated by extraordinary measures. These included an anti-Modernist oath to be sworn by all clergy as well as the establishment of vigilance committees in every diocese to watch out for signs of the heresy. The irony was that the cause of the Modernists — whatever their errors — was not intended as an attack on Catholicism but as an effort to affirm and defend the relevance and vitality of Catholicism in the modern world.

In the aftermath of the encyclical Tyrrell and several others were excommunicated and their works banned. Tyrrell died two years later, still protesting his faith and loyalty to the church. Petre, who regarded her friend as a saint and martyr, assumed the role of his literary executor. She oversaw the editing and publication of his autobiography and a series of other posthumous books. This was regarded as a sign of defiance by her bishop, who insisted that she too swear the "anti-Modernist" oath. As a laywoman, Petre refused to comply with this extraordinary command, arguing that such an oath would accord equal authority to these papal documents and the Nicene Creed. "If I am wrong," she wrote, "then I am so deeply, fundamentally wrong, that only God can prove it to me. If I am right, then He will make good to me what I have forfeited before men." As a result, her bishop announced that she too was formally excommunicated in that diocese.

Nevertheless, she did not cease to regard herself as a faithful Catholic. Indeed, she later moved to the Diocese of Westminster in London, where she maintained her practice of daily communion. She lived on for three decades, publishing historical and critical reflections on the Modernist controversy and its principal figures. Late in her long life, she described herself as "a solitary marooned passenger, the sole living representative of what has come to be regarded as the lost cause of Modernism in the Catholic Church." While she never compromised her principles, she likewise never wavered in her loyal commitment to the church. Thus, she might be said to exemplify a spirituality of loyal dissent.

Toward the end of her life, in an assessment of the Modernist cause, she wrote:

Nothing can alter the radical aspirations of the human heart, and it was for these that the Modernist contended, and for the sake of which he endured the cramping torture of ecclesiastical institutions, because in spite of their limitations, he found in them a support in the passage through this dark and troubled life; he found through them, the grace to live, the courage to die.

Maude Petre died on December 16, 1942. She was buried in the Anglican cemetery in Storrington, one grave removed from Father Tyrrell.

See: M. D. Petre, *My Way of Faith* (New York: E. P. Dutton, 1937); Clyde F. Crews, *English Catholic Modernism: Maude Petre's Way of Faith* (South Bend, Ind.: University of Notre Dame Press, 1984).

St. Edith Stein
Carmelite Martyr (1891–1942)

"Do you want to be totally united to the Crucified? If you are serious about this, you will be present, by the power of His Cross, at every front, at every place of sorrow, bringing to those who suffer, healing and salvation."

Edith Stein was born the eleventh child of Orthodox Jewish parents in Breslau, Germany, on October 12, 1891. Her birth fell on Yom Kippur, the Jewish Day of Atonement, a fact whose significance she later noted. Independent by nature and gifted with a prodigious intelligence, Edith had abandoned her family's faith by the time she was thirteen. She declared herself an atheist — only the first of a series of blows to her pious mother — and devoted herself to the study of philosophy. She was accepted as one of the first women students at the University of Göttingen, where she studied under the brilliant Edmund Husserl, father of phenomenology. Stein became one of his star pupils, so respected by Husserl that he invited her to become his assistant at the University of Freiburg. There she completed her doctorate at the age of twenty-three, writing a dissertation on the nature of empathy.

There was a strong ethical dimension to the phenomenological school, and a number of Husserl's disciples were professing Christians. In the years after World War I Stein herself began to feel a growing interest in religion. This culminated one night in 1921 when she happened upon the autobiography of St. Teresa of Avila, the sixteenth-century Carmelite mystic. With fascination she read through the night and by morning concluded, "This is the truth." She was baptized as a Catholic on the following New Year's Day.

Edith's mother wept when she heard the news of her daughter's conversion. Faced with Edith's resolution, however, she had little choice but to acquiesce. Edith continued to accompany her mother to synagogue, feeling that in accepting Christ she had been reunited, by a mysterious path, with her Jewish roots.

Stein initially believed that with her conversion she should abandon thoughts of a scholarly career. For eight years she taught in a Dominican school for girls. But her study of Thomas Aquinas eventually rekindled her interest in academic pursuits. After preparing a scholarly work integrating phenomenology with scholasticism, she obtained an academic post in Munster in 1932.

This position, however, would be short-lived. As the Nazis rose to power, Stein almost immediately felt the reverberations of anti-Semitism. With unusual foresight, she recognized the destination of this campaign of hatred. Somewhat audaciously, she wrote to seek an audience with Pope Pius XI, hoping to alert him to the peril facing the Jews. Her request was not answered. Meanwhile, with the regrets of the university administration, she was dismissed from the teaching position she had barely begun.

Already Stein understood the terrible storm that was approaching, and she felt in some way that her Jewish-Christian identity imposed a unique vocation. While praying at the Carmelite convent in Cologne, she later wrote,

> I spoke with the Savior to tell him that I realized it was his Cross that was now being laid upon the Jewish people, that the few who understood this had the responsibility of carrying it in the name of all, and that I myself was willing to do this, if he would only show me how.

For the meantime, the loss of her job enabled her to pursue her growing attraction to religious life. She applied to enter the Carmelite convent in Cologne. Once again her mother wept — this time accusing her of abandoning her people in time of persecution. It was a bitter charge, and one that would cloud their parting. After spending a final evening with her mother in the synagogue, Edith bade her farewell. None of her family was present on April 15, 1934, to witness her formal clothing in the Carmelite habit. She took as her religious name Sister Teresa Benedicta a Cruce — Blessed by the Cross. It was a name, she later explained, chosen to refer "to the fate of the people of God, which even then was beginning to reveal itself."

In 1938 the all-out war against the Jews was declared on November 8, the *Kristallnacht*. Believing that her presence in the convent endangered her Sisters, Stein allowed herself to be smuggled out of the country to a

Carmelite convent in Holland. She had no thought of escaping the fate of her people. In fact, she prepared a solemn prayer which she delivered to her prioress, "offering myself to the Heart of Jesus as a sacrifice of atonement" for the Jewish people, for the aversion of war, and for the sanctification of her Carmelite family. Having contemplated and faced the reality of death, she was delivered from further anxiety, and thus prepared to await the end.

In 1940 the Nazis occupied Holland. Despite her cloistered status, Stein was required to wear the Yellow Star of David on her habit. Soon the deportations began. All the while Stein hurried to finish her study of the mystical theology of St. John of the Cross. She was consoled by the presence of her sister Rosa, who by this time had also converted and joined her in the convent as a laywoman.

The Germans had indicated a willingness to spare Jewish-Christians, provided the churches kept silent. When on July 26, 1942, a statement by the Catholic bishops of Holland denouncing the persecution of the Jews was read from pulpits throughout the country, the Nazis retaliated in rage. Within a week all Jewish Catholics, including members of religious orders, were under arrest. For Stein and her sister the end came on August 2, when the Gestapo arrived at their convent. Rosa was distraught, but Edith reassured her: "Come, Rosa. We're going for our people."

Survivors of the following days describe the nun's courage and composure despite her clear certainty of the fate that awaited her. She occupied herself with prayer while caring for the terrified children and consoling mothers separated from their husbands. Someone described her as a "Pietà without the Christ."

From a detention camp in Holland she followed the same route as millions of others: the wretched journey by sealed boxcar, the arrival half-starved at a strange camp amid snarling dogs and cursing guards, the infamous "selection," then the stripping, then the brisk walk to the shower room, from which none emerged.

Edith Stein died in the gas chamber of Auschwitz on August 9, 1942. In 1998 she was canonized as a confessor and martyr of the church by Pope John Paul II, an event that provoked considerable controversy. Many Jews complained that Stein, like six million others, had died as a Jew, and not for her Christian faith. There is a truth to this. But what is remarkable about Stein is not the manner of her death but her understanding of that death — in solidarity with her people, as an act of atonement for the evil of her time, and as a conscious identification with the cross of Christ.

See: Waltraud Herbstrith, *Edith Stein: A Biography* (New York: Harper & Row, 1983); *Edith Stein: Essential Writings,* ed. John Sullivan (Maryknoll, N.Y.: Orbis Books, 2002).

Adrienne von Speyr
Mystic (1902–1967)

"It was made clear to me time and again that I was being set apart, held in reserve for something."

Adrienne von Speyr was born in Switzerland to a family who boasted many generations of doctors, clergymen, and bankers. From an early age she was determined to become a doctor — an unusual ambition for a girl of her time. But she was unusual in other ways as well. Even as a young child she enjoyed mystical experiences — conversations with the Mother of God and with saints and angels — that set her apart from her solidly Protestant milieu. She quickly learned not to share these experiences with others. When, for example, she described how St. Ignatius of Loyola had appeared to her and offered to lead her by the hand, her family reacted with understandable alarm.

Adrienne continued with her education and medical training. In 1927 she married an older widower who had two children. Soon after this she began her medical practice. But her husband's sudden death in 1934 left her devastated, uncertain about the meaning of life and how she could carry on. The great turning point in her life came in 1940 when she was introduced to Hans Urs von Balthasar, a Jesuit priest and the Catholic chaplain of the University of Basel. In their very first conversation she brought up a question that had troubled her: What did it mean to submit to the will of God? In answering her, as von Balthasar later reflected, "I inadvertently touched a switch that at one flick turned on all the lights in the hall. Adrienne seemed to be freed from chains of restraint and was carried away on a flood of prayer as though a dam had burst." Her decision to become a Catholic occurred at that moment, and she was baptized a few weeks later.

If von Balthasar's influence on Adrienne was remarkable, perhaps even more remarkable was the effect that she — a fresh convert with no theological training — would have on him. Von Balthasar had been groping for a new style of doing theology — one more affective, based on experiential insight rather than reason, concerned more with holiness than with intellectual comprehension. He was the first to recognize von Speyr's spiritual gifts, particularly her capacity to integrate mystical insight with active engagement in the world. Though he would become over time one of the most influential Catholic theologians of the twentieth century (and the reported favorite of Pope John Paul II), he would later acknowledge of Adrienne, "On the whole I received far more from her, theologically, than she from me." Not only did she influence many of the great decisions of his life, he wrote, "but I also strove to bring my way of looking at Christian revelation into conformity with hers."

Von Speyr's family was initially shocked by her conversion. But outwardly her life continued much as before. She maintained a thriving medical practice, seeing up to eighty patients a day, before illness eventually forced her to retire. None but her confessor, von Balthasar, knew the extent of her mystical experiences. She had regular visions of Mary and the saints. She spent much of the night in prayer, "traveling," as she put it, to remote corners of the globe — to distant churches, prisons, convents, war zones, and concentration camps — that she could afterward describe in vivid detail. Miraculous cures occurred among her patients. Furthermore she enjoyed a remarkable gift for interpreting scripture. Long after illness left her too weak to write, she dictated thousands of pages of commentary to von Balthasar, who by this time had become both her devotee and amanuensis.

But these gifts came at a price. Soon after her conversion she was visited by an angel who asked if she was ready to consent to whatever God might ordain for her. Such consent, she believed — whether by Mary, Jesus, or the saints — was the very hinge of the spiritual life, the attitude that alone made everything possible. She could not but answer yes.

Thereafter, every year during Holy Week, she relived the sufferings of Christ, both physical and spiritual. In 1942 she received the stigmata, the physical marks of Christ's wounds on her hands. She had several heart attacks that weakened her so much that she could no longer work. She suffered from diabetes and eventually went blind. Still her spiritual labors — through prayer, meditation, and the scores of books she dictated — continued until the end. Prayer, she told von Balthasar, is a vessel that carries us "beyond all concepts, on God's endless sea."

She died on September 17, 1967.

See: Hans Urs von Balthasar, *First Glance at Adrienne von Speyr* (San Francisco: Ignatius Press, 1991).

Mothers of the Disappeared
Argentina (1977–1983)

"When everyone was terrorized we didn't stay at home crying — we went to the streets to confront them directly. We were mad, but it was the only way to stay sane."

The military coup in Argentina on March 24, 1976, did not come as a surprise. After a period of economic crisis and political instability, many middle-class Argentines had openly expressed their hope that military rule would herald a return to stability and order. When it occurred, even the country's Catholic bishops extended their blessing, reassured by the generals' promises to safeguard the values of "Christianity, patriotism, and the family." Few anticipated the savage repression that was to follow.

In the name of their "war against subversion" the military unleashed a wave of terror against all "unpatriotic" individuals and organizations, including labor unions, political activists, university students, and human rights groups. But the Argentine generals, having studied the lessons of previous military dictatorships, had determined to carry out their repression quietly and largely out of sight. Rather than filling stadiums with political prisoners or leaving mutilated bodies on the side of the road, they perfected the practice of kidnapping their victims from their own homes, murdering them in secret, and leaving no evidence behind. In this manner some fifteen to thirty thousand men and women joined the *desaparecidos* — the ranks of the "disappeared."

The aim of this repression was to silence all protest, and it very nearly succeeded. Political opposition evaporated. The press was silent. Church leaders remained willfully blind. It fell to a group of women to find the courage to break this silence. These were the so-called Mothers of the Disappeared.

Their common experience brought them together. Many of them had seen sons or daughters kidnapped by security agents in the middle of the night. Desperately, they had kept their vigils, waiting for a call, a message, a sound of returning footsteps at the door. They had made the circuit of jails, military installations, and hospitals, hoping to find someone who could at least confirm their children's survival, if not their whereabouts. In vain they had pleaded with judges, government officials, and even bishops for some assistance. And everywhere they had been turned away, often with cruel cynicism: "Perhaps their sons had fled to Cuba; perhaps their daughters had run away to become prostitutes. . . . " Friends and neighbors had drifted away, not wanting to get involved, fearful of guilt by association, and troubled by the nagging suspicion that nobody gets arrested for no reason; surely these young people *must have done something.*

In their grief the Mothers found each other — women who shared the same pain and anguish. At first they came together for mutual support, and then they demanded to be heard. It began with a silent vigil in the Plaza de Mayo, a public square in Buenos Aires that faces the Ministry of the Interior. The vigil became a weekly event. Each Thursday, scores of these middle-aged women, the *Madres de Plaza de Mayo,* stood silently, identified only by their white kerchiefs, and sometimes by the pictures they held of their missing children.

It was illegal to hold any public protest during the state of siege. But the generals did not know how to respond to this mute outcry. They resorted to ridicule; they called them the "crazy women," *las locas de Plaza de Mayo.* Then they resorted to bullying and terror. The Mothers began to receive threatening phone calls and letters. Several times the whole group of them was arrested, loaded onto buses, and detained overnight. Some of the Mothers were physically attacked by government thugs. Several of them were kidnapped and disappeared. But the threats only strengthened their resolve.

What gave them such courage? According to one of the mothers, "When a woman gives birth to a child, she gives life and at the same time, when they cut the cord, she gives freedom. We were fighting for life and for freedom. It was our insistence, our refusal to give up, that made us effective." As another put it simply, "When a mother loses a child that pain is stronger than fear or terror."

Despite the news blackout in Argentina, the Mothers' protest was publicized throughout the world. Tourists sought them out, and visiting dignitaries joined them in solidarity. They were a constant thorn in the government's side. At a time when the truth was everywhere suppressed, the Mothers and their silent vigil became the visible conscience of the nation. In a widely circulated declaration the Mothers proclaimed their commitment to "an Argentina where there is justice, where nobody can be detained and disappear as has happened to our children, where the law is respected, and where it is possible to live in liberty, tolerance, and respect."

In 1983 the military, by this time thoroughly discredited, yielded power to a civilian government. The Mothers' hopes were temporarily elevated by the dream that thousands of young people would emerge at last from the darkness of their secret cells. But there was only a terrible silence, and they had to face the truth — that their sons and daughters would never return. Some of the Mothers struggled on to recover their missing grandchildren — the babies born in detention to their pregnant daughters and often adopted by military families. Others continued the struggle to bring the guilty to justice. As one of them said, "The struggle goes beyond the lives of our children. It's about the future of our country."

See: Jo Fisher, *Mothers of the Disappeared* (Boston: Sound End Press, 1989).

Martyrs of El Mozote
El Salvador (d. 1981)

"I was afraid that I would cry out, that I would scream, that I would go crazy. I couldn't stand it, and I prayed to God to help me. I promised God that if He helped me I would tell the world what happened here."
— Rufina Amaya

On December 10, 1981, scores of Salvadoran troops, part of the elite, U.S.-trained Atlacatl Battalion, entered the town of El Mozote, a small hamlet in the Salvadoran province of Morazán. Their mission was code-named "Rescue." Its objective was to pursue guerrilla troops, cut off their supply lines, and eliminate suspected subversives.

No one had ever accused the people of El Mozote of being subversives. They were, in fact, something of an anomaly in this province, otherwise largely under guerrilla control. More than half of the townspeople were born-again evangelicals, a fact that may have accounted for their determination to remain neutral in the ongoing civil war in El Salvador. On the day of Operation Rescue the town was in fact swollen with refugees from the countryside, drawn by the belief that El Mozote would provide a safe haven amid the encircling fighting. They were wrong.

On the first day the soldiers gathered the townspeople and roughly interrogated them for information about the guerrillas. The people had no information to give. At some point the decision was made simply to destroy the town. For the next two days the soldiers systematically gathered the townspeople into small groups of men, women, and children and massacred the lot of them. It was exhausting work, carried out with extraordinary brutality. All the while the air was filled with screams and cries, punctuated by bursts of gun fire. Having begun the task, the soldiers were determined to leave no survivors. But they failed.

A peasant woman, Rufina Amaya, was put at the end of a line of women taken out to be executed. She had already seen her husband decapitated. When she arrived at the site where she was to be killed, Rufina fell to her knees: "I was crying and begging God to forgive my sins. Though I was almost at the feet of the soldiers I wasn't begging them — I was begging God." But in a moment when the soldiers weren't looking she seized the opportunity to crawl away and hide herself in some bushes. She remained there for days — shivering, thirsty, bleeding — watching and listening as the soldiers completed their mission. The children were the last to go. Rufina had to listen to the sounds of her own children being killed, biting her tongue to keep from screaming.

That night she overheard some of the soldiers discussing the faith of the people they had killed. One young girl in particular remained on their minds. While they had raped her repeatedly she had continued to sing hymns. Even after they shot her in the chest she sang. They shot her again, and still she sang. And then "their wonder began to turn to fear — until finally they had unsheathed their machetes and hacked through her neck, and at last the singing stopped."

Rufina alone survived to tell the world what had happened at El Mozote, where as many as a thousand people were killed. It was the largest massacre in modern Latin American history.

For more than a decade, years after the end of the civil war, the town of El Mozote remained abandoned. In the meantime forensic investigators, sponsored by a U.N. Truth Commission, sifted through the gruesome evidence, confirming Rufina's account of the terrible events she had witnessed. Eventually people began to return and rebuild. But not Rufina. She could not bring herself to return. She lived on in a nearby town, where she remarried and bore new children. But despite the pain of her memories she kept her pledge to recount the story of the massacre to any who asked.

A memorial in the town square of El Mozote bears the inscription: "They did not die, they are with us, with you, and with all humanity."

See: Mark Danner, "The Truth of El Mozote," *The New Yorker* (December 6, 1993).

Martyrs of El Mozote

Jessica Powers
Carmelite Poet (1905–1988)

Deep in the soul the acres lie
of virgin lands, of sacred wood
where waits the Spirit. Each soul bears
this trackless solitude.

Jessica Powers was born and raised in Cat Tail Valley in rural Wisconsin. From an early age her spirit was marked by the beauty of nature, by the sounds of killdeers and whippoorwills, and the long stretches of open space. But she was marked too by the austerity and loneliness of country living, especially the cold and darkness of long winters, and the painful struggle to eke out a living. As she wrote in one of her poems:

> My valley is a woman unconsoled.
> Her bluffs are amethyst, the tinge of grief;
> her tamarack swamps are sad.
> There is no dark tale that she was not told;
> there is no sorrow that she has not had.
> She has no mood of mirth, however brief.

Her early life was shaped by a double loss — the death of her older sister when Jessica was eleven, followed two years later by the death of her father. Nevertheless, her keen intelligence and literary talents emerged early. Her English teacher, a nun, recognized and encouraged her poetic talents. But dreams of getting an education and exploring the world were put on hold after the death of her mother, when she was twenty. It fell to her to look after her brothers and oversee management of the family farm.

This period of her life would last eleven years. But all the while, as she maintained the cycle of daily chores, she continued to nourish an inner life and a hope of finding her place in the world. She also wrote scores of poems, many of them published in newspapers and magazines.

> They tell me this is all of life
> It will not matter much
> If I can never walk to reach
> The world beyond my touch.

> They tell me any sun-drugged land
> Has nothing more to give.
> But I know well my destiny
> Is not this life I live.

Her opportunity arrived in 1936 when, by happy coincidence, both her brothers suddenly married. Free at last, she immediately departed for New York. While supporting herself as a housekeeper and au pair, she quickly found a community of Catholic literary friends. Her first book, *The Lantern Burns*, appeared in 1939.

Just as she was achieving some recognition as a poet, she surprised her friends and family with the news that she had decided to become a Carmelite nun. This vocation had been quietly growing in her heart for some time, ever since she first bought a book of poems by St. John of the Cross "and carried them home as if I'd just purchased heaven." As America was entering a new world war, Powers was disappearing behind the strict enclosure of a new Carmel in Milwaukee. There she became Sister Miriam of the Holy Spirit.

In this austere, silent community, Powers spent the rest of her life, struggling to attend to signs of grace and, through her poetry, to make them visible to a wounded world.

> There is a homelessness never to be clearly defined.
> It is more than having no place of one's own, no bed or chair....

> It is the pain of the mystic suddenly thrown
> back from the noon of God to the night of his own humanity.
> It is his grief; it is the grief of all those praying
> in finite words to an Infinity
> Whom, if they saw, they could not comprehend;
> > Whom they cannot see.

Most of her days were occupied with prayer, simple labor, and the liturgical disciplines of Carmelite life. She served three terms as prioress of her community, oversaw the move to a new rural location, and adjusted with difficulty to the radical upheavals in religious life following Vatican II. But through her confessional poetry she allowed her devoted readers to accompany her on her spiritual journey.

> I am alone in the dark, and I am thinking
> what darkness would be mine if I could see
> the ruin I wrought in every place I wandered

Jessica Powers

and if I could not be
aware of One who follows after me.
Whom do I love, O God, when I love Thee?

In this same poem she addresses God as "The great Undoer who has torn apart / the walls I built against a human heart, / the Mender who has sewn together the hedges / through which I broke when I went seeking ill, / the Love who follows and forgives me still." In the final line, she declares, "God is the repairer of fences, turning my paths into rest."

Jessica Powers died on August 18, 1988, at the age of eighty-three.

See: Dolores R. Leckey, *Winter Music: A Life of Jessica Powers* (Lanham, Md.: Sheed & Ward, 1992); *Selected Poetry of Jessica Powers,* ed. Regina Siegfried and Robert Morneau (Kansas City, Mo.: Sheed & Ward, 1989).

Karla Faye Tucker
Penitent (1959–1998)

"If this man were a prophet, he would have known who and what sort of woman this is who is touching him, for she is a sinner."   — Luke 8:39

"When you've done something like I've done and you've been forgiven for it and you're loved — that has a way of so changing you. I have experienced real love. I know what forgiveness is, even when I've done something so horrible. I know that because God forgave me when I accepted what Jesus did on the cross. When I leave here I'm going to be with Him."

On February 3, 1998, Karla Faye Tucker became the first woman to be executed by the State of Texas in over a hundred years. A considerable crowd kept vigil that day outside the Huntsville correctional unit, their signs and banners reflecting two contrasting realities about Tucker's life. There were those who remembered the woman she had been — the cold-hearted "pickax murderess" who had brutally murdered two people fifteen years before. But among the crowd were an equal number drawn by the story of the woman she had become — a "born-again" Christian, whose remorse for her actions was as evident as the joy and love she shared with everyone she encountered.

Many prisoners "find religion" after being arrested for their crimes. Stories of such conversions often invite cynical reactions. But few who met Karla ever doubted her sincerity. She never sought to minimize the horror of her actions or her own responsibility for the choices that had brought her to her fate. Prosecutors, prison officials, and even the policemen who had arrested her all testified to her transformation and hoped she would not die. They were joined in that hope by an unlikely host of advocates, ranging from Pope John Paul II to evangelist Pat Robertson. As for Karla, she had embraced the words of St. Paul: "If we live, we live to the Lord, and if we die, we die to the Lord; so then, whether we live or whether we die, we are the Lord's."

Certainly it would be hard to imagine a more unlikely contrast between the early Karla Faye and the woman of her final years. A drug addict from the age of eleven, she had begun prostituting herself at the age of fourteen — schooled by her mother, also a drug addict. She was a wild outlaw, a part-time groupie, attracted to bikers and "manly men" who knew how to live on the edge of danger. One night in 1983, when Karla was twenty-four, she and her boyfriend set out to steal motorcycle parts from a man they both disliked. Wired on speed and the thrill of being bad they ended up killing the man and his girlfriend with hideous cruelty. Their subsequent boasting to friends led to their arrest. Both were tried and sentenced to death for capital murder.

While in jail awaiting her trial, Karla was moved by curiosity to attend a meeting with a prison ministry group. Members of the group shared their own experiences of prison, prostitution, drugs, and violence, and Karla observed that "they had a peace and joy — something that was real. I had never seen that in anybody." She found herself wanting "to feel what they're feeling." That night, not knowing that Bibles were free for the asking, she stole one and snuck it back into her cell. As she began to read she experienced for the first time the full magnitude of her actions, the realization that "I had brutally murdered two people and there were people out there hurting because of me." On her knees, she asked God "to come into my heart and forgive me for what I had done." And almost at once she felt an incredible infusion of God's love. "He reached down inside of me and ripped out that violence at the very roots and poured Himself in."

The difference in Karla was immediately obvious. Testifying in the sentencing phase of her trial, she fully confessed her actions and made no effort to minimize or mitigate her responsibility. She plunged herself into prison ministry, doing all she could to serve her follow prisoners and to "save other lives" from the weight of sin and despair. She became a beacon of hope to everyone she touched. "I was in the wilderness, but it was by no means dry," she said, "because there's always a well of living water bubbling up. Circumstances don't dictate my joy. The joy bubbles over, no matter what."

Her journey on death row lasted fourteen years. Though she was prepared to accept whatever happened, she did not want to die. She cooperated in her appeals, right to the end, grateful for every day of life. She fell in love with a member of her prison ministry team, and they were legally married, though they would never be alone together. "I love life now," she said. "Instead of taking lives I just want to share the life in me."

But eventually her appeals were exhausted. Her execution date was set. Governor George W. Bush refused her plea for a final stay. Karla told her friends not to mourn. She was "going home to Jesus."

After her death one of her ministers said, "Karla was a murderer who said yes to God. She passed every test; she did not stumble once through the most severe trials. She walked with the glory of God upon her, with clarity and joy, never doubting His faithfulness. She used her time in prison to train for her final moments. Every day God put before her life and death. Each time she chose life, and that choice resulted in the joy we saw in her. As she became a stronger Christian, she ministered that strength and joy to anyone who would receive it, always pointing to him and away from herself."

As Sister Helen Prejean has said, our lives are more than "the worst thing we ever did." Karla Faye Tucker's worst thing cost her her life. And yet she bore witness to the gospel message that God's love is greater than any sin, and that it is freely offered to any who will accept it. Such love has the power to transform us, to make us into new creatures. For that reason, Karla Faye believed, there is hope — even for a murderer like St. Paul, even for the criminal crucified beside Jesus, who received the promise, "Truly, I say to you, today you will be with me in Paradise."

See: Linda Strom, *Karla Faye Tucker Set Free* (Colorado Springs, Colo.: Water-Brook Press, 2000); Beverly Lowry, *Crossed Over: A Murder, a Memoir* (New York: Alfred A. Knopf, 1992).

BLESSED ARE
THE MEEK

*A desperate mother • an ailing woman • a nun • a mystical anchoress •
a reclusive poet • a "little flower" • a spiritual director • a missionary •
a witness to the Holocaust • four child martyrs of the civil rights struggle*

In a world that prizes "self-assertion," "self-fulfillment," and every other form of self-aggrandizement, meekness is not a highly touted virtue. But here, as elsewhere, Jesus turns the usual hierarchies on their head. The first shall be last; those who would be the first of all must become the servants of all.

There is a power in meekness that has nothing to do with groveling submission. Some translations refer to these blessed as "the gentle," or even "the nonviolent," thus suggesting the strength that is hidden in apparent weakness.

St. Therese of Lisieux described her path as the Little Way, or the way of spiritual childhood. Those on this path seek no great name for themselves. And yet, as Jesus promised, it is they, and not today's rulers or celebrities, who "shall inherit the earth."

The Syrophoenician Woman
Faithful Witness (first century)

"But immediately a woman, whose little daughter was possessed by an unclean spirit, heard of him, and came and fell down at his feet."
—Mark 7:25

The Gospels record numerous occasions on which Jesus confronted his disciples and others with the liberating implications of his message. But there is at least one story in which the challenge was reversed. The story of an unnamed gentile woman, identified only by her Syrophoenician origins, recalls an instance in which it was Jesus himself who was moved to act upon the universal logic of the gospel.

As related by Mark, this woman accosted Jesus in a private home, begging him to cast out a demon from her sick daughter. Surely she knew that her action seriously violated the social and religious codes of Jewish society. If so, she was probably better inured than the modern reader to Jesus' insulting rebuff: "Let the children first be fed for it is not right to take the children's bread and throw it to the dogs." Rather than take offense, however, the woman persisted in her request, cleverly returning Jesus' words with a challenge he could not resist: "Yes, Lord; yet even the dogs under the table eat the children's crumbs."

There are few encounters in which Jesus does not have the last word. But this is one. Apparently persuaded by the woman's claim, he answered her request: "For this saying you may go your way; the demon has left your daughter."

The unnamed Syrophoenician woman deserves to be remembered as one of the foremothers of the gentile church who intuited, even while Jesus lived, that his gospel was for everyone. She may also be honored as an example of the countless women who, having refused to accept their marginalization as the final word, have challenged the church to comprehend the universal and liberating logic of salvation.

The Woman with a Flow of Blood
(first century)

"If I touch even his garments, I shall be made well."

One day as Jesus passed through a crowd, a woman pressed her way unnoticed through the protective circle of disciples and touched his garment. Immediately Jesus perceived that "power had gone forth from him." He stopped. Facing the crowd, he asked, "Who touched my garments?" With fear and trembling the woman stepped forward, fell before him, and told her story. She had suffered for twelve years from a "flow of blood."

In making this humiliating confession she might well have braced herself against the revulsion of the crowd. More than a simple physical infirmity, such a condition would have rendered her unclean in the eyes of the law. She was an outcast, an untouchable; her very touch had the power of defilement. And yet having heard reports of Jesus' healing miracles she had dared to touch his garment, trusting that this alone would heal her. By this action she had understood, in a way that the disciples as yet did not, that the power of Jesus was at the service of love. And in touching his garment she had immediately felt herself to be healed.

There was no special saving power in physical proximity to Christ. Among those who heard him preach were the ones who plotted his death. Judas dipped his hand into the same bowl as Jesus before he went out to betray him. It was not enough to touch him, for so did the many others who jostled against him in the crowd, and so did those others who later stripped and scourged him and nailed him to a cross.

Christ was present in that crowd in all his love and power. But it was the faith of a poor, frightened, sick, untouchable woman who recognized that power and so awakened it with a touch and brought it into full view.

Jesus listened to her story. According to the codes of ritual purity he should have been shocked. But he was not. He was able to distinguish in this woman's presumptuous gesture the authentic act of faith. "Daughter," he said, "it is your faith that has made you well."

See: Mark 5:25–34; Hisako Kinukawa, *Women and Jesus in Mark: A Japanese Feminist Perspective* (Maryknoll, N.Y.: Orbis Books, 1994).

St. Lydia
"Worshiper of God" (first century)

"So they went out of the prison and visited Lydia; and when they had seen the brethren, they exhorted them and departed."   — Acts 17:40

Evidence of the role of women in the early church is sketchy at best. The Acts of the Apostles and the letters of St. Paul largely relegate women to minor roles. Those women such as St. Lydia, singled out for particular mention, provide some hint of a wider, forgotten history.

Lydia enters the story of the church when St. Paul and his traveling companion Timothy first ventured onto European soil. After arriving in the city of Philippi in Macedonia, the missionaries went down to the riverside where they "supposed there was a place of prayer" (a synagogue). Their audience turned out to consist entirely of women, including one named Lydia from the city of Thyatira. She was "a seller of purple goods, who was a worshiper of God." From these somewhat mysterious details we may infer that she was a businesswoman of some means (a dealer in expensive purple-dyed fabric) and that she was "a God-fearer" — a Gentile who respected Jewish religious law.

Lydia responded immediately to the good news: "The Lord opened her heart to give heed to what was said by Paul," as a result of which she was baptized along with her entire household — the first Christian converts in Europe. She in turn pressed Paul to remain in her house: "If you have judged me to be faithful to the Lord, come to my house and stay." To this, the narrator of Acts replies in the first person: "And she prevailed upon us."

The Christian movement originated in such "house churches" as Lydia's. So it is reasonable to remember her as one of the founders of the church in Europe. Paul's letter to the "saints in Christ Jesus who are in Philippi," written from his imprisonment in Rome, does not mention Lydia by name. But it does reflect the special place this church occupied in his heart. "For God is my witness," he wrote, "how I yearn for you all with the affection of Christ Jesus.... Rejoice in the Lord always; again I will say, Rejoice."

See: Acts 16:14–15

St. Scholastica
Nun (d. 543)

"I asked my Lord, and He listened to me."

This holy woman was the twin sister of St. Benedict, founder of Western monasticism. Our knowledge of her story depends on two chapters in the famous life of Benedict by St. Gregory the Great. There we learn that she entered religious life at an early age and apparently rose to the office of abbess in a convent near her brother's monastery at Monte Cassino. Gregory's account of Scholastica is largely given over to a story of her last days. It illustrates the affectionate and yet somewhat competitive relationship between the siblings. More importantly, it provides a monastic parable about the power and virtue of love versus a rigid devotion to rules.

It seems that Benedict and Scholastica had a custom of meeting once a year in a house somewhere between their respective monasteries. There they would spend the whole day "praising God and talking of spiritual matters." One year they met as usual. But when, as dusk began to fall, Benedict made preparations to leave, his sister begged him to spend the night that they might "talk until morning about the joys of life in heaven." Benedict refused, citing the rules of his monastery from which it was "impossible" to deviate. To this answer Scholastica responded by simply lowering her head in prayer. Immediately the heavens erupted in thunder and released such a flood of rain that travel was obviously impossible. "May almighty God spare you, Sister," Benedict cried in alarm. "What have you done?" Scholastica answered simply, "I asked you, but you were unwilling to listen to me. I asked my Lord and He listened to me."

And so Scholastica had her desire fulfilled: "They spent the whole night awake, and had their fill of talk about spiritual matters." St. Gregory comments thus on Scholastica's victory over her brother in this case: "As John says, 'God is love,' and she justly overcame him by the greater strength of her love."

It was to be their last meeting. Three days later, as Benedict stood in his cell, he had a vision of his sister's soul leaving her body and rising to heaven in the form of a dove. Without delay he dispatched several monks to retrieve her body. They found her dead, just as Benedict had foreseen. Her body was carried to the monastery and placed in a tomb that Benedict had prepared for himself. There, in time, he joined her.

See: Gregory the Great, *Dialogues, Book II: Saint Benedict,* trans. Myra Uhlfelder (Indianapolis: Bobbs-Merrill Educational Publishing, 1967).

St. Dymphna
Martyr (d. 650?)

"O God, we humbly beseech You through Your servant, St. Dymphna, who sealed with her blood the love she bore You, to grant relief to those who suffer from mental afflictions and nervous disorders, especially [Name]."
— Prayer to St. Dymphna

In thirteenth-century Gheel, a town twenty-five miles from Antwerp in present-day Belgium, a sarcophagus was found to contain the remains of a seventh-century Christian martyr named St. Dymphna. This occasion was accompanied, it is said, by the miraculous healing of many local epileptics and others suffering from mental disturbances. From that time on, Gheel became a refuge for the mentally ill. The town went on to become famous for a remarkable program of treatment that involved housing mental patients in the homes of farmers and other local residents, allowing them to take part in family life and to perform chores and simple labor. And St. Dymphna came to be invoked as the patron of the mentally ill.

St. Dymphna herself was not insane. But like many women in the annals of the saints, she tended — like a magnet — to draw out the insanity of the world around her.

According to legend, Dymphna was the daughter of a pagan Irish king and a Christian princess, who died when she was a child. As Dymphna grew older, her father conceived an unnatural obsession with the girl, who bore an extraordinary resemblance to his departed wife. When he proposed that Dymphna should become his bride, she fled the court along with a small retinue that included her confessor and her father's jester. Eventually the party landed in Antwerp and made their way to Gheel, where they lived for a time as hermits.

In the meantime, however, the king's desire had turned to rage. He tracked down the refugees and insisted that Dymphna accompany him home. When she refused his advances, he first killed the priest and then turned his sword on Dymphna herself. She was buried by the local people, whose love she had earned by her care for the poor and the sick. They remembered and honored her as a martyr.

The only Life of St. Dymphna was composed by a priest in the thirteenth century. Otherwise there is scant evidence of her actual existence. And yet there was sufficient power in her story to heal afflicted minds and to inspire an entire town to take on her compassionate witness.

Mechthild of Magdeburg
Beguine Mystic (1210?–1282?)

"Fish cannot drown in water,
Birds cannot sink in air,
Gold cannot perish
In the refiner's fire.
This has God given to all creatures,
To foster and seek their own nature.
How then can I withstand mine?"

Mechthild of Magdeburg, a German mystic of the thirteenth century, is known to us entirely through her book *The Flowing Light of the Godhead*. Written in her own hand in the vernacular dialect of her native Saxony, her book is a kind of spiritual journal, a work in progress, to which she continuously returned, adding and amending, over the course of her life.

Mechthild was evidently born of a wealthy family somewhere near the town of Magdeburg in Saxony. At the age of twelve she received a mystical vision, the first of a series of "greetings of God" that would continue daily for the rest of her life. She later described the effects of such visitations: "The true greeting of God, which comes from the heavenly flood out of the spring of the flowing Trinity, has such power that it takes all strength from the body and lays the soul bare to itself. Thus it sees itself as one of the blessed and receives in itself divine glory."

Around the age of twenty Mechthild decided to leave her family and travel to Magdeburg, where she knew virtually no one. Rather than enter a convent she joined a household of Beguines. The Beguines were a movement of women who tried to fashion an independent religious life, without rules or enclosure or ecclesiastical approval. They flourished in the Low Countries and Germany in the thirteenth century and provided an attractive haven for religious visionaries like Mechthild.

Virtually nothing is known of how Mechthild spent her many years in the Beguinage, though it may be supposed that like other members of the community she passed her days in prayer, simple labor, and service to the poor. All the while she left a written trail of her inner spiritual journey. Her book combines a number of genres — mystical love poems describing the soul's communion with God, dialogues with Christ, as well as vivid accounts of her visions of paradise, hell, and the destiny of all creatures.

Among other things, Mechthild's book discloses her gift for gentle spiritual direction:

> What hinders spiritual people most of all from complete perfection is that they pay so little attention to small sins. I tell you in truth: when I hold back a smile which would harm no one, or have a sourness in my heart which I tell to no one, or feel some impatience with my own pain, then my soul becomes so dark... and my heart so cold that I must weep greatly and lament pitiably and yearn greatly and humbly confess all my lack of virtue.

At the same time Mechthild turned a critical eye on what she termed "poor Christianity." "I, poor woman, was so bold in my prayer that I impudently took corrupt Christianity into the arms of my soul and lifted it in lamentation."

Sections of Mechthild's book were copied and circulated widely, apparently winning her a loyal following. At the same time her writings invited criticism from those she called "my pharisees." So vehement were her detractors that she described herself as "a post or target at which people throw stones." She was in turn unsparing in her criticism of ecclesial worldliness and corruption:

> Alas! Crown of holy Church, how tarnished you have become. Your precious stones have fallen from you because you are weak and you disgrace the holy Christian faith.... Alas, crown of holy priesthood, you have disappeared, and you have nothing left but your external shape — namely, priestly power — with this you do battle against God and His chosen friends.... For our Lord speaks thus: I will touch the heart of the pope in Rome with great sadness and in this sadness I will speak to him and lament to him that My shepherds from Jerusalem have become murderers and wolves.

Mechthild of Magdeburg

These were, to say the least, risky sentiments. While the Beguines afforded a certain liberty, they also provided little protection. It is therefore not surprising to learn that Mechthild eventually left her community. Sometime around 1270 she settled in the Cistercian convent at Helfta. She was by this time ill and virtually blind. Nevertheless, in that extraordinary community, which already included two other mystics, Mechtild of Hackeborn and St. Gertrude of Helfta, she was apparently welcomed and cared for until her death.

Mechthild's life of intimacy with God brought with it much loneliness and estrangement from the world. She accepted the price along with the rewards of her vocation:

> Ever longing in the soul,
> Ever suffering in the body,
> Ever pain in the senses...
> Those who have given themselves utterly to God
> Know well what I mean.

But for one who remained faithful, suffering was not the last word.

> See there within the flesh
> Like a bright wick englazed
> The soul God's finger lit
> To give her liberty,
> And joy and power and love,
> To make her crystal, like
> As maybe, to Himself.

See: John Howard, "The German Mystic: Mechthild of Magdeburg," in *Medieval Women Mystics*, ed. Katharina M. Wilson (Athens: University of Georgia Press, 1984); Carol Lee Flinders, *Enduring Grace: Living Portraits of Seven Women Mystics* (San Francisco: HarperSanFrancisco, 1993).

Bd. Margaret Ebner
Mystic (1291–1351)

"The Name Jesus Christus blossoms within me during the season of Advent with especially sweet grace, and I can do nothing except what is given me with Jesus and from Jesus and in Jesus."

From the age of fifteen until her death fifty years later Margaret Ebner lived as a Dominican nun in a monastery near Dillingen on the Danube in present-day Germany. Like many members of her community, she came endowed by her patrician family with an excellent education. This prepared her well for the primary occupation of the monastery: hand-copying manuscripts, such as the works of Thomas Aquinas. For the first twenty years of her life, as she would later recall, she lived without any true "awareness of herself." But this began to change in 1312 on "the feast of SS. Vedastus and Amandus," when she was overcome by a mysterious illness that in its various forms would dominate her life for the next fourteen years. For years at a time she was unable to get out of bed. She shunned all company. Her only consolation was found in reciting the Our Father.

Margaret's acute suffering brought her to a state of deep depression that lifted only on the day she was first introduced to a new confessor, a secular priest named Henry of Nördlingen, who was the leader of a pious fellowship called the "Friends of God." As Margaret later wrote, "When the Friend of God came to me — I saw in all truthfulness that it seemed to me as if God had sent His dear angel in the light of truth. . . . When I left him that evening the grace of God was so alive in me from speaking with him that I could scarcely wait for daybreak in order to visit him again. . . . I did not even notice my body, and it seemed to me as if I were floating upward." From that time on she "continued to live all the time in noticeable joy."

The meeting was equally fateful for Henry. In his many letters he described her as "the faithful physician of my wounded heart," "the chosen joy of my heart," "the most interior good of my soul that I have on earth," and "my faithful power in God." The greater change, however, was evident in Margaret. Not only did she recover from her infirmities, but her whole personality was transformed. "Sorrow became non-sorrow," and she seemed to live each day in the presence of the heavenly life. From a once-conventional nun, distinguished only by her strange sufferings, she emerged as a prophet and visionary, whose pronouncements and counsel were heeded far beyond the walls of her monastery. Henry, at first her spiritual teacher, then her friend, and ultimately her devoted pupil, was left to wonder. She had "mastered the steps of the dance of a true life to the sweet piping" of Christ, he wrote. Her "prophetic voice makes me speechless."

Margaret's world was rent by violence and turmoil. Her monastery was caught in the middle of a power struggle between the pope and the emperor. Wars and smaller skirmishes erupted throughout Europe in these decades. The Black Plague would reduce the population by as much as half. All this, she was given to believe, was "because of the great faults and sins of Christendom."

Nevertheless, Margaret had the ability to see the world in its ultimate dimension — suffused by the divine presence. Sometimes it seemed to her as if a "light was given to me that shoots out from my eyes like flames." For long periods she was seized by raptures, or thrust into the presence of Christ's Passion or scenes from his childhood. She was buffeted between periods of "binding Silence" when she could not speak a word, and other periods when she was given to ecstatic "Outcries" or uncontrollable "Speakings" of the Name of Jesus that left her physically exhausted.

Henry asked her to write down her visions and spiritual adventures. It is by this collection of her *Revelations* that she is chiefly remembered. In 1979 she became the first saint to be beatified by Pope John Paul II.

See: Margaret Ebner, *Major Works,* Classics of Western Spirituality (New York: Paulist, 1993).

Bd. Julian of Norwich
Mystic (1342–1416)

"As truly as God is our Father, so truly is God our Mother. Our Father wills, our Mother works, our good Lord the Holy Spirit confirms."

The late fourteenth century was a time of terrible upheaval. With the Black Plague, the Hundred Years' War, and the crisis of church authority occasioned by the long papal schism, Europe was burdened by an atmosphere of anxiety. Intense concern about the prospects for personal salvation, coupled with doubts about the efficacy of the church and its prescribed channels of spirituality, led to a proliferation of new forms of religious expression. Much of the new spirituality emerged from laypeople aspiring to lives of holiness outside of conventional religious orders.

The yearning for a personal, experiential faith contributed to a flowering of nonmonastic Christian mysticism. Fourteenth-century England produced a significant number of mystical classics, written in the vernacular, often by laypeople living as solitaries, and addressed to other laypeople seeking a more intimate relationship with God. The *Showings* of Julian of Norwich is one — and perhaps the greatest — of these works.

We know little of Julian's biography; her name itself is uncertain, possibly being taken from the church of St. Julian in Norwich, to which she attached herself in her later life as an enclosed anchoress. As an anchoress, she would have been literally sealed in a dwelling attached to the wall of a church. Her cell would have allowed a view of the church interior, as well as an outside window for the delivery of food and the reception of visitors seeking spiritual counsel. She may also have enjoyed a garden and the companionship of a cat. Otherwise, her life was devoted to prayer and reflection.

What may today seem like an extreme form of rejection of the world was recognized in her own time as serving an important social function. In any case, her writings testify to the profound love and compassion that were the fruit of her solitary existence. For other details of her life we are entirely dependent on the testimony of her *Showings*.

Thus we learn that she was born in 1342. At some point in her youth she prayed that she might be granted three graces: recollection of Christ's passion; bodily sickness; and "three wounds" of contrition, compassion, and longing for God. Her prayer was answered at the age of thirty when she fell so seriously ill that she was given the last rites of the church. She did not die, but as she lay gazing on a crucifix, she experienced sixteen distinct revelations concerning Christ's passion, after which her sickness left her completely. She recorded these revelations in two versions written some twenty years apart.

In Julian's first revelation she beholds Christ's crown of thorns, the effects of which are described with clinical exactness: "the red blood running down from under the crown, hot and flowing freely and copiously, a living stream." Yet this vision, while "hideous and fearful," is also "sweet and lovely." This unexpected conjunction of adjectives underlines the most distinctive quality of Julian's work. For her the cross becomes a source not of terror and anguish but of consolation, a sign of Christ's "friendliness" and extreme "courtesy." In that the one who is highest has assumed the point reserved for the lowest, God pays the honor of a king who condescends to familiarity with a servant. Physically she sees a bleeding head. Spiritually she sees into the depth of God's love and goodness.

This single vision proves an extraordinarily rich soil, yielding reflection on a range of theological issues, including the value of creation, the power of atonement, and the impotence of evil. Creation amounts to no more than a hazelnut in the hand of God. Physically it is nothing. But spiritually its value is measured against God's love and the price God has paid for it in blood. Thus, to gaze into the heart of darkness itself is to enter the mysterious immensity of God's goodness. The smaller our value the greater is God's love. For all its weakness and sin, God suffered for this world; Christ's blood was its price. And in the end God's suffering is turned to joy. For our Creator, who is also our Protector, is also our Lover, working good through all manner of things. The logic of joy and mercy is predetermined even before Christ suffered his crown of thorns. We are "soul and body, clad and enclosed in the goodness of God."

There are many themes in Julian's writings that speak directly to the heart of contemporary spirituality. Among these is her frequent recourse to feminine images of God. Jesus, she says, is our true Mother, who bears us in the womb of his love and nourishes us with his own flesh. Throughout her writings, the affirmation of the goodness of creation and her stress on the beauty, friendliness, and love of God contrast sharply with a theology that lays stress on the anger and omnipotent judgment of God over a sinful world.

Julian did not directly address the major political and ecclesial crises. But it cannot be said that she was remote from the concerns of her day. In an age of anxious uncertainty, Christians were desperate to seek assurances of salvation, of the meaning of suffering, and of the power and goodness of God. Julian's answers spoke directly to these issues. Her central insight was that the God who created us out of love and who redeemed us by suffering love, also sustains us and wills to be united with us in the end. This love, and not sin, fundamentally determines our existence. Evil has no independent status; whatever we may suffer, God has already suffered. "The worst," as she noted, "has already happened and been repaired." As for our suffering in this life, insofar as we share Christ's passion we may look forward as well to sharing his joy in heaven. Thus she could say, in her most famous and characteristic words, "All shall be well, all shall be well, and all manner of things shall be well."

See: Julian of Norwich, *Showings,* trans. James Walsh, S.J., Classics of Western Spirituality (New York: Paulist, 1978).

Emily Dickinson
Poet (1830–1886)

I'm Nobody! Who are you?
Are you — Nobody — Too?

Emily Dickinson was born in 1830 in Amherst, Massachusetts. She briefly attended the Mount Holyoke Female Seminary, but returned home after only one year, perhaps put off by the strong atmosphere of evangelical revival. Many members of her family, including her father, a distinguished figure in Amherst, were caught up in this spiritual renewal. But Emily herself seems to have resisted the impulse. In one of her poems she described her reasons for avoiding church services:

> Some keep the Sabbath going to Church —
> I keep it, staying at home —
> With a Bobolink for a Chorister —
> And an Orchard, for a Dome — ...
>
> God preaches, a noted Clergyman —
> And the sermon is never long.
> So instead of getting to Heaven, at last —
> I'm going, all along.

Though in her youth Emily made a number of trips to Washington, Boston, and Philadelphia, at a certain point she effectively withdrew to her home and adopted the life of a recluse, hermit, or stationary pilgrim, depending on one's point of view. To her neighbors she was simply an eccentric, famous for dressing only in white and for her passion for seclusion. She described herself in these terms: "small, like the wren; and my hair is bold like the chestnut burr; and my eyes, like the sherry in the glass, that the guest leaves."

Many theories have been offered for her withdrawal: disappointed love; a feminist protest against the constraints on women; the necessary solitude for her vocation as a writer; or simple agoraphobia. There is no easy way of resolving this mystery. While she maintained a lively correspondence and counted many friends, she enjoyed little personal contact beyond her family. During her final illness she permitted a doctor to "examine" her only from the hallway by watching her pass back and forth in front of her door.

How did she spend her time? After her death in 1886 her family discovered in her drawers a collection of poems — 1,775 in all — carefully written by hand and organized in notebooks. She had shared her poems with only a few friends and published only a handful in her life, though all the while writing with furious concentration. The first selections were published four years after her death; the complete edition in 1955. This work secured her reputation as one of the most significant figures in American literature.

Dickinson's poems were deceptively simple, many following the cheerful rhythms of popular hymns. But they reflected a complex and deeply personal approach to the world. A great number of them addressed her effort to define her relationship with God — not according to the doctrines of Puritan religion, but on her own terms, wavering frequently between doubt and faith.

She was a great poet of nature. Her careful observations about bees, birds, and flowers of every kind showed her capacity to see the universe in a grain of sand. For Dickinson these details of the natural order served as a harbor, opening up to speculative musings on eternity. But it was the subject of death — the border between the individual and infinity — that seems to have captured her imagination most of all. Throughout her poems, death appears as a friend and guide, a source of pain but also the conductor to new life. Death is "the supple Suitor/ That wins at last." As she wrote in one of her most famous poems,

> Because I could not stop for Death —
> He kindly stopped for me —
> The Carriage held but just ourselves —
> And Immortality . . .

The loss of many friends and family members, the separation from those she loved, the vast bloody backdrop of the Civil War, all provided a sweeping panorama, carefully surveyed from the seclusion of her room. The written word was her point of contact: "This is my letter to the World / That never wrote to Me." Of poetry she wrote, "If I read a book and it makes my whole body so cold no fire can ever warm me, I know that is poetry. If I feel physically as if the top of my head were taken off, I know that is poetry."

Few in Dickinson's life ever suspected the fire that warmed her heart. But in measuring the meaning of a life, she adopted the long view:

Each life converges to some centre
Expressed or still —
Exists in every human nature
A goal —

Admitted scarcely to itself, it may be —
Too fair
For credibility's temerity
To dare. . . .

Ungained, it may be, by life's low venture,
But then —
Eternity enables the endeavoring
Again.

On May 14, 1886, she wrote to friends, "Little Cousins, — Called back. Emily." She died the next day.

See: The Selected Poems & Letters of Emily Dickinson (Garden City, N.Y.: Doubleday, 1959).

St. Therese of Lisieux
Doctor of the Church (1873–1897)

*"I am only a very little soul,
who can only offer very little things to our Lord."*

The story of St. Therese is lacking in outward drama. She was born in 1873 to a middle-class family in Lisieux, a small town in Normandy. Her mother died when she was four, and Therese and her four older sisters were left in the care of their father, a watchmaker and a man of marked piety. Therese, it seems, was his favorite child. When she was fifteen she received a special dispensation (in light of her young age) to enter the Carmelite convent of Lisieux, where two of her sisters had already preceded her. The rest of her short life was spent within the cloister of this obscure convent. She died of tuberculosis on September 30, 1897, at the age of twenty-four. It might be supposed that the memory of such a short and uneventful life would remain within the walls of the convent. Instead, her name quickly circled the globe. In response to popular acclamation, her canonization was processed with remarkable speed. She was declared a saint in 1925. Her feast is on October 1.

What lay behind these developments was the posthumous publication of her autobiography, *The Story of a Soul*, in which she described her experience and her distinctive insights into the spiritual life. It is a book that might well have been subtitled "The Making of a Saint," for essentially it is about the path to holiness in everyday life. Despite the somewhat cloying and sentimental style of her provincial piety, Therese presents herself as a woman possessed of a will of steel. As a child she had determined to set her sights on the goal of sanctity, and she went on to pursue this objective with courageous tenacity. She called her method of spirituality "the Little Way." Simply put, this meant performing her everyday actions and suffering each petty insult or injury in the presence and love of God.

As a teenager she had literally stormed heaven to win acceptance into the Carmelite convent. Once inside, as her book reveals, she was not content merely to fulfill the letter of her religious rule. Seemingly driven by an inner sense that little time was available, she tried to accelerate the process of sanctification. Devoting herself body and soul to Christ she offered her life as a victim of love for the salvation of souls. So acute was her belief in the Mystical Body of Christ that she believed each act of devotion, each moment of suffering patiently endured, might be credited to other souls in greater need.

Therese considered herself to be of little account — literally a "Little Flower" — though for this reason no less precious in the eyes of God. She also called her Little Way the way of spiritual childhood. But she believed that this way might transform any situation into a profound arena for holiness, and that one might thus, through the effect of subtle ripples, make a significant contribution to transforming the world.

Therese writes of her feeling that she was called to all vocations. She felt a powerful vocation to be a priest—but also a warrior, an apostle, a Doctor of the Church, and a martyr. "I would like to perform the most heroic deeds. I feel I have the courage of a Crusader. I should like to die on the battlefield in defense of the church. If only I were a priest!" The passage of time has not dulled the challenge of this heartfelt confession. But ultimately Therese came to realize that her vocation was nothing less than Charity itself, a virtue embracing every other vocation. "My vocation is love!...In the heart of the Church, who is my Mother, *I will be love*. So I shall be everything and so my dreams will be fulfilled!" At another point she described her mission as simply "to make Love loved."

In 1894 Therese woke on the morning of Good Friday to find her mouth filled with blood. She rejoiced privately in the thought that she might soon be on her way to heaven. "I was absolutely sure that, on this anniversary of His death, my Beloved had let me hear His first call, like a gentle, far-off murmur which heralded His joyful arrival." But instead this sign simply heralded the onset of a protracted period of agonizing pain as well as spiritual desolation. Before the end her sufferings would constitute a virtual crucifixion.

Therese wrote her autobiography in obedience to the request of her superior. The last chapters were literally written *in extremis.* During this time her physical torment was aggravated by periods of intense spiritual suffering. Her consciousness was flooded with terrifying images and at times she came close to despair. By continuing to pray and to hold fast to the image of Christ she eventually passed through this dark night. When she died, surrounded by her Carmelite Sisters, her last words were, "Oh, I love Him!...My God...I love You."

The publication of Therese's autobiography immediately struck a responsive chord, especially among the "simple faithful." Few are they who are called to do great things, to witness before kings and princes, or to shoulder the cross of martyrdom. And yet, as Therese demonstrated, there is a principle of continuity between our response to the everyday situations in which we find ourselves and the "great" arenas in which the saints and martyrs have offered their witness. According to Therese, each moment, accepted and lived in a spirit of love, is an occasion for heroism and a potential step along the path to sanctity.

In the years following her death, Therese was credited with an extraordinary number of miracles. It was remembered that she had once said, "After my death I will let fall a shower of roses. I will spend my heaven in doing good upon earth."

See: The Autobiography of St. Therese of Lisieux: The Story of a Soul (Garden City, N.Y.: Image, 1957); Dorothy Day, *Therese* (Springfield, Ill.: Templegate Publishers, 1960); *St. Thérèse of Lisieux: Essential Writings,* ed. Mary Frohlich (Maryknoll, N.Y.: Orbis Books, 2003).

Mary Slessor
Missionary (1848–1915)

"Lord, the task is impossible for me, but not for Thee. Lead the way and I will follow."

Mary Slessor, a "wee, red-haired lass" from Dundee, Scotland, was born on December 2, 1848. Her father was a shoemaker, and also an alcoholic, frequently unable to work. It fell to her mother to support the family. She was a weaver, and also a devout Presbyterian, who eagerly read each month's issue of the *Missionary Record*. Mary grew up listening to stories of Dr. Livingstone and other tales of missionary adventures among the "heathen." They spoke of a world apart from the slums of Dundee and the mills where Mary began working from the age of eleven. After working twelve hours a day, she took evening classes, and on the weekend taught Sunday school. But all the while she dreamed of Africa.

In 1876, when she was twenty-eight, Mary's application to the Presbyterian mission board was accepted, and she departed for the Calabar River in southern Nigeria. It was a region decimated by centuries of slave trade and constant internecine fighting. The climate was unforgiving — most Westerners considered it unlivable. But Mary quickly made herself at home. Working in her first years in the coastal mission towns, she mastered the difficult Efik language and adapted, as much as possible, to local customs.

Her aim was to awaken the people to a love of Christ. But she did not believe this could be accomplished simply by preaching. Instead she sought to demonstrate her own love for the people, and thus to awaken them to a sense of their own preciousness in the eyes of God. She expressed this particularly through her devotion to women and children, which at times set her in conflict with traditional practices. For instance, she opposed the custom of attributing any misfortune to malign spirits and evil charms. The typical response to any illness or accident was first to identify the responsible malefactor and then to exact punishment. Mary intervened in countless domestic and village disputes, thus preventing needless bloodshed.

The birth of twins was considered a particularly bad omen; both children would be exposed in the wilderness, while their mother might become an untouchable outcast. Mary made it a habit to rescue these twins and their mothers, taking them into her own home. She raised eight children as her own. Eventually, her efforts bore fruit. Through her example, she wrote, "It has dawned on them the fact that life is worth saving, even at the risk of one's own."

In time Mary received permission to extend her ministry upriver, deep into the uncharted jungle where no missionary had dared to travel. There were reports of cannibalism and other horrors. Even her neighboring villagers warned her that she would surely be killed. But she would not be dissuaded. "Why should I fear? I am on a Royal Mission. I am in the service of the King of kings." Inevitably she developed malaria, a condition that often put her out of commission for long periods. Yet she continued her mission, enduring not only illness but every kind of physical danger. The local people were amazed by her courage and stamina; gradually their suspicions gave way to trust and respect. They called her, affectionately, "Ma," or "Mother of All the People."

In the jungle she established a rudimentary hospital and offered primary education. But her deeper purpose was to impart an understanding of God's love and desire for all people to experience life in abundance. Her own love gave credibility to her message. She labored in Calabar for nearly forty years, most of the time working entirely independently. She wrote back to the mission board, appealing to other young women with these words:

> Don't grow up a nervous old maid! Gird yourself for the battle outside somewhere, and keep your heart young. Give up your whole being to create music everywhere, in the light places and in the dark places, and your life will make Melody. I'm a witness to the perfect joy and satisfaction of a single life — with a tail of human tag-rag hanging on. It is rare! It is as exhilarating as an aeroplane or a dirigible or whatever they are that are always trying to get up and are always coming down!
>
> Mine has been such a joyous service, God has been good to me, letting me serve Him in this humble way. I cannot thank Him enough for the honor He conferred upon me when He sent me to the "dark continent."

In 1914 Mary fell ill with a terrible fever. She maintained her confidence until the end. "The time of the singing of birds is where Christ is," she said. "Never talk about the cold hand of death. It is the hand of Christ...Life is so grand and eternity is so real."

Mary Slessor died on January 13, 1915.

See: James Buchan, *The Expendable Mary Slessor* (New York: Seabury, 1981).

Evelyn Underhill
Spiritual Guide (1875–1941)

"It is useless to utter fervent petitions that Thy Kingdom be established and that Thy Will be done, unless we are willing to do something about it ourselves. . . . We are agents of the Creative Spirit in this world. Real advance in the spiritual life means accepting this vocation with all it involves."

Through her voluminous writings, Evelyn Underhill did much to awaken modern interest in the mystical traditions of Christianity. In her scholarly work she illuminated the links between such disparate figures as Meister Eckhart, Julian of Norwich, and John of the Cross. But as a popular writer and spiritual director she went further, showing the relevance of mysticism for ordinary people living in the modern world.

Born on December 6, 1875, Underhill was raised in a comfortable middle-class British home. Though nominally Anglican, she showed no early signs of her later religious yearnings. By her late twenties, however, she had begun to feel a powerful attraction to Roman Catholicism. She regularly attended Catholic services and received religious instruction. But in the end she shrank from formal conversion. One factor was the strong objection of her fiancé, Hubert Stuart Moore, whom she married in 1907. But there were other factors. The harsh papal condemnation of Modernism in that same year made her wary of submitting to church authority.

For some years she reverted to a private faith outside any formal practice apart from her systematic study of the Christian mystics. Such an interest was quite unusual in Underhill's day; in many cases their writings were not even available in English. To the extent that Protestants were even aware of Christian mysticism, they tended to view it as a species of Catholic neurosis, a relic from the Middle Ages. For Catholics, meanwhile, the word "mysticism" shared a corner with supernatural gifts like bilocation or the stigmata — something reserved for God's chosen few, but of little relevance to the ordinary faithful. It was in this context, in 1911, that Underhill published her landmark work, *Mysticism*.

Underhill distinguished mysticism in its pure sense from visions, ecstasies, and "special effects." Mysticism, she wrote, "is the art of union with Reality. The mystic is a person who has attained that union in greater or less degree; or who aims at and believes in such attainment."

The origins of Christian mysticism were in fact in scripture — in the life of Jesus, St. Paul, and the earliest disciples. As such, it was not an extraordinary sideline but an essential expression of the Christian life. It reached its apogee in those great figures like Eckhart and St. Hildegard of Bingen, or the anonymous author of *The Cloud of Unknowing*. But in essence it was available to all believers. Mysticism was simply the experiential dimension of faith, "the soul of religion."

The publication of her book brought her new friends, among them Baron Friedrich von Hügel, a Roman Catholic philosopher whose own work, *The Mystical Element of Religion*, remains a classic in its field. She asked him to become her spiritual director. As such, he criticized her somewhat individualistic approach to spiritual life and urged her to resume the discipline of communal prayer and worship. He also urged her to undertake charitable work among the poor.

She saw his point. "Divorced from all institutional expression mysticism tends to become strange, vague, or merely sentimental," she later wrote. "True mysticism is the soul of religion; but like the soul of man it needs a body if it is to fulfill its mighty destiny." The result was her formal and heartfelt return to the Anglican church.

Underhill went on to write thirty books — some of them further studies of the mystics, but many more on general spiritual themes, directed to a popular audience. As a married laywoman, occupied with the concerns and distractions of ordinary middle-class life, she felt a particular calling to address other laypeople. She wanted to show that growth in the spiritual life was not simply for holy prodigies or those behind the cloister, but should be the aim of every Christian.

Though she maintained her own discipline of prayer, worship, spiritual reading, and charitable work, she never presented herself as a model of heroic piety. In the spiritual life, she observed, some go to God as if "by a moving staircase," or "appear to be whisked past us in a lift." What matter that "we find ourselves on a steep flight of stairs with a bend at the top so that we cannot see how much farther we have to go"? The important thing, she maintained, "is the conviction that all are moving toward God, and, in that journey, accompanied, supported, checked and fed by God." When we realize this, then life, "inner and outer, becomes one single, various act of adoration and self-giving; one undivided response of the creature to the demand and pressure of Creative Love."

Yet she constantly emphasized the practical dimension of spirituality. Our job is not just to gaze with reverent appreciation on God's creation. "He made us in order to use us, and use us in the most profitable way," sometimes in dramatic or heroic fashion, but more often in humble tasks. In our "ordinary mixed life of every day" — this is where we live out our religious vocation. As a spiritual director, Underhill offered similarly homely and practical advice. To one overly scrupulous correspondent she wrote, "Refuse to pander to a morbid interest in your own misdeeds. Pick yourself up, be sorry, shake yourself, and go on again." To another: "Don't saturate yourself the whole time with mystical books. . . . Hot milk and a thoroughly foolish novel are better things for you to go to bed on just now than St. Teresa."

Evelyn Underhill died on June 15, 1941.

See: Christopher J. R. Armstrong, *Evelyn Underhill: An Introduction to Her Life and Writings* (Grand Rapids, Mich.: William B. Eerdmans, 1975); Emilie Griffin, ed., *Evelyn Underhill: Essential Writings* (Maryknoll, N.Y.: Orbis Books, 2003).

Edel Quinn
Missionary of the Legion of Mary (1907–1944)

"We have only this short life in which to prove our love."

The thing that struck most people about Edel Quinn was her extraordinary gaiety and spirit of fun. Some would find that inconsistent with a life of intense religious devotion. But for Edel they were two sides of the same coin. People of all sorts — whether bishops, prostitutes, Irish dock workers, or African peasants — perceived an aura of intense aliveness in her presence that drew them close and enlarged their faith.

She was born and raised in Ireland. After leaving school she took a course as a shorthand typist and went to work to help support her family. Her employer fell in love with her and proposed marriage, but she turned him down, explaining that she planned as soon as possible to enter a contemplative convent. Her parents begged her to delay her vocation, as they needed her help raising her siblings. In the meantime, she became involved with the Legion of Mary, an organization of pious laypeople committed to invigorating the faith of their neighbors through loving service. Before long, Edel had become passionately committed to this work, which occupied all her spare time. One of her particular projects was befriending and rescuing prostitutes — a mission for which she showed surprising aptitude.

By 1932 she was finally ready to enter the Poor Clares. But at the last moment illness intervened. After suffering a hemorrhage, she was discovered to have advanced tuberculosis. She spent a year in a sanitarium, a time she regarded as an opportunity for intense spiritual study and reflection. Eventually, when her condition stabilized, she was allowed to return home and to resume her previous schedule of apostolic activity. In 1936, she jumped at an invitation for Legion workers in East Africa. The Legion was reluctant to entrust such arduous work to a young woman of delicate health. But her enthusiasm won the day.

Arriving in Africa, she established a base of operations in Nairobi, where she found the church rigidly segregated between Europeans and Africans. Everyone said it was useless to try to overcome this breach, but she was not discouraged. "The impossible has happened elsewhere — why not here?" she wrote. "Let us give scope to grace and faith." In fact, within weeks she had established Legion cells throughout Nairobi, and within months they were bringing white and black Catholics together in religious celebrations.

She seemed tireless, covering vast distances throughout East Africa — Kenya, Uganda, Nyasaland, and Tanganyika — much of this in trucks over rough, unpaved roads, and under conditions that would have daunted people of more robust health. Wherever she went, she left a share of her own faith and love. In the words of one bishop, "After a year of Miss Quinn's work the atmosphere of my diocese had changed. Without any noise, she had brought a germ of life.... One could feel the passing of grace. In her presence questions of race and of social rank disappeared. Her coming among us was a direct and special favor from God."

By 1938, however, her health had markedly deteriorated. After she suffered a severe case of malaria, some of her colleagues urged her to leave Africa. But she would hear none of that. She had never been happier, she insisted. Her life was entirely in God's hands. When someone asked her, "Are you naturally lighthearted or do you practice it as a virtue?" she answered, "It is about three-quarters natural."

For the next several years Edel's life was punctuated by incapacitating illness. As soon as she had recovered from one bout she would set back out on the road. But with each cycle she became visibly weaker. She finally died on May 12, 1944, at the age of thirty-seven.

For years after her death, the people she had encountered and touched — however briefly — remembered her as one of the most extraordinary people they had ever known. One bishop summed up his impressions simply: "She was splendid!"

See: Hilda Graef, *Mystics of Our Times* (Garden City, N.Y.: Hanover House, 1962); Leon-Joseph Suenens, *Edel Quinn* (Dublin: C. J. Fallon, 1953).

Anne Frank
Witness of the Holocaust (1929–1945)

"Who would ever think that so much can go on in the soul of a young girl?"

There are some persons whose great gift, in a dark age, is simply to maintain a candlelight of humanity and so to guarantee that darkness should not have the final word. Anne Frank, a Jewish child who perished during the Holocaust, was surely one of these. Her life was extinguished at the age of fifteen — thus contributing to the Nazi dream of a Jewish-free Europe. But her light continued to burn, thus fulfilling her own dream: "I want to go on living after my death."

Anne's story is well known. She was born on June 12, 1929. During the Nazi occupation of Holland, her family and another family, the Van Daams, took shelter in a "secret annex" in her father's office in the center of Amsterdam. They remained sequestered for two years. Keeping still all day, never able to leave their hidden quarters, they relied on the support of Dutch friends to preserve their secret and to bring them supplies and news of the outside world. Anne was thirteen when she entered the annex in July 1942. Besides her schoolbooks and her treasured scrapbook of Hollywood stars, Anne brought along with her a diary she had received for her thirteenth birthday. Addressing her daily entries to an imaginary girlfriend, "Kitty," Anne faithfully kept her diary throughout the course of her captivity. This diary was published after the war and was quickly acclaimed as one of the most deeply affecting artifacts of the Holocaust. But because of Anne's unusual gifts as a writer and because of the extraordinary qualities of her personality, her work merits recognition as a literary classic in its own right and as one of the great moral documents of the twentieth century.

For Anne herself keeping a diary was not simply a distraction but a duty, a responsibility to render her experience and her feelings in the most accurate possible terms. "I want to write, but more than that, I want to bring out all kinds of things that lie buried deep in my heart," she writes in the early pages. With remarkable skill Anne manages to describe the personalities and atmosphere in the annex — the strain of captivity and close quarters and the brave efforts to carry on with life. All this takes place against the backdrop of fear and the constant danger of discovery.

> I see the eight of us with our "Secret Annex" as if we were a little piece of blue heaven, surrounded by heavy black rain clouds. The round, clearly defined spot where we stand is still safe, but the clouds gather more closely about us and the circle which separates us from the approaching danger closes more and more tightly.

The diary is mostly a sharply recorded chronicle of the everyday trials and the modest joys of a young girl's life "underground." But it also contains Anne's remarkably unchildlike reflections on the meaning of life and faith in the face of adversity.

> The best remedy for those who are afraid, lonely, or unhappy is to go outside, somewhere where they can be quiet alone with the heavens, nature, and God. Because only then does one feel that all is as it should be and that God wishes to see people happy, amidst the simple beauty of nature. As long as this exists...I know that there will always be comfort for every sorrow, whatever the circumstances may be.

Lying in bed, she says she ends her evening prayers with the words, "I thank you, God, for all that is good and dear and beautiful," and adds, "I am filled with joy....I don't think of all the misery, but of the beauty that still remains."

Aside from acknowledging the terror that prowls beyond her hiding place, the diary also reflects the mysterious unfolding of Anne's personality, her emergence from childhood, and her growing sense of herself as a young woman with a future and a task in the world.

> I know what I want, I have a goal, an opinion, I have a religion and love. Let me be myself and then I am satisfied. I know that I'm a woman, a woman with inward strength and plenty of courage. If God lets me live...I shall not remain insignificant, I shall work in the world and for mankind! And now I know that first and foremost I shall require courage and cheerfulness.

Rarely has anyone so well defined the virtues required by our age — "courage and cheerfulness" — as this fourteen-year-old girl already living under sentence of death.

In August 1944, soon after Anne's fifteenth birthday, the secret annex was betrayed and all its eight inhabitants were dispersed among the factories of death. Only Otto Frank, Anne's father, survived the war and returned to the old house in Amsterdam. He learned that his wife had died in January 1945 in Auschwitz, while Anne and her sister Margot had died of typhus in Bergen-Belsen in early March. Then he was presented with the diaries of his daughter, lovingly preserved by friends in hopes of her eventual return.

In light of her death it is excruciating to read Anne's intimate confidences, her account of the homey details of life in hiding. But through the girlish record of quarrels with her mother, worries about her studies, and the possibilities for finding romantic happiness with the Van Daams' teenage son, Otto Frank was the first to recognize in his daughter's diary a profound witness to the value of life and the virtue of hope. Words written days before her arrest only gain additional power in the light of her fate:

> In spite of everything I still believe that people are really good at heart.... I see the world gradually being turned into a wilderness, I hear the ever-approaching thunder, which will destroy us too, I can feel the sufferings of millions and yet, if I look up into the heavens, I think that it will all come right.... In the meantime, I must uphold my ideals, for perhaps the time will come when I shall be able to carry them out.

See: *The Diary of Anne Frank* (London: Pan, 1954).

Gabrielle Bossis
Mystic (1874–1950)

"Don't get the idea that a saint is a saint at every moment. But there is always my grace. You must aim at perfection, but the perfection of your own nature. This is the way you will please me."
— Christ's words to Gabrielle Bossis

Gabrielle Bossis was born in Nantes, France, in 1874. As a child she enjoyed a special sense of God's presence. She liked to carry on what she called "simple talks" with Jesus, a practice she continued all her life. Later, when she described this practice to her spiritual director, a Franciscan, he urged her to become a nun. But she was certain this was not Jesus' will for her. Neither was she called to marriage. Instead she determined that her vocation was to live out her dedication to God as a single woman in the world.

Though she came from a wealthy family, she trained as a nurse to be of service to the poor. Her friends knew her as a gregarious and entertaining woman, but few had any knowledge of her rich inner life. When she was sixty-two she took up writing "moral comedies" for the theater. Within a short while she became famous as both a playwright and an actor. It was only at this point that she wondered whether God wanted her to share the fruit of her contemplative life. She began to keep a journal of her colloquies with Christ, a practice she continued up to the end of her life.

After her death on June 9, 1950, her journals were published—to the astonishment of her friends and to the delight of many readers. Though written in the voice of Christ, her journal entries reflect her own joyful and loving attitude, and her experience of the presence of grace. "In your soul there is a door that leads to the contemplation of God," she writes, "but, you must open it."

Christ's message, as conveyed by Bossis, is the imperative to seek his face not only in other people, but in every circumstance, and to respond to him joyfully and with love. "You were touched when you read that I was in the Gospels, hidden in the sacrament of the Word. But how much more I am present in the sacrament of human life!"

Holiness, according to Bossis, is a matter of awakening to the presence of God. This holiness is not expressed so much in pious attitudes as in a certain openness to life. She might have been describing herself: "Don't think that a saint must look saintly in the eyes of humans. Saints have an outer nature, but it is the inner nature that counts. There is a fruit whose rough — even thorny — skin gives no inkling of its sweet and juicy taste. That is how it is for my saints. Their value is in their hearts."

In Bossis's view we are called to express the divine nature in our own lives, to make it visible in our actions. To the extent that we do this we "continue" God's life: "Your life is a gift from me, so I ask you to give it to me through all your actions. Don't you feel the greatness of it — to make God live?"

Gabrielle Bossis

The God she loved was closer than her own heart — hidden in her own yearnings, sufferings, and ideals — but always wanting to be discovered. "Hunt for me everywhere! I'll let myself be captured with such joy! How could you expect to find me if you didn't search? And when you have found me, give me to others. There are people I am waiting to reach only through you. This is the mission foreseen for you from all eternity. Do not be unfaithful to it."

In May 1950 Bossis became seriously ill. The final entry in her journal, in which there is no distinguishing between Christ's voice and her own, was written on May 25, 1950: "Have I come to the end of my life? Is this the moment when I celebrate my first and last Mass? Where are you, Loving Presence? . . . And afterward, what will I be?"

"It will be I. It will be I. Forevermore."

Gabrielle Bossis died on June 9, 1950.

See: Shawn Madigan, C.S.J., editor, *Mystics, Visionaries, and Prophets: A Historical Anthology of Women's Spiritual Writings* (Minneapolis: Augsburg Fortress, 1998).

Martyrs of Birmingham
(d. 1963)

"These children — unoffending; innocent and beautiful — were the victims of one of the most vicious, heinous crimes ever perpetrated against humanity." —Martin Luther King, Jr.

On the morning of September 15, 1963, someone tossed a packet of dynamite sticks through the basement window of the Sixteenth Street Baptist Church in Birmingham, Alabama. Moments later an explosion took the lives of four young girls and seriously injured twenty others. The slain children were Addie Mae Collins, Carole Robertson, and Cynthia Wesley, all fourteen, and Denise McNair, eleven. At the moment of the blast they had just finished their Sunday school lesson and were putting on their choir robes in the basement changing room.

The church bombing was a terrible rejoinder to the uplifting spectacle, only weeks before, of the March on Washington, where Martin Luther King, Jr., had delivered his famous speech, "I Have a Dream." But in Birmingham it also followed an intense summer of demonstrations and civil disobedience. The aim of this campaign, much of it organized in churches like the one on Sixteenth Street, was to challenge the rigidly enforced policies of racial segregation in this city, known as the "Johannesburg of the South." Scenes of fire hoses and attack dogs set upon nonviolent demonstrators had dramatized to the nation both the reality of racism and the hateful violence stirred up by the peaceful cry for justice.

All this seemed to culminate in the explosion on that Sunday morning. The terrible symbolism of such a massacre in church, and the innocence of the young victims, seemed to underscore the spiritual character of the forces engaged in the Birmingham struggle — literally a battle between the Children of Light and the Children of Darkness. Martin Luther King delivered a eulogy at the funeral for the girls. He called them "martyred heroines of a holy crusade for freedom and human dignity." He expressed the hope that their deaths would awaken the conscience of Birmingham and the nation and so douse the flames of hatred and division. "God still has a way of wringing good out of evil," he said hopefully. "History has proven over and over again that unmerited suffering is redemptive." To the parents of the four girls he addressed these words of comfort:

> Your children did not live long, but they lived well. The quantity of their lives was disturbingly small, but the quality of their lives was magnificently big. Where they died and what they were doing when death came will remain a marvelous tribute to each of you and an eternal epitaph to each of them.... They died within the sacred walls of the church after discussing a principle as eternal as love.

See: Henry Hampton and Steve Fayer, *Voices of Freedom* (New York: Bantam, 1990); James M. Washington, ed., *Testament of Hope: Essential Writings of Martin Luther King, Jr.* (San Francisco: Harper & Row, 1986).

Gladys Aylward
Missionary (1902–1970)

"I believe God has called me ... and it is not to walk as other people have walked in a nice rosy way, but just along the way he walked to Calvary. ... One day we will know and understand why."

Gladys Aylward grew up in a working-class home in London. She left school when she was fourteen, with no trade skills and no evident prospect of ever leaving the circumscribed world reserved for her class.

And yet, even from her childhood, she dreamed of becoming a missionary and spreading the name of Jesus to China. It was a fantastic ambition. She tried to win support from the China Inland Mission, but they quickly decided that she lacked the necessary education, that she would never learn Chinese, and that she was better suited to her current employment in domestic service.

But Gladys would not give up. After hearing of an aging missionary named Jeannie Lawson somewhere in China, she became convinced that God intended her to seek out Mrs. Lawson and become her assistant. Thus inspired, she saved every penny and eventually lined up just enough money to book an overland train ticket from Holland, through Germany, Poland, and Russia to China, a distance of some five thousand miles. She had two pounds left over to cover her expenses en route.

She set out in 1930 at the age of twenty-seven. Only tremendous faith or incredible naiveté can account for her plan — to cross Siberia in the depths of winter and to enter Soviet Russia with the occupation "missionary" stamped in her passport, notwithstanding the fact that Russia and China were at war, and that connecting rail lines between them were blocked. And yet somehow, miraculously, she managed it. In the city of Yangcheng, after many months of travel, enduring hunger, cold, and sickness, she even managed to find Mrs. Lawson. The latter took the arrival of this small, inexperienced woman in stride. The older missionary merely advised her to throw away her Western clothes and put on a pair of blue trousers and matching jacket. Gladys did so, adopting what would be her dress for the rest of her life.

Gladys's arrival signaled the moment for Lawson to launch a long-cherished project: to establish an inn where traveling muleteers could rest for the night. Lawson reasoned that these merchants would be attracted by the good, clean service, and once there they could be entertained by stories of Noah and the Ark, Moses and the children of Israel, and the life of Jesus. With help from Gladys and some Chinese companions, her dream was realized. The Inn of Eight Happinesses opened and, just as she had envisioned, it was a great success.

Years passed. When Jeannie Lawson died Gladys wondered whether she could continue without her. By this time she was fluent in Chinese and adept at telling her Christian stories to any who would listen. As she wondered about her next step, she received a surprising request from the local ruler. A new modernizing decree had gone out, forbidding the ancient practice of binding the feet of young girls. The

Mandarin wondered how readily peasants would comply with this innovation. He requested that Gladys accept an appointment as "Foot Inspector of the Mandarin of Yangcheng." Her job was to travel from village to village through the region, ordering families to comply with the new directive. This task proved easy, as most families were only too ready to discard the cruel custom. Nevertheless, her travels made Gladys a well-known and beloved figure, affording her an opportunity to bear witness to the gospel wherever she went.

Determined to claim Chinese citizenship, Gladys burned her British passport. At the same time she acquired a new name. The people called her Ai-weh-deh — "The Small Woman." It was a fitting name for someone who liked to call herself a "Cockney sparrow." But despite her small size and unassuming appearance, there was no mistaking her courage and strong will. On one occasion she intervened in a prison riot and stilled the violence with the simple force of her calm appearance. After listening to the prisoners' complaints, she instructed the warden to improve prison conditions and to provide exercise and work for the miserable inmates. He immediately complied.

Gladys was content with her life. She had established a school and personally adopted several orphans. Inspired by her example, even the Mandarin had adopted her Christian faith. Gladly would she have remained forever in Yangcheng at the Inn of Eight Happinesses. But the conflicts of the world were encroaching, first the battles between Communist and Nationalist forces, followed by the Japanese invasion, which brought even more terrible reports of massacres and atrocities. In the spring of 1938 Japanese planes unleashed their bombs on Yangcheng. Gladys gathered her flock along with one hundred orphaned children and led them to safety in caves outside the city. When she later sneaked back, she found that all who had remained in the city had been slaughtered by the invading troops.

For months Gladys led her army of children through the war zone, sleeping in the open and foraging for food where they could find it. Before long she discovered that the Japanese were distributing flyers with her name on them, charging her with being a spy and offering a reward for her capture. At one point she was wounded by gunfire and nearly captured. But once again, against all odds, she managed to lead her party to safety. Upon arriving in Fufeng, she immediately collapsed, suffering from pneumonia and typhoid. But she gradually recovered and there waited out the rest of the war.

110

Gladys's adventures brought her unexpected fame. After the war she accepted an invitation to return to Britain to lecture and preach. She was there when the Communists seized control of China, making it impossible for her to return to the Chinese mainland. But she could not stay away. In 1957 she left her homeland for good, traveling first to Hong Kong and ultimately to Taiwan, redoubt of the defeated Nationalist forces. There Providence indicated the form of her new mission when she found a pair of orphaned babies abandoned on her doorstep. She carried out her mission of service until her death on New Year's Day, 1970.

See: Catherine Swift, *Gladys Aylward* (Minneapolis: Bethany House Publishers, 1989).

Sister Thea Bowman
African American Franciscan (1937–1990)

"Maybe I'm not making big changes in the world, but if I have somehow helped or encouraged somebody along the journey then I've done what I'm called to do."

Thea Bowman was one of the great treasures of the American Catholic Church. As a Franciscan Sister, she managed, in her manifold witness to the gospel, to integrate the resources of her Catholic faith with her identity as an African American woman. Ablaze with the spirit of love, the memory of struggle, and a faith in God's promises, she impressed her many audiences not just with her message but with her nobility of spirit. No one she encountered, whether school children, college students, cynical journalists, or a convention hall of bishops, could fail to catch a measure of her joy and gratitude for the gift of life. She was a particular inspiration to the black Catholic community, helping them to assert their pride of place among the people of God, while also encouraging them to enrich the wider church with the gifts of their distinctive culture and spirituality.

She was born Bertha Bowman in rural Mississippi in 1937. While attending a parochial school she was baptized as a Catholic at the age of ten. The most formative experience of her childhood came when her parents switched her to a new school run by the Franciscan Sisters of Perpetual Adoration. There she found her love of learning but also her vocation to become a nun. To her family and friends it was an astonishing decision. Nevertheless, she entered the convent when she was sixteen and took the name Sister Thea ("of God").

As the only black face in a white religious order she tended to stand out. But whatever the expectations of her community, she had no desire to "blend in." She brought with her a strong sense of her identity as a black Catholic woman, and over time she came to believe that this identity entailed a very special vocation. She was committed to asserting a black way of being Catholic. Previously black Catholics were expected to conform to the spirituality of the white Euro-American church. The gospel hymns, the spirituals, the dancing, the testifying in the spirit — all features of the Protestant black churches — were foreign in the Catholic Church. But for black Catholics, Sister Thea believed, this accounted for a sense of cultural marginality. Not only should there be room in the Catholic Church for the spiritual traditions of African Americans, but their experience had much to contribute to the wider church. Part of this experience was the history of slavery and oppression. But part of it also was a spirituality of survival and resistance reflected in the tradition of the spirituals, the importance of family, community, celebration, and remembrance.

"What does it mean to be black and Catholic?" she asked. "It means that I come to my church fully functioning. I bring myself, my black self, all that I am, all that I have, all that I hope to become. I bring my whole history, my traditions, my experience, my culture, my African American song and dance and gesture and movement and teaching and preaching and healing and responsibility as gift to the Church."

After earning a doctorate in English, Thea returned to the South to work with the church in Mississippi and Louisiana. In 1980 she helped to found the Institute of Black Catholic Studies at Xavier University in New Orleans. This became the base for her ministry as a speaker and evangelist. Thea was an extraordinary, spellbinding speaker. A combination storyteller, preacher, and performer, she brought to her lectures the atmosphere of a revival meeting. Punctuating her speaking with renditions of the spirituals, she generally had her audiences, black or white, singing along with her before she was finished.

She was invited to speak before hundreds of groups, including the U.S. Catholic bishops at their annual meeting in 1989. In one speech she noted that women were not allowed to preach in the Catholic Church. But this shouldn't stop them from preaching everywhere else! "God has called to us to speak the word that is Christ, that is truth, that is salvation. And if we speak that word in love and faith, with patience and prayer and perseverance, it will take root. It does have power to save us. Call one another! Testify! Teach! Act on the Word! Witness!"

By this time Sister Thea was compelled to bear witness in a different way. She was diagnosed in 1984 as suffering from breast cancer. Though increasingly ill, Thea continued her extensive travels and speaking, even when she was confined to a wheelchair. With her bright African robes and her now-bald head, she was, as always, a striking figure. But now when she sang the spirituals — "Sometimes I feel like a motherless child / A long way from home" — her audience detected an even more personal and poignant confession of faith.

The faith that had sustained the slaves, the hope expressed in the spirituals, the love embodied by St. Francis, now sustained her in her personal way of the cross. And to her other mighty gifts to the church she now added the witness of her courage and trust in God:

When I first found out I had cancer, I didn't know what to pray for. I didn't know if I should pray for healing or life or death. Then I found peace in praying for what my folks call "God's perfect will." As it evolved, my prayer has become, "Lord, let me live until I die." By that I mean I want to live, love, and serve fully until death comes. If that prayer is answered... how long really doesn't matter. Whether it's just a few months or a few years is really immaterial.

Asked how she made sense out of her suffering, she answered, "I don't make sense of suffering. I try to make sense of life.... I try each day to see God's will.... I console myself with the old Negro spiritual: 'Sooner will be done the troubles of this world. I'm going home to live with God.' "

Sister Thea died on March 30, 1990, at the age of fifty-three.

See: Celestine Cepress, ed., *Thea Bowman: Shooting Star* (Winona, Minn.: Saint Mary's Press, 1993).

BLESSED ARE THOSE
WHO HUNGER AND THIRST
FOR RIGHTEOUSNESS

A shameless defender of the oppressed • a mystic and reformer • a martyr of conscience • a pair of abolitionist sisters • an escaped slave • a union leader • a feminist theologian ahead of her time • a civil rights activist • a baroness and friend to the poor

Christ's blessing encompasses all those who stubbornly refuse to accept the world as it is, all those who burn with zeal to see God's will fulfilled "on earth as it is in heaven." This prophetic spirit is reflected in the words of Mary's Magnificat: "He has cast down the mighty from their thrones and exalted the lowly; he has filled the hungry with good things, while the rich he has sent empty away." In this spirit holy women have opposed tyranny and corruption, slavery, sexism, injustice, and discrimination — not even fearing to challenge those religious authorities who claimed God's blessing on the status quo.

Some of these holy women paid a high price for their courage. But in this case Christ's promise to them is actually good news for all humanity: "They shall be satisfied."

Rahab
Faithful Prostitute

"I know that Yahweh, your God, has given this land to you. . . . The news has frightened us, and everyone has lost courage because of you, for Yahweh, your God, is God in heaven above as he is on earth below."

—Joshua 2:9–11

The name of Rahab, a Canaanite prostitute, is an unlikely addition to the list of biblical saints and heroes. And yet St. James singles her out with Abraham as a model of faith in action. The author of Hebrews includes Rahab among the "mighty cloud of witnesses." St. Matthew even includes her name in the genealogy of Jesus.

Rahab's story appears in the book of Joshua in connection with the siege of Jericho. We are told that when Joshua sent spies to look over the Canaanite city, the two men sought shelter in the house of "a harlot whose name was Rahab." Apparently her house, which abutted the walls of Jericho, afforded a useful view of the city and its defenses. When the king's own informants detected the arrival of the men of Israel, he commanded Rahab to deliver them. Instead she hid the spies and lied about their presence. But before doing so she struck a deal with the fugitives. She had heard of the escape of Israel from Egypt and of the prior victories in Canaan. She confessed her fear of Yahweh and expressed her belief that "Yahweh is he who is God in heaven above and on earth below." In exchange for sheltering these spies she exacted a promise that they would protect the lives of her family and herself. And so the two men survived to make their report. Joshua in turn remembered the oath and made certain that Rahab and her family were delivered from the town before it was destroyed. She lived out the rest of her life among the people of Israel.

Evidently the authors of scripture were able to draw various meanings from the story of Rahab. According to James, Rahab illustrates his point about salvation by works: "Was she not justified by her works when she harbored the messengers and sent them out by a different route? Be assured, then, that faith without works is as dead as a body without breath" (James 2:25–26). But there are, as well, other lessons to be drawn from the story of Rahab. Rahab was not a penitent or "reformed prostitute" when she stepped forward to betray her social world and to identify with its enemies. Nevertheless, as one whose profession placed her among the outcasts of society, she had responded with special interest to the story of the Exodus and of the covenant Yahweh had formed with the runaway Hebrew slaves. She chose to defect, to change sides, to worship the God who led slaves to freedom.

Rahab's is the story of a marginalized "outsider" who, by her courageous deeds and faith in the promises of Yahweh, the Lord of history, was raised to a place of honor among God's special servants.

See: Joshua 2, 6; Judette A. Gallares, *Images of Faith: Spirituality of Women in the Old Testament* (Maryknoll, N.Y.: Orbis Books, 1992).

Mary and Elizabeth
Prophetic Mothers (first century)

"Blessed are you among women."

The feast of the Visitation, on May 31, commemorates the extraordinary meeting between two pregnant saints: Mary, the mother of Jesus, and her kinswoman Elizabeth, the mother of John the Baptist.

As recounted in Luke's Gospel, it was Mary who took the initiative for this "visitation," a journey of some distance from Nazareth. From the angel who had announced Mary's own miraculous conception, she had learned that Elizabeth — "she who was called barren" — had also conceived a son "in her old age." The story suggests that Elizabeth's miraculous conception was a kind of guarantee of the promises made to Mary: "For with God nothing will be impossible." That might explain why Mary's first impulse was to hasten to the hill country to visit Elizabeth, to see for herself the woman to whom she was strangely linked in God's mysterious plan.

When Elizabeth hears Mary's greeting she feels the babe in her womb leap for joy. "Blessed are you among women," she exclaims, "and blessed is the fruit of your womb."

Upon receiving this blessing Mary experiences a sudden insight into her own part in the unfolding and realization of all God's promises, especially as these relate to the poor and oppressed. She responds with an extraordinary hymn of praise, the "Magnificat":

> My soul magnifies the Lord,
> and my spirit rejoices in God my Savior,
> for he has regarded the lowliness of his handmaiden....

He has shown might with his arm,
he has scattered the proud in the conceit of their hearts,
he has put down the mighty from their thrones,
and has exalted the lowly;
he has filled the hungry with good things
and the rich he has sent empty away.

It is a remarkable and subversive vision in which the favor of God to two humble women is seen to presage a thorough process of social reversal: Victory to the poor! Defeat to their enemies!

The joy of that encounter is unclouded by any foreshadowing of the price to be paid. There is no hint that the kind of vision evinced in Mary's prayer will one day lead to the untimely death of these two leaping babes. That day is a long way off. For now the feast of the Visitation remembers only the joy, celebrating the sisterhood of two women joined by their faith in the God of the Impossible.

See: Luke 1:39–56.

Lady Godiva of Coventry
Defender of the Poor (eleventh century)

"The Countess Godiva, who was a great lover of God's mother, longing to free the town of Coventry from the oppression of a heavy toll, often with urgent prayers besought her husband that, from regard to Jesus Christ and his mother, he would free the town from that service and from all other heavy burdens." — Roger of Wendover

From ancient times until the present, the church has venerated the story of holy women who "chose death before dishonor." The story of Lady Godiva, who rode naked through the market of Coventry for the sake of the poor, reflects a different kind of honor. Risking shame for the sake of justice, she stripped off the social codes that too often in history have served merely to keep women in their "place."

The earliest written account is from a chronicle by Roger of Wendover, who died in 1236, over a hundred years after the purported events. He tells the story of the countess Godiva, wife of Leofric, the earl of Mercia, who lived in Coventry in the eleventh century. This pious woman, "a great lover of God's mother," importuned her husband to relieve his subjects of their crushing tax burden. Exasperated by her entreaties, he set a challenge she would surely refuse: "Mount your horse and ride naked, before all the people, through the market of this town from one end to the other, and on your return you shall have your request." To his surprise, Godiva took him at his word. Stripping off her robe, she "let down her tresses," mounted her horse, and rode through the marketplace of Coventry. Upon returning to her astonished husband, "she obtained of him what she had asked."

Though historians have doubted most elements of this legend, they have confirmed the existence of Lady Godiva (at least one advantage she enjoys over many venerated saints). She and her husband founded a Benedictine monastery in Coventry and built the church where she was later buried. And yet her story has echoed across the centuries, joining the tales of Ivanhoe, Robin Hood, William Tell, and other legendary champions of justice. Unlike the others, Godiva brandished no weapon. She rode into battle armed only, as St. Paul would put it, with the "sword of the Spirit," clad only with "the breastplate of righteousness."

St. Birgitta of Sweden
Mystic and Prophet (1303–1373)

"My Lord Jesus Christ, with your kindly ears you gladly hear and hearken to all who humbly address you. Blessed, therefore, be those ears of yours; and may they be eternally filled with all honor. Amen."

St. Birgitta of Sweden was one of the great women of the fourteenth century: the wife of a nobleman and the mother of eight children; a nun and founder of monasteries as well as a religious order; a pilgrim who crossed continents and seas; a mystic who filled many volumes with accounts of her visions and colloquies with Christ; a prophet who called kings to justice and popes to live up to their sacred duties.

Birgitta was born to a noble family and raised in privilege and ease. As a child, however, she sensed that God was calling her to some greater purpose. At a young age she experienced her first vision. She saw an altar, and seated above it a woman in a shining dress who said, "Come, Birgitta," and offered her a crown. When she tried to take it, the lady pressed it on her brow and then disappeared. Some years later she had a vision of Christ hanging on the cross. When she asked him who had treated him this way, he answered, "They who despise me and spurn my love for them." From that point she felt herself mystically united with Christ and determined to serve him in every way.

At fourteen she married a young prince named Ulf. It was a happy marriage that lasted twenty-eight years. Respecting the obligations of her noble station, she served as lady in waiting to the queen of Sweden. But she was disgusted by the vanity and frivolity of court life. She made herself unpopular with the king when she saw fit to lecture him on his policies of taxation and the onerous burden his luxuries imposed upon the poor. Whenever she could, she would visit the hospitals, binding the wounds and sores of the patients with her own hands. She was often accompanied on these errands by her young children, since it was her desire, she said, for them to learn "at an early age to serve God and His poor and sick."

Fed up with life in court, she and Ulf embarked upon a long pilgrimage that took them all the way to Compostela in Spain. On the way back Ulf fell ill and eventually died. Birgitta consoled herself by living as a penitent in a convent for four years. She emerged ready to enter an even wider, more public stage in her mission. At this point she was instructed by Christ in a vision to found a new monastery for nuns and monks in Vadstena. By her account Christ was exact in describing the Rule for this new monastery, along with particulars regarding dress, diet, and architecture.

In another vision, Christ conveyed an even more personal message: "You will be my bride; you will see and hear the spiritual truths and penetrate into the celestial secrets, and My spirit will dwell in you until your death." After a pilgrimage to the Holy Land, where she received many dramatic visions of the events of Christ's life — his birth, baptism, ministry, passion, and death — she traveled to Rome, where she lived for the last twenty years of her life.

Wherever Birgitta traveled she spoke out against slavery, injustice, and other threats to the peace. These were dangerous times. She was traversing Europe in the midst of the Hundred Years' War and the Black Death. She raised her voice with the pathos and authority of a biblical prophet. Confronting the corruption and dissolution she encountered in Rome she cried out: "Oh Rome, Rome, be converted and turn to the Lord thy God."

St. Birgitta of Sweden

Part of her reason for visiting Rome was to win official recognition for her religious order. The frequent turnover in papal administrations made this difficult. More difficult was the fact that the popes, seeking to escape political rivalries, had fled Rome for the court in Avignon. Like St. Catherine of Siena after her, Birgitta laid spiritual siege to the pontiff, insisting, by her authority as God's messenger, that he leave the comforts of Avignon and return to his proper seat in Rome. At one point she denounced the pope as "a murderer of souls, worse than Lucifer, more unjust than Pilate, and more merciless than Judas." At another point she warned him that Christ would strike him dead if he did not return. He did not heed her threats. But he did approve the Rule of her new order, the Order of the Most Holy Savior, or Brigettines, as they have come to be called.

During her years in Rome she occupied herself with charitable work among the sick and poor. Throughout this active life she maintained an ongoing dialogue with God, which formed the basis of her voluminous *Revelations*. These revelations consisted of profound theological discourses couched in the form of divine answers to a series of probing questions. Her questions cover an astonishing range, from the mysteries of nature to subtle matters of doctrine. They reveal much about the mind that conceived them:

> Why do animals suffer, though they cannot revel? Why, though they come into life without sin, must they endure pain? Why have you created useless things? Why can one not see souls? Why do some children die before being born, though gifted with a soul, while others live to receive baptism? Why do you permit the ruin of the just, and good fortune for the unbeliever? Why are some troubled beyond measure, while others are, as it were, secure from tribulation? Why are some given intelligence and an incomparable genius for learning while others are like asses without intellect?

Birgitta died on July 23, 1373. A triumphal procession accompanied her body across Europe and back to the abbey in Vadstena, where it was laid to rest.

See: Marguerite Tjader Harris, ed., *Birgitta of Sweden: Life and Selected Revelations,* Classics of Western Spirituality (New York: Paulist, 1990).

St. Joan of Arc
Maid of Orleans (1412?–1431)

"On being asked whether she did not believe that she was subject to the church which is on earth, namely, our Holy Father the Pope, cardinals, archbishops, bishops, and prelates of the church, she replied: 'Yes, but our Lord must be served first.'"

Joan of Arc is one of the most attractive and intriguing heroes of history. Her life has been the subject of countless studies, as well as the inspiration for films, plays, novels, and poems. She has been claimed, variously, as a symbol of patriotism, military valor, feminism, and as a martyr of conscience. At least since 1920, when she was formally canonized, she has also been claimed as a Christian saint. Just what kind of a saint remains the subject of debate. But among canonized saints she enjoys what is probably the unique distinction of having been previously condemned by the church and executed as a heretic. She thus may be legitimately claimed not only as a patron of France, but of all those holy men and women who have been vilified in their own time in the hope of eventual vindication.

Her familiar story remains compelling. As a young peasant girl in southern France, she claimed to hear the voices of the Archangel Michael, later joined by St. Catherine of Alexandria and St. Margaret, charging her with a mission to save France by restoring the Dauphin to his rightful throne and driving the English enemy from French soil. It was partly a reflection of the desperate times that she managed to convince the Dauphin and his advisors to put her in command of his faltering army. She turned the tide of the war by successfully breaking the English siege on Orleans. Dressed in soldier's attire and brandishing the standard, she inspired the French troops to valor and managed a string of military victories that paved the way for the crowning of the Dauphin as Charles VII, king of France.

But from this pinnacle the wheel of fortune quickly turned. In a subsequent battle she was captured by Burgundian troops who sold her to their English allies. She was imprisoned for a year and subjected to an interminable interrogation by an ecclesiastical court sympathetic to the English cause. Though her fate was never in doubt, the court sought desperately to discredit her by finding evidence of heresy or witchcraft. Joan deflected their questions with guileless wit and impressed many with her evident faith and purity of heart. Throughout she held adamantly to the authority of her "voices," and she would not give up her male clothing. These were the bases on which she was eventually convicted.

On May 30, 1431, Joan was publicly burned at the stake. Her ashes were thrown in the Seine. She was nineteen years old.

In 1455 an official ecclesiastical investigation examined Joan's court proceedings and found her innocent of the charges against her. She was canonized 450 years later, a testimony to the longstanding interest in her cause. Even then, however, there was a certain vagueness about the kind of holiness she represented. Not wanting to call her a martyr, the church emphasized instead her piety and virginity.

There is no gainsaying Joan's purity and ardent faith. This accounts in part for the perennial fascination with her story: she epitomizes the confrontation between purity and the corruptions of power. But unlike traditional saints, she employed her piety not so much in the service of the church but in the cause of national liberation. She represents a kind of political holiness, not a "church" piety or the mystical rapture of the convent, but a mysticism expressed in commitment to the world and engagement in the events of history. In this, she was more like the Maccabean martyrs of Israel than her virginal patrons Sts. Catherine and Margaret. It is useless to speculate what supposed interest these saints might have had in the dynastic fortunes of France. But for us that is not the issue; Joan's "voices" spoke to her alone, and what is important is the courage of her response. Thus she inspires us to attend to the voices of our own angels and to respond with equal faith.

An illiterate peasant girl, a shepherd, a "nobody," she heeded a religious call to save her country when all the "somebodies" of her time proved unable or unwilling to meet the challenge. She stood up before princes of the church and state and the most learned authorities of her world and refused to compromise her conscience or deny her special vocation. She paid the ultimate price for her stand. And in doing so she won a prize far more valuable than the gratitude of the Dauphin or the keys of Orleans.

See: Marina Warner, *Joan of Arc: The Image of Female Heroism* (New York: Alfred A. Knopf, 1981).

St. Teresa of Avila
Mystic, Doctor of the Church (1515–1582)

"Let nothing disturb you, nothing dismay you. All things are passing, God never changes. Patient endurance attains all things....God alone suffices."

By any standard, Teresa of Avila is one of the towering figures in Christian history. In a time and place (sixteenth-century Spain) that paid little attention to the voice of any woman, Teresa managed to outshine nearly all her contemporaries. She was a mystic, a religious reformer, the founder of seventeen convents, the author of four books, and one of the outstanding masters of Christian prayer. In light of these accomplishments it is not surprising to learn that she possessed a vivid and charismatic personality. She could be at turns charming, imperious, irreverent, and impossible, depending on the circumstances and the provocation. But there was little doubt among any she encountered that her courage and wisdom were rooted in a special relationship with God.

Teresa was born in the fortress city of Avila in 1515. Her father, a wealthy merchant, had married into the aristocracy. Nevertheless, the family's social standing was tenuous. Teresa's grandfather was a *converso*, one of the many Spanish Jews who converted to Christianity under threat of exile. In later years such a pedigree reinforced the suspicions of those otherwise inclined to fault her program or her leadership. Teresa's mother died when she was fourteen, and her father arranged for her education in a local convent. By the time she was twenty she had decided to become a nun, a vocation motivated, she later recognized, much more by the fear of purgatory than by the love of God. Her father opposed this plan, but Teresa, with characteristic willfulness, disobeyed his wishes and ran off to the Carmelite convent in Avila. Within a year she had become so ill that her father came to take her home. Her condition deteriorated to the point that she fell into a coma and was thought to be dead. Although she recovered, her convalescence was long and painful. For three years she was virtually paralyzed from the waist down. Eventually she was well enough to return to her monastery, but her spiritual life had grown tepid and superficial.

Her progress was not helped by the lax conditions of the convent. The strictness of the original Carmelite rule had been so mitigated over the years that the convent in Avila had come to resemble a boarding house for wealthy maidens more than a house of prayer. The enclosure was

St. Teresa of Avila

not seriously maintained, and the nuns spent much of their time in the parlor entertaining visitors and gentlemen callers. In this atmosphere Teresa's natural charm and extroverted personality brought her much attention.

At the age of thirty-nine, however, Teresa had an experience of conversion. It was sparked when she happened to glance, one day, at an image of the suffering Christ on the cross. Instantly she was filled with loathing for the mediocrity of her spiritual life, and she determined to devote herself more seriously to a life of prayer. Almost immediately upon this resolution she began to experience the sensation of God's love, transforming her from within. She decided to establish a new reformed Carmelite house, returning to the spirit of the original primitive Rule of Carmel. After strenuous lobbying she finally won permission to undertake this initiative. Her new convent was founded in Avila in 1562.

Her new community was known as the Discalced (shoeless) Carmelites. In fact the nuns wore hemp sandals, but their name referred to the strict poverty that was a feature of Teresa's reform. Her nuns were to seek no endowments but to live entirely by alms and their own labor. A strict enclosure was to be maintained, along with a vegetarian diet and a rigorous schedule of prayer.

From Avila Teresa went on to establish sixteen other convents in Spain. In the meantime she had to endure opposition from within her Carmelite family, suspicion from members of the hierarchy, and eventually formal investigation by the dreaded Spanish Inquisition. Not so many years had passed since the Spanish victory over the Moors and the expulsion of the Jews in 1492. Spain at this time was exultantly and aggressively Catholic. Along with this came a fanatical suspicion of anything that smacked of Protestantism. As a woman and reformer, who based her authority on private visions, Teresa's activities entailed considerable risk. Her confessor and colleague, John of the Cross, with whom she helped to inspire a male branch of the Discalced Carmelites, had a direct taste of these dangers when he was for a time imprisoned in the dungeon of the "Calced" Carmelite monastery in Toledo.

Teresa blithely surmounted all obstacles in her path. When asked how she intended to found a monastery with only a handful of ducats in her purse, she answered, "Teresa and this money are indeed nothing; but God, Teresa, and these ducats suffice." The Inquisition was not her only concern. She also endured sickness, hunger, and poverty along the way. A particular mortification was the misery and hazards of travel at a time when donkey carts were the standard mode of transportation. One time her cart overturned, throwing her into a muddy river. When she complained to God about this ordeal, she heard a voice from within her say, "This is how I treat my friends." "Yes, my Lord," she answered, "and that is why you have so few of them."

Teresa's public accomplishments are all the more remarkable in light of the intensity of her life of prayer. Among all the saints there are few to rival her in the variety and depth of her mystical experiences. As she advanced in life she experienced frequent ecstasies in which it seemed her heart had been pierced by God's love. She described this and other experiences in great detail in her autobiography, along with several other volumes on prayer and mystical spirituality. And yet for someone who had achieved a virtually unique degree of communion with God, she remained fully able to speak in common terms: "Prayer, in my view, is nothing but friendly intercourse, and frequent solitary converse, with Him Who we know loves us." Having achieved the most rarefied heights of spiritual wisdom, Teresa retained the ability to counsel "everyday" Christians. In a maxim she left for her Sisters she wrote, "Remember that you have only one soul; that you have only one death to die; that you have only one life, which is short and has to be lived by you alone; and that there is only one glory, which is eternal. If you do this, there will be many things about which you care nothing."

Teresa died in 1582. She was canonized forty years later. In 1970 she was the first woman to be named a Doctor of the Church.

See: The Life of Teresa of Avila, ed. E. Allison Peers (Garden City, N.Y.: Image, 1960); Tessa Bielecki, ed., Teresa of Avila: Mystical Writings (New York: Crossroad, 1994); John Beevers, St. Teresa of Avila (Garden City, N.Y.: Doubleday, 1961).

Anne Hutchinson
Puritan Prophet (1591–1643)

"It was never in my heart to slight any man, but only that man should be kept in his own place and not set in the room of God."

The Puritans who settled Massachusetts in the 1630s were motivated in part by a desire to escape religious persecution. But they did not come to create a haven of religious freedom. On the contrary, they believed their holy commonwealth would stand as "a city on a hill," a beacon of purified Christianity in which biblical values of piety and sobriety would govern the conduct of its members. Severe punishment awaited those who fell short of these standards, a fate that was extended too to those who criticized the Puritan code. Rarely was there ever such a concentration of persons so godly, so sober, and so eager to cast the first stone. Among the most famous victims of Puritan justice was Anne Hutchinson, a mystic and healer, whose particular heresy was to maintain that it was a blessing and not a curse to be a woman.

Anne Hutchinson arrived in Boston in 1634, accompanied by her husband, William, a prosperous businessman, and their several children. They were committed Puritans, though of the two Anne was by far the more zealous. She was an unusually independent woman for her times, a skilled midwife with a particular gift for herbal treatments. She was also an avid student of the Bible, which she freely interpreted in the light of what she termed divine inspiration. Though she generally adhered to the principles of Puritan orthodoxy, she held extremely advanced notions about the equality and rights of women. These positions had put her in some tension not only with the established church of England but also with her own coreligionists. Nevertheless, she had decided to emigrate in the belief that New England afforded greater religious freedom as well as wider opportunities for women.

In Boston the Hutchinsons quickly achieved a prominent social position. Anne's services as a midwife were in great demand, and many a family soon found themselves in her debt. Before long she also began inviting women to join her in her home for prayer and religious conversation. In time these meetings became very popular, attracting as many as eighty participants a week. Hutchinson would present a text from the Bible and offer her own commentary. Often her spiritual interpretation differed widely from the learned but legalistic reading offered from the Sunday pulpit. In particular, Hutchinson constantly challenged the standard interpretation of the story of Adam and Eve. This was a vital text for the Puritans, key to the doctrine of original sin. But it was regularly cited to assign special blame to women as the source of sin and to justify the extremely patriarchal structure of Puritan society.

Increasingly, the ministers opposed Hutchinson's meetings, ostensibly on the grounds that such "unauthorized" religious gatherings might confuse the faithful. But gradually the opposition was expressed in openly misogynistic terms. Hutchinson was a modern "Jezebel" who was infecting women with perverse and "abominable" ideas regarding their dignity and rights. Anne paid no attention to her critics. When they cited the biblical texts on the need for women to keep silent in church she rejoined with a verse from Titus permitting that "the elder women should instruct the younger."

In 1637 she was brought to trial for her subversive views. She was forty-six at the time and advanced in her fifteenth pregnancy. Nevertheless she was forced to stand for several days before a board of male interrogators as they tried desperately to get her to admit her secret blasphemies. They accused her of violating the fifth commandment — to "honor thy father and mother" — by encouraging dissent against the fathers of the commonwealth. It was charged that by attending her gatherings women were being tempted to neglect the care of their own families.

Anne deftly parried and defended herself until it was clear that there was no escape from the court's predetermined judgment. Cornered, she addressed the court with her own judgment:

> You have no power over my body, neither can you do me any harm. I fear none but the great Jehovah, which hath foretold me of these things, and I do verily believe that he will deliver me out of your hands.... Therefore, take heed how you proceed against me; for I know that for this you go about to do to me, God will ruin you and your posterity, and this whole state.

This outburst brought forth angry jeers. She was called a heretic and an instrument of the devil. In the words of one minister, "You have stepped out of your place, you have rather been a husband than a wife, a preacher than a hearer, and a magistrate than a subject."

Anne was held in prison during the cold winter months. Her family and a stream of sympathizers continued to visit her, and to them she continued freely to impart her spiritual teaching. In the spring she was banished from the commonwealth along with her youngest children. After seven days of difficult travel through the wilderness they arrived in Rhode Island. There they were reunited with William Hutchinson, who had gone ahead to establish a homestead. But soon after her arrival, Anne suffered a painful miscarriage. In Boston the details were gleefully recounted by her persecutors, who saw in her misfortune a vivid confirmation of God's judgment.

In 1642 William Hutchinson died. He had been a devoted husband throughout his wife's ordeal. When the authorities had tried to pressure him to disavow his wife's teachings, he had said "he was more nearly tied to his wife than to the church; he thought her to be a dear saint and servant of God." Alone with six of her children Anne decided to leave

Rhode Island, to go as far she could from the long arm of the Mass-achusetts authorities. She got as far as the Dutch settlement on Long Island. There sometime in the summer of 1643 she and her children were massacred by Indians.

See: Selma R. Williams, *Divine Rebel: The Life of Anne Marbury Hutchinson* (New York: Holt, Rinehart and Winston, 1981).

Sor Juana Inés de la Cruz
Poet and Scholar (1651–1694)

"From the moment I was first illuminated by the light of reason, my incli-nation toward letters has been so vehement that not even the admonitions of others... nor my own meditations... have been sufficient to cause me to forswear this natural impulse that God placed in me."

Sor (Sister) Juana Inés de la Cruz was a seventeenth-century nun, the first great poet of Latin America, and one of the earliest champions of equality for women in the church. She has been called a genius, a saint, a heretic, and an early feminist. The degree to which she may have reconciled these various identities is the source of her attraction and, ultimately, her mystery.

Juana was born on November 12, 1651, in Mexico, then called New Spain, in a small town not far from Mexico City. Raised by her mother's family — her parents were evidently unmarried — she displayed from her earliest childhood an extraordinary passion for knowledge. She learned to read and write by the time she was four and mastered Latin after only twenty lessons. As she recalled of her childhood, "In me the desire for learning was stronger than the desire for eating." By the time she was sixteen her reputation for brilliance, augmented by her famous beauty, had brought Juana to the attention of the viceregal court. She lived there for several years as a lady-in-waiting and became a popular member of elite society. But then suddenly, at the age of nineteen, she turned her back on the court and entered the Convent of St. Jerome in Mexico City.

There is no evidence that she was motivated by great piety. In fact she was later frank in describing her repugnance for "certain conditions" of convent life. Nevertheless, she said, "given the total antipathy I felt for marriage, I deemed convent life the least unsuitable and the most honorable I could elect if I were to insure my salvation." No doubt it was in part the name of St. Jerome, translator of the Bible and patron of all scholars, that dictated her choice of a convent.

Happily, the convent lived up to the promise of its name. Within the cloister she was able to amass one of the great personal libraries of her day — several thousand volumes — and to indulge her voracious appetite for learning of every sort. She could discourse intelligently on history, rhetoric, philosophy, art, architecture, geometry, astronomy, and many other fields. At the same time she wrote volumes of poems — passionate love poems, religious allegories, historical odes. These constitute one of the great literary outputs of the baroque era. She wrote plays, musical librettos, and scholarly monographs. All these were well known in the viceregal court, and her fame extended to Spain.

The watershed in her life occurred in 1690 when she first ventured to write on matters of theology. She was moved to cross this threshold by reading a forty-year-old sermon by a famous preacher that struck her as idiotic. In response she wrote a long and brilliant critique, certainly the first theological work by a woman in the New World. This elicited an open letter from the bishop of Puebla, who praised her orthodoxy and her insight, but then condescendingly urged her to restrict herself to activities more becoming to a member of her sex.

This released a tightly wound coil in Sor Juana. After several months she responded with a lengthy treatise. In this letter, composed with devastating irony and self-restraint, she defended her compulsion to learn as a God-given calling, one that she was powerless to deny. Even if she were deprived of books, she said, all the world was her university: "There is no creature, however lowly, in which one cannot recognize that *God made me;* there is none that does not astound reason if properly meditated on." At the same time she championed the equal rights of women to learning with an erudite appeal to Aristotle and Cicero, scripture, her patron St. Jerome, his holy helper, St. Paula, and all other learned women saints. "You foolish men," she wrote, "accusing women for lacking reason when you yourselves are the reason for the lack."

It was a bold and unprecedented manifesto. In the eyes of many church authorities it was also outrageously presumptuous. What happened next is not in doubt, though the meaning of it is open to interpretation. After Sor Juana's "Response," her confessor would have no more to do with her. Soon after she made a public renewal of her vows and consecrated herself to the Immaculate Conception of the Virgin Mary — a document she signed with her own blood. She then dispersed her famous and beloved library, distributing the proceeds among the poor. She wrote no more. In 1694, while nursing her sister nuns during a virulent outbreak of plague, she succumbed to the dread disease and quickly died on April 17.

Some critics have seen in Juana's last years the marks of a profound conversion; her silence is akin to that of Thomas Aquinas, when he realized that all his great words were as straw. The proof is in the mystical charity she displayed in her final days. Others, including Octavio Paz, see her actions as a humiliating exercise in self-abnegation, an expression of her powerlessness as a woman. Just as her options dictated that she enter the convent in order to be a scholar, so her options as a woman religious dictated that she renounce her learning — renounce herself — in order to stay alive. The issue was not her orthodoxy. The issue was her gender. The alternative was the Inquisition.

Still, the mystery lingers. Though not conventionally pious, Juana embraced the religious life as a means of pursuing the call to learning — a vocation she believed to come from God. Ultimately it proved difficult, if not impossible, to negotiate the claims of these vocations. And so the question remains: Did Sor Juana's elected silence represent an act of faithful submission or a betrayal of herself, her true vocation, and thus of God? Which was ultimately the greater rebellion: to stand up to church authorities or to submit? Her only answer is silence. No one can answer the riddle of Sor Juana who has not tried to walk her path.

See: A Woman of Genius: The Intellectual Autobiography of Sor Juana Inés de la Cruz (Salisbury, Conn.: Lime Rock, 1982); Octavio Paz, Sor Juana (Cambridge, Mass.: Harvard University Press, 1988); Michelle A. Gonzalez, Sor Juana: Beauty and Justice in the Americas (Maryknoll, N.Y.: Orbis Books, 2003).

Margaret Fell
Quaker (1614–1702)

"And this hath been the only ground and cause of our sufferings, because we obeyed the command of Christ and observed the apostle's doctrine and practice; and not for any other cause or end have our sufferings been, but for conscience' sake...."

Margaret Fell was one of earliest champions of the Quaker movement — formally known as the Society of Friends — which had its origins in the conversion of George Fox in 1646. After experiencing the seed of God in his own soul, Fox realized that he had no need of special guides or mediators. His mission was to heed the Inner Light and to awaken others to a similar consciousness. Fox's message, which he delivered through public preaching, or by standing in church to address challenging "queries" to the presiding minister, quickly attracted many followers. Among them, women played a particularly prominent role.

Fox believed that the Inner Light was equally present in men and women. He permitted women to preach and to engage in the religious instruction of men. The Quakers rejected all social distinction. They wore plain clothes to obliterate any sign of status or rank, and they addressed everyone — whether fellow Quakers, magistrates, or kings — by the familiar *thee* and *thou*. Such deviant behavior offended both the religious and political establishments, for which reason Fox and his followers suffered harsh persecution. In this, too, women claimed an equal share.

Margaret Fell, one of the most important figures in the rise of Quakerism, was born in 1614 to a wealthy family in Lancashire. When she was in her teens she married Thomas Fell, a judge, many years her elder. They lived on his estate, Swarthmore, a great house with thirteen fireplaces. As Fell was frequently called away on business, Margaret managed the estate, while raising nine children.

Apparently Margaret liked to welcome traveling clergymen to her home. That is how she happened to meet George Fox, who visited Swarthmore in 1652 while Judge Fell was away. Margaret was greatly taken with Fox's teaching, and by the time her husband returned she had become his ardent follower. Though Fell himself remained unconvinced, he did not stand in the way of his wife's Quaker practice.

In the following years Swarthmore became a center of Quaker worship and organization. Margaret served Fox as secretary and assistant, organizing his affairs, circulating his writings, and defending him when he was frequently in jail. When Judge Fell died in 1658, Margaret inherited the Swarthmore estate. But without her husband's protection she was far more vulnerable.

In 1662 an anti-Quaker law was enacted, threatening imprisonment to any who would not take an oath to the king. On the basis of Jesus' commandment in scripture, Quakers refused to take oaths of any kind — insisting simply that their "nay be nay," and their "aye be aye." For disobedience to this act, Fox and many Quakers were imprisoned under terrible conditions. In 1664 Margaret joined them. Regarding the oath, Margaret's answer was, "This shall I say, as for my allegiance, I love, own, and honor the King and desire his peace and welfare; and that we may live a peaceable, a quiet and a godly life under his government, according to the Scriptures; and this is my allegiance to the King. As for the oath itself, Christ Jesus, the King of Kings, hath commanded me not to swear at all, neither by heaven, nor by earth, nor by any other Oath." When hearing the sentence — life in prison — she answered, "Although I am out of the King's protection, yet I am not out of the protection of the Almighty God." She remained in prison for more than four years.

While in prison Margaret wrote a powerful pamphlet on women's preaching, showing how this was "justified, proved, and allowed of by the Scriptures, all such as speak by the Spirit and Power of the Lord Jesus." This theological tract, one of the first of its kind, begins by recalling that women, as well as men, were created in the image of God. Although the Fall introduced division into the world, this was repaired by the Resurrection of Christ. In fact, Christ and the prophets refer to the church as a woman, "and those that speak against this Woman's speaking, speak against the Church of Christ." Jesus made no attempt to silence the Samaritan woman or Martha or Mary Magdalene, who addressed him on theological matters. Nor would he allow his disciples to criticize the woman who anointed him with precious oil. Margaret went on to recall the faithful women who accompanied Christ on the way of the cross. "Thus, we see that Jesus owned the Love and Grace that appeared in Women, and did not despise it: and by what is recorded in the Scriptures, he received as much Love, Kindness, Compassion, and tender Dealing toward him from Women, as he did from any others, both in his Life time, and also after they had exercised their Cruelty upon him."

Addressing the scriptural texts that enjoin women to keep silent in church, Margaret explained these texts as applying only to a specific local situation. They did not suggest an eternal or universal principle. They referred to women *under the Law*, but not to those women who now lived by the Spirit. Furthermore, these texts paled in significance beside those texts that spoke of the church as a whole receiving the gift of the Holy Spirit, and of those women who labored beside Paul in building the early church. And so, she concludes in her address to the "Ministers of Darkness": "Let this serve to stop that opposing Spirit that would limit the Power and Spirit of the Lord Jesus, whose Spirit is poured upon all Flesh, both Sons and Daughters, now in his Resurrection."

In 1669 Margaret Fell and George Fox were married. Between their various terms of imprisonment and Fox's increasingly wide-ranging

travels to America and elsewhere, they spent relatively little time together. Fox died in London in 1691. Margaret lived on at Swarthmore
until her own death in 1702. Her final words were, "I am at peace."

See: D. Elton Trueblood, *The People Called Quakers* (New York: Harper & Row,
1968).

Sarah Grimké (1792–1873) and Angelina Grimké (1805–1879)
Abolitionists and Feminists

*"I ask no favors for my sex. I surrender not our claim to equality. All I
ask of our brethren is that they take their feet off our necks, and permit us
to stand upright on the ground which God has designed us to occupy."*

Despite the thirteen years' difference between them, the sisters Sarah
and Angelina Grimké were exceptionally close. At Angelina's birth
Sarah begged to serve as her sister's godmother, a responsibility she
took so seriously that Angelina would forever call her Mother. They
remained inseparable for most of their lives — united, among other
things, in their common commitment to justice and human dignity.

Raised in a prominent Charleston family in South Carolina, the
Grimké sisters grew up on a plantation with many slaves. From an early
age, however, Sarah chafed against the confining strictures of her world.
She abhorred the institution of slavery and questioned the hypocrisy of
a "Christian society" that could tolerate such injustice. As soon as she
was able she imparted the same convictions to her younger sister.

After the death of their father, Sarah fled Charleston for the relative freedom of Philadelphia. For some time she had been attracted
to Quakerism, an interest sparked in part by her reading of John
Woolman's antislavery *Journal.* In Philadelphia she immersed herself in
Quaker life, and even attracted the attention of a young widower who
asked her hand in marriage. She struggled over this proposal but eventually turned it down. Marriage, she believed, was a "snare of Satan"
that would inevitably interfere with the larger task — whatever that
might be — to which God was calling her.

Though different in character from her sister — less dour and intro-
spective — Angelina felt her own call to Quakerism. As was the case

with Sarah, Angelina's conversion was strongly influenced by her abolitionist convictions. And yet, after joining her sister in Philadelphia, she
became increasingly worried that the Quakers were not ardent enough
in their antislavery convictions. Many Friends seemed to take a "live
and let live" attitude toward the persistence of slavery — something
Angelina found intolerable. And yet she was at a loss to know what
she could do.

In 1835, after reading an issue of William Lloyd Garrison's radical
abolitionist journal, *The Liberator,* Angelina was inspired to write him a
letter of support. "Respected friend," she wrote, "the ground on which
you stand is holy ground; never, never surrender it. If you surrender
it, the hope of the slave is extinguished.... If persecution is the means
which God has ordained for the accomplishment of this great end,
EMANCIPATION; then...I feel as if I could say, LET IT COME; for
it is my deep, solemn deliberate conviction, that this is a cause worth
dying for."

After Garrison published Angelina's letter she was widely celebrated
as a brave new voice in the abolitionist cause. The fact that she was a
Southerner from a slaveholding family underscored her eloquence. But
it also assured her outcast status; she could never return home. More
hurtful was the hostility of fellow Quakers, who warned her against
consorting with dangerous radicals. Increasingly estranged from the
Quaker establishment, the Grimkés soon found wider fellowship in
the Philadelphia Female Anti-Slavery Society. Once again, it was the
younger sister who precipitated their move toward public leadership.

Angelina conceived the idea of writing "An Appeal to the Christian
Women of the Southern States," hoping to set before her sisters in the
South "the awful responsibility resting on them at this crisis; for if the
women of the South do not rise in the strength of the Lord to plead with
their husbands, brothers, and sons, that country must witness the most
awful scenes of murder and blood."

Few copies of Angelina's appeal made it to the South; most were
confiscated and burned before they could be distributed. But her appeal struck a particular chord among a different audience — Northern
women who were amazed by Angelina's bold call to assume their role
as actors in history. Sarah followed with an appeal to Southern clergymen, deftly unraveling the specious theological and biblical arguments
used to justify slavery. Before long the Grimké sisters were among the
most sought-after speakers on the abolitionist circuit.

But with their increasing prominence in the abolitionist cause, the sisters became steadily sensitized to the oppression of women. There was a deep connection, they argued, between the bondage and subjugation of black Americans and the overt as well as subtle measures contrived to keep women silent and *in their place.* As Angelina put it, "The rights of the slave and the woman blend like the colors of the rainbow."

In the first feminist manifesto in American history, Sarah's "Letters on the Equality of the Sexes and the Condition of Women," she wrote: "I have sometimes been astonished and grieved at the servitude of women.... A woman who is asked to sign a petition for the abolition of slavery...not infrequently replies, 'My husband does not approve of it.' She merges her rights and her duties in her husband, and thus virtually chooses him for a savior and a king, and rejects Christ as her Ruler and Redeemer."

Some abolitionists feared that this infusion of feminist principles would divide the antislavery cause. Nevertheless, in 1838 the sisters made history when they were invited to present their views on slavery before the state legislature of Massachusetts. It was the first time any government body in the United States had invited a woman to testify. Rising before a hushed audience, Angelina delivered one of her most eloquent speeches:

> I stand before you as a Southerner, exiled from the land of my birth by the sound of the lash and the piteous cry of the slave. I stand before you as a repentant slaveholder. I stand before you as a moral being, and as a moral being I feel that I owe it to the suffering slave and the deluded master, to my country and to the world, to do all that I can to overturn a system of complicated crimes, built upon the broken hearts and the prostrate bodies of my countrymen in chains and cemented by the blood, sweat, and tears of my sisters in bonds.

This speech was perhaps the high point of the sisters' influence. That same year they effectively retired from public life. Ironically, this retirement was precipitated by Angelina's marriage to Thomas Weld, a prominent abolitionist and aspiring politician. Angelina was increasingly occupied by domestic duties and childrearing; Sarah, who had rejected marriage as a distraction from her mission, remained at Angelina's side. And yet they lived to see the end of slavery and the rise of a women's movement in America — the two causes for which they had dedicated their lives and helped lay the foundation.

See: Mark Perry, *Lift Up Thy Voice: The Grimké Family's Journey from Slaveholders to Civil Rights Leaders* (New York: Viking, 2001).

Lucretia Mott
Abolitionist and Feminist (1793–1880)

"It is time that Christians were judged more by their likeness to Christ than their notions of Christ."

At the historic 1848 Women's Rights Convention in Seneca Falls, New York, Lucretia Mott read aloud a new revolutionary manifesto. Adapting the words of the American Declaration of Independence, it began, "We hold these truths to be self-evident: that all men *and women* are created equal." By the addition of two words these women had corrected the foundational document of American democracy. But in a deeper sense they had righted an imbalance of historic proportions and thus opened a new chapter in the annals of civilization.

The Seneca Falls convention was the idea of two women, Lucretia Mott and Elizabeth Cady Stanton, both Quakers, who had met while attending the World Anti-Slavery Convention in London in 1840. Though women were a major force in the abolitionist movement, the male-dominated convention had refused to recognize them as official delegates. This exclusion proved a radicalizing event for both women, a catalyst in their decision to combine opposition to slavery with struggle for the rights of women. For Mott both positions resonated with her Quaker faith, which upheld the indwelling of the divine light in each human being. On this basis she devoted her life to the cause of liberty and the equality of all persons before God.

Lucretia, the daughter of a whaling captain, was born in Nantucket and educated in a Quaker school in New York before settling with her family in Pennsylvania. Her marriage in 1811 to James Mott began an unusually close partnership. Her husband, a successful merchant, supported Lucretia in all her causes and followed her about on her travels. He even consented to chair the convention at Seneca Falls when none of the women felt qualified for the task. Lucretia bore six children. The death of her first son, Tommy, prompted a period of deep religious introspection. Afterward, in Quaker meeting, she spoke with such depth and insight that she was formally recognized as a minister.

This was a time of rising tensions within the Quaker communities. While "orthodox" Friends put more emphasis on order and the authority of scripture, Lucretia sympathized with the teaching of Elias Hicks, who stressed the authority of the Spirit in the hearts of the faithful. Hicks was also an ardent abolitionist. The Motts followed his lead in refusing any commerce in the fruits of slavery. They wore linen or wool instead of cotton from Southern plantations; they used maple sugar instead of cane sugar. Increasingly, this antislavery message found its way into Lucretia's preaching, drawing complaints from Quaker elders who urged her to avoid such "divisive" social issues.

It was in 1830, however, after meeting the radical abolitionist William Lloyd Garrison, that Lucretia threw herself fully into the struggle against slavery. After creating a stir when she rose to speak at a national antislavery convention in Philadelphia, she proceeded to found the Philadelphia Female Anti-Slavery Society. In the opening words of its constitution, she wrote, "We deem it our duty, as professing Christians, to manifest our abhorrence of the flagrant injustice and deep sin of slavery by united and vigorous actions."

The work of such abolitionist societies provoked a violent backlash, even in liberal Philadelphia. In 1838 during the Anti-Slavery Convention of American Women, a violent mob of several thousand attacked the meeting, driving the delegates out by force, and burning down the building.

The antislavery convention in London in 1840, from which she and other women were excluded, prompted the next stage in Mott's journey. Increasingly her preaching reflected a new feminist energy: "I long for the time when my sisters will rise, and occupy the sphere to which they are called by their high nature and destiny." Her prophetic teaching ruffled feathers within Quaker circles and beyond. Nevertheless, she appealed to the spirit of Jesus — a spirit of liberation, justice, and equality — against the dry power of doctrine, creed, and what she called "priestcraft." By this she referred not simply to ecclesiastical authority, but more generally to the power of men to define and enforce the "will of God." And yet she continued to claim loyalty to her Quaker roots, and indeed to keep faith with the "eternal doctrine preached by Jesus . . . that the kingdom is with man, that there is his sacred and divine temple."

The Seneca Falls convention in 1848 marked the birth of the women's movement in America. Its resolutions — which elicited widespread mirth and sarcasm among those newspapers that even acknowledged the event — called for recognition of the equality of all men and women, including the extension of universal suffrage. To the question "What does woman want?" Mott answered: "She asks nothing as a favor, but as a right, she wants to be acknowledged a moral, responsible being. She is seeking not to be governed by laws in the making of which she has no voice."

She continued to connect the antislavery cause with the promotion of women's rights. In time, however, the work of the abolitionists was overtaken by the Civil War and the Emancipation Proclamation of 1863. She rejoiced in the "Jubilee": "In our more sanguine moments we never expected to see the consummation now attained." Yet she could not help protesting vigorously that in extending the vote to freed slaves, the Constitution still excluded half the population, whether black or white. (Women's suffrage would not come until 1920.)

In her later years Mott was glad to cede leadership to a new generation of women. She lived to the age of eighty-seven, dying peacefully on November 11, 1880. Days before her death she received word of a resolution passed at a national women's rights convention:

Resolved, that this convention presents its greetings to its venerable early leader and friend, Lucretia Mott, whose life in its rounded perfection as wife, mother, preacher, and reformer is the prophecy of the future of woman. The large liberty which the Society of Friends has always given to women has been justified in her example. Have we not a right to believe that the larger measure of freedom we are here to claim will be alike blessed to all American women?

See: Margaret Hope Bacon, *Valiant Friend: The Life of Lucretia Mott* (New York: Walker and Company, 1980).

Sojourner Truth
Abolitionist Preacher (1797–1883)

"What we give the poor, we lend to the Lord."

Sojourner Truth was born a slave in Hurley, New York, around the year 1797 (her master did not record the exact date of her birth). Her parents named her Isabella, a name she abandoned at the age of forty-six when she took up her calling as a prophet and preacher.

Her first language was Dutch, the language of her master. It marked her English with a strong accent, just as her back ever bore the mark of beatings she received as a child of bondage. In her youth she was bought and sold a number of times. Some of her owners were relatively benign, while others were harsh and cruel. She was the ninth child born to her parents, but she never knew her brothers and sisters — all of them sold away to different owners.

Despite Isabella's sufferings, her mother raised her to believe in "a God who hears and sees everything you think and do." Her mother told her, "When you are beaten or cruelly treated, or you fall into any kind of trouble, you must ask his help. He will always hear you and help you." Indeed, throughout her life Isabella carried on a continuous conversation with God. Later she used to begin her speeches with the phrase, "Children, I speak to God and God speaks to me." She poured out her sufferings to God, and God told her that she would be free.

As a young woman Isabella was given in marriage to an older slave, with whom she bore five children. But early one morning in 1826 she walked away from her master's farm and stole herself from slavery, taking only her infant daughter and leaving her other four children behind.

She worked as a servant in and about New York City for a number of years. But by 1843 Isabella became convinced that God was calling her to some greater mission. So she set off on foot and left New York, carrying her few possessions in a pillow case, unsure about her destination, determined to be a preacher. With her new freedom she felt it was time to replace her slave name. After appealing to God for inspiration, she chose the name Sojourner Truth, which reflected her calling to travel "up and down the land, showing the people their sins and being a sign unto them."

As Sojourner Truth she commenced an itinerant ministry of the word, preaching from the scriptures she had practically learned by heart and delivering God's judgment against the evils of slavery. Her autobiography, *The Narrative of Sojourner Truth*, which she dictated and published in 1847, became a powerful weapon in the abolitionist cause. Yet, as eloquent and effective a speaker as she was in the antislavery movement, Truth divided her energies with the growing movement for women's rights. Many abolitionists were wary of the feminist movement, worried about compromising the struggle against slavery by linking it with another unpopular cause. But Truth insisted that there was no separating the issues. "If colored men get their rights, and not colored women," she said, "colored men will be masters over the women, and it will be just as bad as before."

In a time when the country was increasingly divided over the issue of slavery, Truth's appearances were often met with violent mobs. She never let fear or conflict silence her. More than once she tamed a hostile audience with her disarming wit. When an angry heckler once declared, "Old woman, I don't care any more for your talk than I do for the bite of a flea," she replied, "The Lord willing, I'll keep you scratching."

She never doubted that the end of slavery would come at last. When the great abolitionist Frederick Douglass once ended a speech on a discouraging note, Truth interjected with forthright confidence, "Frederick, is God dead?" In the end, however, the conflict over slavery led to bloody civil war. Truth lent her energies to supporting the war effort, especially by visiting black troops who were fighting in the Union Army. In 1864 she traveled to Washington to meet Abraham Lincoln and to encourage him in the struggle. Moved by the sufferings of the many ex-slaves who had crowded into squalid refugee camps in Washington, she decided to stay on in the capital and minister to their needs. She was there when the war ended at last, and on December 12, 1865, when Congress ratified the Thirteenth Amendment to the Constitution, abolishing slavery in the United States.

She continued to struggle for freedom and equality until the day she died on November 26, 1883, at the age of eighty-six. She was widely acclaimed as one of the most influential women of her day: an illiterate black woman, a political activist without office, a preacher without credentials save for her penetrating and holistic vision of God's justice.

In one of her most famous speeches, she rose in a women's rights meeting to respond to those men who had spoken with patronizing solicitude of women's weakness and consequent subordination to men:

> I have plowed and planted and gathered into barns, and no man could head me — and ain't I a woman? I have born'd five children and seen 'em mos' all sold off into slavery, and when I cried out with a mother's grief, none but Jesus heard — and ain't I a woman?...Den dat little man in black dar, he say women can't have as much rights as man, 'cause Christ warn't a woman. Whar did your Christ come from? *Whar did your Christ come from?* From God and a woman! Man had nothing to do with him!

A few days before she died, Truth said to a friend, "I'm not going to die, honey. I'm going home like a shooting star." Her star still shines.

See: Joyce Hollyday et al., "'Ain't I a Woman?' Sojourner Truth," special issue of *Sojourners* (December 1986); Peter Krass, *Sojourner Truth* (New York: Chelsea House, 1988).

Pandita Ramabai
Indian Christian and Reformer (1858–1922)

"People must not only hear about the kingdom of God, but must see it in actual operation, on a small scale perhaps and in imperfect form, but a real demonstration nevertheless."

Pandita Ramabai, a poet, scholar, and champion of the rights of women, has been acclaimed as a "mother of modern India." In her own time she struggled hard, as a Christian convert, to define her own identity and spiritual path, in the process drawing criticism from Hindus and fellow Christians alike. She remains an intriguing example of the effort to bridge the spiritual traditions of the East and West; both sides felt the challenge posed by this courageous and independent woman.

Ramabai was born in Karnataka in 1858. She was the daughter of a wealthy Brahmin scholar and his much younger wife. Though her father was a devout and orthodox Hindu he scandalized his high-caste friends by teaching his wife and later his daughters to read the Sanskrit classics. This talent later stood her well, when most of her family perished during a great famine. At the age of sixteen, Ramabai walked across India, visiting the holy Hindu shrines and attracting astonished audiences to her recitation of Sanskrit poetry. Her knowledge of Sanskrit, the sacred language of Hinduism, eventually won her fame and honor. She was given the honorific title "Pandita," mistress of wisdom.

She married at the age of twenty-two, but her husband died of cholera after only sixteen months, leaving her alone with an infant daughter, Manorama. Her travels in India and now her present circumstances sensitized her to the bleak plight of widows and orphans. The practice among higher castes of betrothing young girls to much older men (her own mother had been nine, her father over forty, at the time of their marriage) had contributed to the vast number of widows, women without status or protection. Ramabai set out to do something about this social problem, establishing centers for widows and orphans in Poona

Pandita Ramabai

and later Bombay, where the women were given basic education and training in marketable skills. Soon Ramabai had become the leading advocate for the rights and welfare of women in India.

Her work brought her into contact with Christian missionaries. In 1883 she accepted an invitation by a congregation of Anglican nuns to visit England. For some time Ramabai had felt a distance from her Hindu upbringing, both on spiritual grounds and on the basis of her perception of the status of women in India. While in England she undertook a serious study of the Bible and eventually asked to be baptized.

News of her conversion provoked angry public controversy in India. Ramabai herself wrestled with her strong aversion to the cultural imperialism of foreign missionaries in India. She was determined that becoming a Christian should not be construed as a denial of her Indian culture and roots. The gospel of Christ represented for her the purest expression of her own spiritual intuitions, in particular her growing belief that to serve women and the poor was a religious and not simply a social work.

She returned to India and continued her charitable work, among other things founding a center for unwed mothers, a program for famine relief, and a series of schools for poor girls. Now, ironically, it was her fellow Christians who became her public critics. They charged that because she made no effort to convert the poor women in her centers her own conversion was only superficial. They also pressed for proof of her doctrinal orthodoxy. Ramabai refused to be drawn into theological or confessional debates. "I am, it is true, a member of the Church of Christ, but I am not bound to accept every word that falls down from the lips of priests or bishops.... I have just with great efforts freed myself from the yoke of the Indian priestly tribe, so I am not at present willing to place myself under another similar yoke."

Ramabai criticized the profusion of Christian denominations, a fact, she believed, that was bewildering to the poor. The spirit of Christ as reflected in the Bible sufficed to satisfy her own religious questions. From that source she learned that the heart of true religion was the love of God and the love of one's neighbor as oneself. That she live by this creed, she insisted, was all that anyone had a right to ask of her. In later years she prayed not for the conversion of Hindus but for the conversion of Indian Christians.

She died on April 5, 1922, at the age of sixty-four.

See: S. M. Adhav, *Pandita Ramabai* (Madras: Christian Literature Society, 1979).

Mother Jones
Labor Agitator (1830–1930)

"Pray for the dead, and fight like hell for the living."

Mary Harris Jones bore four children and saw them all cut down by yellow fever. But it was her activities in the second half of her life as a tireless agitator, advocate for the oppressed, and general "hell-raiser," that earned her the affectionate title Mother Jones. Where did she live? "I live in the United States," she told a Congressional Committee, "but I do not know exactly where. My address is wherever there is a fight against oppression. I abide where there is a fight against wrong."

Among the "respectable pirates" who owned the coal mines, railroads, and steel mills, her name was spoken with contempt. But to the great masses who labored in the darkness of the anthracite pits, or coughed out their youth working sixty-five hours a week in the mills, she was indeed a mother, and more — a ministering angel. With her black dress, white hair, and quaint glasses, she might have passed for anyone's grandmother — until she opened her mouth. Describing her life's work, she said, "I have tried to educate the worker to a sense of the wrongs he has had to suffer, and does suffer — and to stir up the oppressed to a point of getting off their knees and demanding that which I believe to be rightfully theirs." But woe to anyone who called her a "lady": "God Almighty created women," she said, "but it was the Rockefeller thieves who created ladies."

Born in 1830 to a family of landless peasants in County Cork, Ireland, Mary Harris had rebellion in her blood. "I belong to a class," she would later say, "which has been robbed, exploited, and plundered down through many long centuries. And because I belong to that class, I have an impulse to go and help break the chains." After her grandfather was arrested and hanged as a rebel, her family emigrated to America in 1841. Mary was educated as a teacher and eventually settled in Memphis, Tennessee, where in 1860 she married an iron molder and union man named George Jones. It was there, while the Civil War raged around them, that she bore her children and experienced her only spell of family life. In 1867 an outbreak of yellow fever struck the city with terrible suddenness. Within quick succession Mary lost each of her children, and then her husband, leaving her alone and widowed at the age of thirty-seven.

Moving to Chicago, she worked as a seamstress. She was present to witness the great fire of 1871, which destroyed a hundred thousand homes. She herself was among the homeless. It was while walking one night among the ruined streets that she came upon a meeting of the Knights of Labor, an idealistic organization whose motto was "An injury to one is an injury to all." Intrigued by what she heard, Mary then and there devoted herself to the cause of workers' rights.

The postwar boom was followed by a harsh depression. All across the nation hundreds of thousands were out of work and left to beg or starve. Demonstrations and bloody riots erupted in New York, Chicago, and other cities. Protesters marched under the slogan "Bread or blood." As a traveling organizer for the Knights of Labor, Mary was in Philadelphia when troops fired into a crowd, killing twenty-six people. In labor disputes around the country, federal troops and state militia effectively served as employees of the railroad companies and the factory bosses.

Mary worked in relative obscurity for many years before she achieved her full fame in the 1890s as an agitator for the United Mine Workers. From Virginia to Pennsylvania, West Virginia, and out to Colorado, "Mother Jones" became a legendary figure. Her presence and fiery oratory could move men and women to tears and then embolden them to action. The sight of her white hair could shame armed deputies into lowering their rifles at her approach. One time in Colorado she walked up to a machine gun, poised to open fire on a line of demonstrators; placing her hand over the barrel, she simply turned it toward the ground and walked on past.

Knowing full well the power of her presence, the bosses and their government friends constantly tried to stifle her voice. She was repeatedly, and illegally, detained by company guards, militia, and federal troops. Sometimes this meant being hustled out of town on the next train. But well into her eighties she was imprisoned in makeshift jails and holding cells — what she called "bastilles." In one case she was held incommunicado for six weeks in a dark, underground cellar, fed on bread and water, and left to fight off the cellar rats with a broken bottle.

None of this deterred her. She emerged every time indomitable and undefeated. Decades after most organizers had retired from the fight, burned out, or died, Mother Jones continued her mission. To interfere with strike-breaking scab labor, she organized women into "bucket and broom brigades" who would stir up so much noise that mules would refuse to enter the mines. To raise awareness of exploitative child labor, she led a procession of three hundred young textile workers on a "Children's Crusade," marching from Philadelphia to New York. Stopping at meetings along the way, she would introduce girls and boys with mutilated hands, "tiny babies of six years old with faces of sixty who did an eight-hour shift for ten cents a day." In a letter to President Roosevelt, she wrote, "We ask you, Mr. President, if our commercial greatness has not cost us too much by being built on the quivering hearts of helpless children. We are now marching toward you in the hope that your tender heart will counsel with us to abolish this crime."

Mother Jones was raised in the Catholic Church. By and large she had little use for the ministers of organized religion, who preached a gospel of "pie in the sky when you die." But her speech was steeped in the language of the prophets and the revolutionary message of the Gospels. "The labor movement was not created by man," she said to a group of workers. "The labor movement, my friends, was a command from God Almighty. He commanded the prophet to redeem the Israelites that were in bondage; he organized the men into a union and led them out of the land of bondage and robbery and plunder into the land of freedom." Of those who enjoyed fancy luxuries, bought with the blood of the poor, she said, "I wish I was God Almighty! I would throw down something some night from heaven and get rid of the whole blood-sucking bunch."

Mother Jones never did retire. She lived to turn one hundred, and then died on November 30, 1930. On the eve of her death she expressed the wish that she could "live another hundred years in order to fight to the end that there would be no more machine guns and no more sobbing of little children."

See: Mother Jones Speaks: Collected Speeches and Writings, ed. Philip S. Foner (New York: Pathfinder Press, 1983); Linda Atkinson, *Mother Jones: The Most Dangerous Woman in America* (New York: Crown, 1978).

Simone Weil
Philosopher and Mystic (1909–1943)

"Today it is not nearly enough merely to be a saint; but we must have the saintliness demanded by the present moment, a new saintliness."

Simone Weil was born in France in 1909; her parents were well-educated, nonreligious Jews. From her early childhood she gave evidence of qualities that would characterize her later life: a brilliant mind, a steel will, and an acutely sensitive conscience. She studied philosophy at the elite École Normale Supérieur in preparation for a teaching career. But her intellectual interests ranged over many fields, including literature, history, political theory, and mathematics. For a time she was engaged in the world of radical politics. But she became strongly critical of the authoritarian tendencies of Marxism and the sectarian squabbles of left-wing intellectuals.

Weil taught in a series of high schools where she was regarded as an idiosyncratic but popular teacher. She got herself into some trouble, however, by trying to divide her time with teaching in a labor college and also engaging in trade union activity. Feeling a tremendous need to share the experience of the working class, she took a year's leave of absence from her job to work in a series of factories. In 1936 she again left her teaching to join the Republican cause in the Spanish Civil War, where she served with an anarchist brigade. Her life was probably spared by an accidental injury that forced her return to France.

Weil's life was marked by many instances of her impulse to sacrifice and to share the suffering of others. In retrospect it is possible to interpret her various intellectual and political explorations as steps on a deeply spiritual quest. Nevertheless, a significant turning point in her life came in the late 1930s through a series of experiences that brought her latent spiritual inclinations to the fore. While watching a religious procession in a Portuguese fishing village, she felt the conviction arise within her "that Christianity is preeminently the religion of slaves, that slaves cannot help belonging to it, and I among others." Later in a chapel in Assisi she felt, for the first time, the compulsion to fall to her knees in prayer. And then in 1938 came the experience that "marked her forever." She was spending Holy Week at the Benedictine monastery in Solesmes, following the liturgical services. At the time she was suffering a particularly devastating round of headaches, a condition to which she was prone. In the darkness of the chapel she recited the poem "Love" by the English metaphysical poet George Herbert, trying, through a tremendous effort of attention, to identify the pain she was suffering with the passion of Christ. In this effort she suddenly felt that "Christ himself came down and took possession of me."

From that time on her thinking became increasingly Christ-centered. She resumed her study of philosophy, history, and science, but now her angle of vision was trained on the meaning of God's intervention in history through the Incarnation and the cross. She immersed herself in the New Testament, attended Mass, studied the mystics, and brought herself, as she said, to the "threshold of the church" — to the point, that is, of struggling for the rest of her life with the question of whether to seek baptism. And yet she did not cross the threshold.

In 1940, as a Jew, she was fired from her teaching position by the Vichy government. She went to Marseilles with her family and sought work in the countryside harvesting grapes. In 1942 she left France and made her way to America. Instantly, however, she regretted the move, feeling her place was back in France, sharing the suffering of her people. She managed to return as far as England, where she contributed her services to the Free French organization. But her efforts to find a way of getting back into occupied France were rebuffed. In the spring of 1943 she collapsed at her desk. She was hospitalized with tuberculosis, a condition that might have improved had she been willing to cooperate with her treatment. However she insisted on eating no more than was available, under rationing, to those in occupied France. She died on August 24 at the age of thirty-four.

There is no question that Simone Weil considered herself a Christian. "Nothing that is Catholic, nothing that is Christian," she wrote, was alien to her. And yet she chose not be baptized, convinced that she was thus obedient to a vocation to be a Christian outside the church — to place herself at the intersection of Christianity and all that stands outside. "I cannot help wondering whether in these days when so large a proportion of humanity is submerged in materialism, God does not want there to be some men and women who have given themselves to him and to Christ and who yet remain outside the church." She could not bear the thought of separating herself from the "immense and unfortunate multitude of unbelievers."

There were other reservations that held her back from formal conversion. At heart she was attracted to the pure spirituality she perceived in Greek philosophy and in the Hellenistic dimension of the New Testament; she was in equal measure thoroughly repulsed by everything contaminated, as she saw it, by the spirit of Imperial Rome — a territorial, legalistic, and nationalistic spirit which she detected in the Catholic Church as well.

Weil was by all accounts a difficult and complex person, given to categorical and exasperating judgments. There is much in her writing that shows a distasteful disregard for bodily existence; this, and her philosophical repudiation of the Old Testament, are symptoms of a tendency to gnosticism, which has led some to question whether she was not really farther from orthodox Christianity than she even supposed.

Nevertheless, there is a rarefied integrity to Weil's life that has made her one of the most compelling religious figures of the twentieth century. She represents a type of noninstitutionally sanctioned sanctity, an engaged mysticism that takes into account the pathos of the human condition and the particular horrors of the modern age.

One thinks of her in connection with another French maid, Joan of Arc, who also died among the English. Like Joan she defied the wisdom of the world, clinging to her vision of truth in a spirit of utter purity, obedience, and a humility so extreme that it bordered on arrogance. In any age she would have pursued her vocation with the same determination — spurred on by a private voice, her own or Another's. In any age, one feels, she would have burned at the stake, whether of her own or another's devising.

See: Simone Weil, *Waiting for God* (New York: Harper & Row, 1973); Robert Coles, *Simone Weil: A Modern Pilgrimage* (Reading, Mass.: Addison-Wesley, 1987); *Simone Weil: Writings*, ed. Eric Springsted (Maryknoll, N.Y.: Orbis Books, 1998).

Viola Liuzzo
Martyr for Civil Rights (1925–1965)

"It's everybody's fight. There are too many people who just stand around talking."

Selma, Alabama, was the site of one of the great campaigns of the civil rights struggle, a place where white supremacists had drawn a line, determined to suppress the growing cry for freedom. In February 1965, after a young black activist named Jimmie Lee Jackson was clubbed to death by state troopers, civil rights leaders called for a march from Selma to the state capital in Montgomery. In reply Governor George Wallace announced that he would not only refuse to meet the demonstrators but would ban the march as a threat to public safety. The battle lines were drawn.

On March 7 six hundred demonstrators set off to begin the fifty-mile march. As they crossed the Edmund Pettus Bridge over the Alabama River they met a phalanx of heavily armed state troopers. When the demonstrators refused an order to turn around, the troopers rushed into the crowd, wildly swinging their clubs and whips. Another wave of troopers on horseback trampled over the falling marchers. The day would be remembered as Bloody Sunday.

Among the millions of Americans who watched this scene on television was a white, thirty-nine-year-old housewife and mother of five, Viola Liuzzo of Detroit. Viola herself had known personal struggle, pulling herself out of the poverty of her childhood and confronting a number of painful dead ends. Leaving school after tenth grade, she was twice married and divorced by the time she was twenty-five. But with her marriage in 1950 to Jim Liuzzo, an official with the Teamsters union, and her conversion to Catholicism, her life had taken on a steadily deeper focus. She had completed evening courses at a career training school and by 1964 had enrolled in part-time studies at Wayne State University.

Friends recalled her as a person of boundless energy and generosity, always seeking ways to be helpful. They also teased her for her indignation over social injustice. Like many Americans she was shocked by the images of hatred and violence unfolding in the South. After viewing the debacle of Bloody Sunday, she joined other students from Wayne State in a protest march — her first — on the steps of the Federal Building in Detroit, where they raised placards and sang "We Shall Overcome."

On March 21 another march was scheduled from Selma — this time with federal support and the protection of National Guard troops. When a call went out for volunteers to join the march, many hundreds from around the country responded. Viola Liuzzo was among them. One of the northern ministers who organized the effort remembered her as an "ordinary" person. Yet she impressed him as someone prepared to take a risk for what she believed in. She was a person seeking the truth, he said, searching for "the manifestation of God in a broad rather than in a narrow way."

Fearing her family's efforts to dissuade her, Viola didn't tell them in advance of her plans. Instead she simply arranged with a friend for the care of her children, packed a shopping bag full of clothes into her blue Oldsmobile sedan, and headed to Alabama. Calling her husband from the road, she begged him to understand that this was something she had to do.

Her family never saw her again.

By the day of the march, over three thousand people had gathered in Selma. Viola was part of that great mass, though she did not walk the whole way. She put herself at the service of the organizers, offering to do anything that might be helpful, whether assisting in the first-aid station or ferrying people to and fro in her car. This "people's army" of marchers was a dramatic sight. Famous leaders of the civil rights movement were joined by ordinary people, black and white, from every class and background. Priests and rabbis, nuns in their distinctive habits, students and workers from around the country — all had gathered to bear witness to justice and equality and against the forces of hatred. This time the march ended peacefully in Montgomery, with speeches by Rosa Parks and Martin Luther King, who thrilled the crowd with his vision of the coming day of freedom: "How long will it take? Not long, because truth pressed to earth will rise again."

Rather than head home right away, Viola offered to stay on and offer her services as a chauffeur. That night she was ferrying a young black civil rights worker, Leroy Moton, on the road back to Selma. At a certain point they realized they were being followed. Even when she accelerated to ninety miles per hour, the pursuing car kept pace. Finally it drew up beside her. In the next moment a fusillade of bullets pierced Viola's car. One of them hit her in the skull, killing her instantly, as her car rolled off the road. Miraculously, Moton survived, playing dead when the assailants circled back to inspect their work.

The next day President Johnson spoke to the nation. "Mrs. Liuzzo went to Alabama to serve the struggle for justice," he said. "She was murdered by the enemies of justice, who for decades have used the rope and the gun and the tar and feathers to terrorize their neighbors." He vowed that justice would be done.

In fact, with surprising speed, three men were promptly arrested — all of them members of the Ku Klux Klan. It turned out that a fourth passenger in the car that night had been a long-time FBI informant. Nevertheless, despite his testimony and other overwhelming evidence, an all-white jury acquitted the defendants on murder charges. Only later did a federal jury find them guilty of violating Viola Liuzzo's civil rights. They were ultimately sentenced to ten years in prison.

Not everyone honored Liuzzo's actions. Scurrilous rumors were circulated about her character: after all, what business did a white woman have to be caught alone in a car with a young black man? Even some of her Detroit neighbors spat epithets at her children as they walked to school. As one of her sons would later say, "I've been labeled all my life a 'nigger lover' because of what my mother did. If that's what I am, then God love it."

But for another America, those who shared Dr. King's vision of justice and the dignity of all God's children, Viola's sacrifice would be remembered as a singular milestone on the long march to freedom.

See: Beatrice Siegel, *Murder on the Highway: The Viola Liuzzo Story* (New York: Four Winds Press, 1993).

Fannie Lou Hamer
Prophet of Freedom (1917–1977)

"I am sick and tired of being sick and tired."

Fannie Lou Hamer was born the daughter of sharecroppers in the Mississippi Delta, a poor black woman in the poorest region of America. And yet she rose up from obscurity to challenge the mighty rulers of her day, a towering prophet whose eloquence and courage helped guide and inspire the struggle for freedom.

Until 1962 her life was little different from that of other poor black women in rural Mississippi. One of twenty children in her family, she was educated to the fourth grade and, like her parents before her, fell into the life of sharecropping. This system allowed poor farmers to work a piece of the plantation owner's land in exchange for payment of a share of their crop. In practice, it was a system of debt slavery that combined with segregation and brute force to keep the black population poor and powerless. Looking back on her own twenty years of sharecropping, Hamer later said, "Sometimes I be working in the fields and I get so tired, I say to the people picking cotton with us, 'Hard as we have to work for nothing, there must be some way we can change this.'"

The way opened up for Hamer when she attended a civil rights rally in 1962 and heard a preacher issue a call for blacks to register to vote. At the age of forty-five Hamer answered the call, though it meant overcoming numerous threats and obstacles and resulted in the eviction of her family from their plantation home. Hamer took this as a sign to commit herself to full-time work for the freedom movement, serving as a field secretary for the Student Nonviolent Coordinating Committee and quickly rising to a position of leadership.

For a black person in 1963 to challenge the system of segregation in Mississippi was literally to court death. Hamer, like other activists in the movement, faced this reality on a daily basis. In the summer of 1963 she was part of a group arrested in Charleston, South Carolina, after they illegally entered the side of a bus terminal reserved for whites. While in jail she was savagely beaten, emerging with a damaged kidney and her eyesight permanently impaired.

In 1964 Hamer led a "Freedom Delegation" from Mississippi to the National Convention of the Democratic Party in Atlantic City. There they tried unsuccessfully to challenge the credentials of the official

Fannie Lou Hamer

white delegation. President Lyndon Johnson would tolerate no such embarrassment to the party bosses of the South, and the Freedom Delegation was evicted. But Hamer touched the conscience of the nation with her eloquent account of the oppression of blacks in the segregated South and their nonviolent struggle to affirm their dignity and their rights.

In later years, Hamer's concerns grew beyond civil rights to include early opposition to the Vietnam War and efforts to forge a coalition among all poor and working people in America — the Poor People's Campaign that Martin Luther King left uncompleted. In all these endeavors, Hamer was sustained by her deep biblical faith in the God of the oppressed. "We have to realize," she once observed,

> just how grave the problem is in the United States today, and I think the sixth chapter of Ephesians, the eleventh and twelfth verses help us to know ... what it is we are up against. It says, "Put on the whole armor of God, that ye may be able to stand against the wiles of the devil. For we wrestle not against flesh and blood but against principalities, against powers, against the rulers of the darkness of this world, against spiritual wickedness in high places." This is what I think about when I think of my own work in the fight for freedom.

In the nonviolent freedom struggle of the 1960s ordinary people — men, women, and children — became saints and prophets. Inspired by a vision of justice and freedom, sustained by faith, they found the strength to confront their fears and stand up to dogs, fire hoses, clubs, and bombs. In the ranks of this extraordinary movement Hamer was a rock who did as much as anyone of her time to redeem the promise of the gospel and the ideals of America. She said,

> Christianity is being concerned about your fellow man, not building a million-dollar church while people are starving right around the corner. Christ was a revolutionary person, out there where it was happening. That's what God is all about, and that's where I get my strength.

Hamer died of breast cancer on March 14, 1977.

See: Danny Collum et al., "Fannie Lou Hamer: Prophet of Freedom," *Sojourners* (December 1982).

Catherine de Hueck Doherty
Founder of Madonna House (1896–1985)

"The hunger for God can only be satisfied by a love that is face to face, person to person. It is only in the eyes of another that we can find the Icon of Christ. We must make the other person aware we love him. If we do, he will know that God loves him. He will never hunger again."

Catherine Kolyschkine, as she was first named, was born in Russia on the feast of the Assumption in 1896. Her father, a wealthy diplomat and industrialist, was half-Polish and Catholic, and so Catherine was raised in the Catholic Church. When she was fifteen she married Baron Boris de Hueck, which made her a baroness. No sooner had she made this entry into the aristocracy than Russia was plunged into the First World War. While the baron served as an officer on the front, Catherine worked as a nurse. They watched as the starving and demoralized Russian army began to retreat, presaging the collapse of the tsarist empire in the October Revolution of 1917.

Though Catherine and Boris were reunited, their situation, as aristocrats, was perilous. Deprived of food rations, they came close to starving before risking a hazardous flight across the border to Finland. By 1920 they had arrived with their newborn son in Canada. Still in desperate financial straits, Catherine traveled to New York in search of work. She held a number of low-paying jobs. Finally, while working as a department store sales clerk, she was approached by a woman who asked if it was true that she was a Russian baroness, and would she be interested in lecturing about her experiences. Catherine immediately agreed, and soon she was on a lecture circuit, making $300 a week describing her harrowing escape from communism. During this time her marriage collapsed. It seemed that she had finally put the memory of poverty and hunger behind her. She had a luxurious apartment, a fancy car, and a country house in Graymoor—all that communism had taken away from her. And yet her conscience was clouded by a nagging doubt, a feeling that it was just such a materialistic life and the failure of Christian values that had fed the communist revolution.

At the peak of her success she felt the pull of the gospel verse, "Go, sell what you have and give to the poor. Then come follow me." So in 1930 she gave up her worldly goods and moved into an apartment in the slums of Toronto, committed to living "the gospel without compromise." With the support of the archbishop, she came to establish

Catherine de Hueck Doherty

Friendship House, a storefront center for the works of mercy, where the hungry were fed and the homeless were welcomed. Catherine's program of action was simple and unsystematic. It was merely a matter of living among the poor with an open door and an open heart. There was no need to seek out people in need. They came to her.

She received encouragement in these years from Dorothy Day, whose Catholic Worker movement was operating on similar principles in New York's Bowery. In 1937 Catherine herself moved to New York to establish a Friendship House in Harlem. She had come to feel that the sin of racial prejudice and the consequent segregation of whites and blacks was the greatest countersign to the gospel. Friendship House was a sign of interracial justice and reconciliation.

Among those moved by her example was the young Thomas Merton, who heard Catherine speak in 1938 and who joined her for a time in Harlem. Years later, in his autobiography, he described her message:

> Catholics are worried about Communism: and they have a right to be.... But few Catholics stop to think that Communism would make very little progress in the world, or none at all, if Catholics really lived up to their obligations, and really did the things Christ came on earth to teach them to do: that is, if they really loved one another, and saw Christ in one another, and lived as saints, and did something to win justice for the poor.

Catherine was a large woman whose bearing of authority, commanding presence, and thick Russian accent all seemed appropriate to the title of Baroness. That is indeed how most people addressed her. But to her friends she was simply "the B." She was famous for her earthy humor and her righteous anger. When a society woman sniffed contemptuously, "You smell of the Negro," Catherine retorted, "And you stink of hell!"

Nevertheless, her imperious style of leadership led to tensions. In 1946 Catherine resigned from Friendship House. By this time she had married a famous journalist, Eddie Doherty. Together they moved back to Ontario, Canada, and settled on a piece of land in the forests of Combermere. Catherine established a new community called Madonna House, which became a place of prayer and retreat. At Madonna House she returned full circle to the atmosphere of Russian spirituality she had known in her youth. Out of this came her best-selling book, *Poustinia*. The "poustinia," the Russian word for desert, is a place of silence and withdrawal from the compulsions of the world, a place to listen to God. It could be a hut in the forest, a special room in our apartment, or even a special place within our hearts, to which from time to time we might retreat. Through Madonna House and the communities it inspired around the world, Catherine promoted the two principles by which she lived — a commitment to the social apostolate in the world and the need to root such a commitment in a life of prayer and the spirit of Christ.

She died on December 14, 1985.

See: Catherine de Hueck Doherty, *Poustinia* (Notre Dame, Ind.: Ave Maria Press, 1975); *Fragments of My Life* (Notre Dame, Ind.: Ave Maria Press, 1979).

Catherine de Hueck Doherty

BLESSED ARE
THE MERCIFUL

A holy abbess • a widowed nun • a prison reformer • a nurse • a liberator
of the enslaved • an Orthodox martyr • a friend of ragpickers • a witness
of divine compassion • a righteous gentile • a missionary of charity

According to tradition, the works of mercy include feeding the hungry, clothing the naked, and sheltering the homeless. Many saints, particularly women, defined their mission in terms of these works, whether caring for the poor, nursing the sick, or comforting the dying. But the quality of true mercy is determined less by the physical gesture than by the love that inspires it. The poor know the difference. Mercy asks nothing in return — neither the gratitude, freedom, nor self-respect of its recipients. It is inspired simply by a recognition of shared humanity — the ability to see in the face of a stranger a friend, a neighbor, another self, another Christ.

To anyone who has ever been in need of help or compassion, there is no more miraculous sacrament of God's love than an act of kindness given freely, gratuitously, with no strings attached. Those who extend such gifts are promised a most appropriate reward: "They will be shown mercy."

St. Brigid of Ireland
Abbess of Kildare (c. 450–525)

"I would like a great lake of beer for the King of the kings; I would like the people of heaven to be drinking it through time eternal."

Brigid lived in the era when traditional Irish religion was giving way to the formal institution of Christianity. The lives and legends of holy Brigid reflect that uneasy ebb and flow. It has been noted that in ancient times Brigid was, in fact, the name of the Celtic sun goddess. This has given rise to the suggestion that in St. Brigid, a nun and abbess of the fifth century, we find the repository of primeval religious memories and traditions. In any case, it seems that with the cult of St. Brigid (called "The Mary of the Gael") the Irish people maintained an image of the maternal face of God with which to complement the more patriarchal religion of St. Patrick and subsequent missionaries.

As best as can be discerned through the mists of legend, it is believed that Brigid was born into slavery and was later converted to Christianity by St. Patrick sometime in her childhood. She was granted her freedom when it proved impossible to curb her enthusiasm for giving alms; it seems she would otherwise have impoverished her master through such unauthorized largesse.

The themes of generosity and compassion are the feature of miracles without number. Brigid's only desire was "to satisfy the poor, to expel every hardship, to spare every miserable soul." (That there remained any miserable souls in Ireland is hard to believe, given the extent of her recorded miracles.) Many of her marvels have a particularly maternal character, reflecting her propensity to nourish and give succor. Thus, she supplied beer out of her one barrel to eighteen churches, which sufficed from Maundy Thursday to the end of the paschal time. Once when a leprous woman asked for milk, there being none at hand she gave her cold water, but the water turned into milk, and when she had drunk it the woman was healed.

Brigid became a nun and ultimately abbess of Kildare, which was a double monastery, consisting of both men and women. Through her fame as a spiritual teacher the Abbey of Kildare became a center for pilgrims. So great was the authority of Brigid, it seems, that she even induced a bishop to join her community and to share her leadership. According to legend — which the church, for obvious reasons, has strenuously resisted — the bishop came to ordain Brigid as a fellow bishop.

Some chroniclers cite this in a matter-of-fact way (it is, after all, scarcely less credible than many of the reports of Brigid's career). Others report the story while trying in some way to mitigate the scandal. It is suggested, for instance, that the bishop was so "intoxicated with the grace of God" that he didn't know what he was doing. Whatever the historical facts, the persistence of such a tale says a good deal about Brigid's status in the Irish conscience, and perhaps the effort to rectify the exclusion of such an extraordinary woman from the ranks of apostolic authority.

See: Hugh de Blacam, *The Saints of Ireland* (Milwaukee: Bruce, 1942); Mary Condren, *The Serpent and the Goddess: Women, Religion, and Power in Celtic Ireland* (San Francisco: Harper & Row, 1989).

St. Mechtild of Hackeborn
Nun and Mystic (1241–1298)

"She gave teaching with such abundance that such a one has never been seen in the monastery and we fear, alas, will never be seen again."
— St. Gertrude

St. Mechtild was one of a trio of extraordinary mystics who inhabited the same Benedictine convent in Saxony in the late thirteenth century. Aside from Mechtild of Hackeborn, who first came to the convent of Helfta when she was seven, there was also the ex-Beguine Mechthild of Magdeburg and the younger Gertrude the Great. None of these women held any notable office in their community, and yet they exerted spiritual authority far beyond the convent as a result of their visions and their wide reputation for holiness.

Mechtild of Hackeborn and Gertrude were particularly close. Gertrude had been donated to the convent at the age of five, and Mechtild, fifteen years her senior, had been largely responsible for her upbringing. As nuns and mystics they both developed a similar spirituality, emphasizing an affective devotion to the humanity of Christ and a strong focus on the Eucharist.

In the case of Mechtild, her first mystical vision occurred while receiving communion. Christ appeared to her, held her hands, and left his imprint on her heart "like a seal in wax." Christ furthermore presented his own heart to her in the form of a cup and said, "By my heart you will praise me always; go, offer to all the saints the drink of life from my heart that they may be happily inebriated with it."

Mechtild had a great devotion to the humanity of Christ, for this humanity was the "door" by which human beings and, indeed, all creation entered into union with divinity. In one extraordinary vision she perceived that "the smallest details of creation are reflected in the Holy Trinity by means of the humanity of Christ, because it is from the same earth that produced them that Christ drew his humanity."

As a result of her visions, Mechtild wielded tremendous authority within her community and beyond. She was regarded as a prophet, teacher, and counselor, "a tender mother of the unfortunate by her continual prayers, her zealous instruction, and her consolations." The teachings and visions of St. Mechtild were carefully recorded by her spiritual daughter and lifelong friend, St. Gertrude, in a work entitled *The Book of Special Grace*. She died on November 19, 1298.

See: Caroline Walker Bynum, *Jesus as Mother: Studies in the Spirituality of the High Middle Ages* (Berkeley: University of California Press, 1982).

St. Louise de Marillac
Co-Founder of the Daughters of Charity
(1591–1660)

"Love the poor, honor them, as you would honor Christ."

Louise de Marillac was raised and educated by her widowed father, a distinguished country gentleman. His death, when she was fifteen, left her in desperate social straits, a situation alleviated only by her consent to marry a gentleman named Antony Le Gras, secretary to the household of the French queen. With him she bore a son, Michel. It was evidently a happy marriage. Nevertheless, she was visited periodically with anxious regrets that she had suppressed a vocation to religious life. When her husband was struck by a debilitating illness, Louise nursed him with great devotion. Even before his death, however, she privately vowed that she would not remarry but would instead devote her life to the service of God.

After the death of Le Gras Louise withdrew from public life, awaiting some sign of her vocation. This came with her introduction in 1623 to

Father Vincent de Paul, who consented to become her spiritual director and with whom she went on to form one of the great partnerships in the history of religious life.

Monsieur Vincent, as he was widely known, had organized an extraordinary range of charitable projects. These included a circle of aristocratic ladies who joined to work in the Parisian slums among the sick and destitute. Louise readily committed herself to this work. But with time it became clear that the needs of the poor required more effective service than could be provided by such well-intentioned but part-time volunteers. Vincent and Louise formed the notion of a community of women completely committed to loving service to the poor. Thus were born the Daughters of Charity.

From the beginning, Vincent did not conceive of the community as a religious congregation. "Your convent," he wrote, "will be the house of the sick; your cell, a hired room; your chapel, the parish church; your cloister, the streets of the city or the wards of the hospital; your enclosure, obedience; your grating, the fear of God; your veil, holy modesty." Nevertheless, the Daughters were later recognized by Rome as a religious congregation, with members annually renewing vows of poverty, chastity, and obedience. Such recognition of a congregation of women living outside of an enclosed convent and engaged in apostolic work in the world was a novel and remarkable achievement. Although the gray habits and white headdresses later became a distinctive emblem of the Sisters of Charity, at the time their dress was indistinguishable from the garb of peasant women. In their spiritual formation the Sisters were constantly reminded that the poor were their masters. In them they would encounter the face of Christ. And so they should never hesitate to leave off from other spiritual obligations should they be summoned by those in need. They should realize that in leaving off their prayers or even the Mass to go to the poor they would be going, as it were, "from God to God."

The numbers and works of the Daughters expanded quickly. Soon their communities had spread throughout France and other parts of Europe. With members drawn particularly from among the peasant class, they could be found administering hospitals, orphanages, and schools for the poor, as well as ministering to prisoners and galley slaves and visiting the poor in their squalid hovels. Louise herself cared for the victims of the plague during an epidemic in Paris.

Louise de Marillac was by all accounts a valiant and inspired leader, whose voluminous correspondence with her beloved friend and mentor reveals at the same time her refinement and acute spiritual wisdom. One source of anxiety was her slow-witted son, Michel, to whom, naively, she attributed a vocation to the priesthood. Vincent gently persuaded her that the boy felt no such calling. Michel eventually married and went on to become a civil servant. Years later Louise was happy to receive him with his wife and child at her deathbed. She was deprived, however, of the consoling presence of her friend, Monsieur Vincent, whose age and infirmity kept him from her side. He sent her word that they would soon be reunited in heaven.

Toward the close of her life Louise worried about the future of her congregation. She was afraid in particular that the Sisters would lose touch with the radical spirit of service in the world and become "institutionalized," like so many other religious communities. Vincent shared this concern. Whereas the aim of most religious was their own perfection, he conceived that "these Daughters are used...for the salvation and comfort of the neighbor." Repeatedly, Louise admonished her Sisters to be "diligent in serving the poor...to love the poor, honor them, my children, as you would honor Christ Himself."

She died on March 15, 1660. Vincent de Paul followed her six months later. Louise was canonized in 1934, by which time the Sisters of Charity numbered more than fifty thousand around the world.

See: J. Calvet, *Louise de Marillac: A Portrait* (New York: P. J. Kenedy & Sons, 1959); Joseph I. Dirvin, C.M., *Louise de Marillac* (New York: Farrar, Straus & Giroux, 1970).

St. Joan Delanou

Founder of the Sisters of St. Anne
of the Providence of Saumur (1666–1736)

"Inasmuch as you did these things
for the least of my brothers and sisters..."
—Matthew 25:40

As a shopkeeper in Saumur, France, Joan Delanou was a notorious miser. She hoarded every cent she earned, angrily drove beggars from her door, and caused scandal by keeping her shop open on Sundays and feast days. Into this self-enclosed life, however, the influence of grace effected an extraordinary conversion.

It began when Joan provided lodging to a strange old woman, a widow named Frances Souchet, who spent her time traveling the countryside and visiting holy shrines. Her shabby appearance and her habit of muttering to herself led many to believe she was a bit mad. Souchet told Joan that she was sent from God. Nevertheless, she paid for her room, and that was enough reason for Joan to tolerate her company.

As time passed the presence of the old woman worked a strange influence on her landlord. Joan no longer found the same pleasure in counting her savings. She ceased to keep her shop open on Sunday, and instead she began to accompany her lodger to weekly Mass. Meanwhile Madame Souchet continued her strange pronouncements: *"He says this..." "He says that..."* It gradually dawned on Joan that this woman was a messenger from God sent to bear a warning and challenge: "I was hungry, and you did not feed me; thirsty, and you did not give me drink; I was a stranger, and you offered me no shelter...." At once she decided to amend her life.

She began by taking in a homeless family with six children. Others gradually found their way to her door. Her home became known as Providence House. Madame Souchet remained a welcome guest, continuing to provide her spiritual counsel. When Joan worried about how to support her groaning household, the old woman offered assurance: "The king of France won't give you his purse; but the King of kings will always keep His open for you."

Eventually she received something more precious than gold: willing helpers. She took this as a sign that she ought to found a religious congregation, dedicated to service of the poor and sick. And so on the feast of St. Anne, July 26, 1704, she and her associates took religious vows and assumed the name Sisters of St. Anne. Joan eventually became known as Sister Joan-of-the-Cross. Within a decade her community had grown and acquired several adjoining buildings with enough room for over a hundred orphans, as well as the sick and aged. Joan acquired a wide reputation for holiness. Only her confessors knew the extent of her private austerities, not to mention the physical pain and spiritual torments that regularly assailed her in later years. By the time she died on August 17, 1736, at the age of seventy, she was the best loved person in Saumur. She was canonized in 1982.

Nano Nagle
Founder of the Presentation Sisters (1718–1784)

"I think any little labor I have, the Almighty has given me health to go through it; and if I did not make use of it in his service, he may soon deprive me of it."

Honora Nagle, known as Nano, was born in Ballygriffin, a small town in County Cork, Ireland, in 1718. She came from a wealthy family, though like all Irish Catholics she felt the repressive burden of England's penal laws. These punitive restrictions on the faith and liberties of Irish Catholics were designed, in small ways and large, to demoralize and weaken a defeated people. Enacted in the 1690s, these laws banished all bishops and religious orders from Ireland and abolished all Catholic schools. No Catholic could vote or serve on a jury, or acquire property from a Protestant neighbor, or bequeath land to an eldest son, unless the son himself was a Protestant. As Edmund Burke observed, this system of law was "a machine of subtle invention, the best adapted to the oppression, impoverishment, and degradation of a people, the debasement of human nature itself, which has ever been conceived by the perverted ingenuity of man."

This was the world in which Nano Nagle was born. Her early education was in one of the illegal "hedge schools" that proliferated in the countryside. Eventually, though, her family found the means to send her to Paris, where she enjoyed the pleasures of high society and the glittering court of King Louis XV. She was, in her own words, "a lover of the world, of dress, and of vanity." The death of her parents, however, brought her back to Ireland, where for the first time she began to appreciate the misery of her people and felt a calling to some higher purpose. Religious life was an option. She returned to France and entered an Ursuline convent. But her spiritual director convinced her that her mission was home in Ireland.

Returning to Cork she established the first of a network of illegal schools. Meeting in a mud shack, risking imprisonment and even death, should she be discovered, Nagle eventually attracted two hundred girls to the new school. She offered basic education, along with religious instruction and training in practical skills. With the support of other helpers, her work steadily expanded to a series of schools. But with this success her vision only grew larger. She decided to establish a religious order devoted to serving the poor in every way. In 1775 she founded the Society of the Charitable Instruction, which eventually became the Presentation Order, a congregation numbering many thousands, which later spread to the West Indies and North America.

By the time of her death on April 26, 1784, her work was known and revered throughout Ireland. The inscription on her gravestone read in part, "Here lie, waiting, 'tis hoped, a glorious resurrection, the remains of Miss Honora Nagle...whose life and fortune were always devoted to the service of God and of the poor; whose piety, humility, and self-denial made a most salutary impression on an admiring public; and whose charity and zeal were most singularly and successfully exercised for more than thirty years in the instruction of multitudes of poor children, rearing them true servants of God, and useful members of society."

But perhaps her life is best summed up in her own motto: "Not words, but deeds."

See: M. Rosaria O'Callaghan, *Flame of Love: A Biography of Nano Nagle* (Milwaukee: Bruce Press, 1960).

St. Elizabeth Ann Seton
Founder of the Daughters of Charity
of St. Joseph (1774–1821)

"God is with us — and if sufferings abound in us, his Consolations also greatly abound, and far exceed all utterance."

For generations of poor and immigrant Catholics, the parochial school system, staffed largely by dedicated nuns, was the entry point to education and assimilation into American life. This outstanding feature of American Catholicism was created by many people. But it arose largely from the foundation established by one woman, Elizabeth Ann Seton, a Catholic convert and the first canonized saint born in the United States.

Elizabeth Ann Bayley was born two years before the American Revolution to a prosperous and staunchly Episcopalian family in New York City. At the age of twenty she married a successful shipping merchant named William Magee Seton. Together they had five children. But her fortunes underwent a drastic change, first when her husband's business failed, then when he was stricken with tuberculosis. In a desperate effort to improve his health in a sunnier clime, Elizabeth, William, and their eldest daughter embarked for Italy. It was a difficult voyage. Upon arrival, their ship was placed in quarantine for a month. William's health steadily deteriorated until eventually he died.

Accepting the hospitality of Italian friends, Elizabeth chose to remain in Italy for some months. She was so touched and consoled by her hosts' faith that she found herself attracted to the Catholic Church. By the time she returned to New York she had determined to become a Catholic. It was a radical step. So intense was the anti-Catholic feeling among her family and social circle that she was effectively abandoned. By the time she was formally received into the church in 1805 she was left penniless with the care of her five children.

A way out was provided when a priest in Baltimore invited her to come and start a school in his parish. In Maryland, the one state in America founded by Catholics, Elizabeth finally found a home. In short order she attracted other women to help her with her school. The thought occurred to them of starting a religious congregation devoted to the care and education of children. In 1809, with support from Bishop John Carroll (the first Catholic bishop in the United States), the women took religious vows and formed the Daughters of Charity of St. Joseph. Elizabeth Seton — now Mother Seton — became their first superior.

As the first religious congregation founded in the United States, Mother Seton and her Sisters had to grope their way through unknown territory. Though they modeled themselves on the Daughters of Charity of Sts. Vincent de Paul and Louise de Marillac, they had few precedents or examples to guide them. Certainly Mother Seton, a convert of only four years and still in charge of her family, brought no previous experience in religious life. For some years, until she found her balance, she suffered under the rigid spiritual direction of priests who tried to control and shape the direction of her order.

Her greatest personal trial came in 1812 following the death of her sixteen-year-old daughter, Anna. For six months she was devastated by a grief that came close to despair. As she later wrote, "After Anna was taken I was so often expecting to lose my senses and my head was so disordered that unless for the daily duties always before me I did not know much of what I did or what I left undone." But eventually she pulled through, helped in part by a good priest who convinced her that hers was a "celestial commission"; as a mother of her Daughters of Charity, she would do so much good for "God and souls through this short life."

St. Elizabeth Ann Seton

In the years to come her practical good sense, abiding faith, and deep maternal instincts steadily guided the growth and spirituality of her community. Before long, schools and orphanages under her direction opened in several cities. By the time of her death on January 4, 1821, there were twenty such houses across the country — part of the great infrastructure of charity and service that would, before long, meet the vast wave of Catholic immigrants.

Mother Seton died at the age of forty-seven. Toward the end she wrote, "I am sick, but not dying; troubled on every side, but not distressed; perplexed, but not despairing; afflicted, but not forsaken; cast down, but not destroyed; knowing the affliction of this life is but for a moment, for the glory and the life to come will be eternal."

Over a thousand of her Sisters were present in Rome in 1975 to witness her canonization.

See: *Elizabeth Ann Seton: Selected Writings,* ed. Kelly and Annabelle Melville (New York: Paulist, 1987).

Elizabeth Fry
Quaker Reformer (1780–1845)

"My mind is in a state of fermentation.
I believe I am going to be religious or some such thing."

Elizabeth Fry was raised in a prosperous Quaker family, the Gurneys of Norwich, England. Her family represented the more "lax" end of the Quaker spectrum; thus, the children were allowed to sing and dance and wear bright clothes to Meeting. As Elizabeth grew up, however, she was increasingly attracted to the more austere devotional habits of the "Plain Quakers." When she was seventeen an encounter with a Quaker abolitionist from the United States stimulated her desire to pursue a path of godly service. Afterward she wrote in her journal, "I wish the state of enthusiasm I am now in may last, for today I *have felt* there is a *God. I have been devotional,* and my mind has been led away from the follies that it is mostly wrapt up in."

Within two years she was married to Joseph Fry, and her life was subsequently absorbed in the responsibilities of a growing family. Ultimately, she bore eleven children over a period of twenty-one years. This life was not without its rewards. But after twelve years of marriage, she felt that she was missing out on her true vocation. In her diary she wrote, "I fear that my life is slipping away to little purpose."

It was soon afterward that she accepted the invitation of another Quaker to visit the infamous Newgate prison. There she witnessed conditions that filled her with shame and indignation. Women and their young children were crowded into fetid cells, "tried and untried, misdemeanants and felons" together, "in rags and dirt...sleeping without bedding on the floor." In one cell she saw two women strip the clothing off a dead baby to dress another infant.

This was the beginning of a cause, public and private, that Fry pursued for the rest of her life. She began by returning to the prison with clean clothing and straw for the women to lie on. Although the jailers tried to obstruct her efforts, claiming that the women were incorrigible savages, Fry was determined to respond to them in a manner befitting their humanity. When she asked them whether they would like her to provide instruction to their children, they responded eagerly, with many of the illiterate women pressing in to benefit from her lessons.

With the support of a committee of other Quaker women Fry launched a campaign for general prison reform. This achieved many results, including provisions for larger living quarters, better food, fresh air, and the supply of sewing materials to provide the women with some occupation and a means of earning money. Over the years Fry was tireless in her efforts, which eventually extended throughout England and Scotland. There were some who criticized her on the grounds that her devotion to this cause entailed the neglect of her family. She too upbraided herself at times. As she wrote in her journal in 1817,

> My mind too much tossed by a variety of interests and duties — husband, children, household, accounts, Meetings, the church, near relations, friends, and Newgate — most of these things press a good deal upon me. I hope I am not undertaking too much, but it is a little like being in the whirlwind and in the storm.

Her efforts also elicited public opposition from those who felt that to humanize the prisons was to undermine their deterrent value, thus "removing the dread of punishment in the criminal classes." But Fry was motivated by the conviction that prisoners, regardless of their crimes, were human beings who bore within them the spark of the divine image. It was sacrilege to treat them with no more than punitive cruelty.

Fry continued to live in the whirlwind and pressed on with her cause, in season and out, until the end of her life on October 12, 1845.

See: D. Elton Trueblood, *The People Called Quakers* (New York: Harper & Row, 1966); George Anderson, "Elizabeth Fry: Timeless Reformer," *America* (October 14, 1995).

Bd. Anne-Marie Javouhey
Founder, Sisters of St. Joseph of Cluny (1779–1851)

"The Cross is found wherever there are servants of God, and I rejoice to be reckoned among them."

Anne-Marie Javouhey — Nanette as she was called — was the eldest daughter of a prosperous farmer in Burgundy. The first stirring of her religious vocation occurred when she was a child, though the timing could not have been more inauspicious. The revolutionary regime in France had outlawed all religious congregations, part of a deliberate effort to suppress the Catholic faith. Nevertheless Nanette would conduct secret catechism classes for her neighboring children and shelter clandestine priests who passed through her village. One of these priests persuaded her reluctant father to let her make private religious vows in anticipation of the day when convents might return to France.

When that day finally arrived, Nanette entered a restored convent of the Sisters of Charity. But she withdrew on the eve of her final vows, swayed in part by a mysterious dream or vision — she herself could not say which. She had awakened one night to find her cell illuminated by a strange light. She was surrounded by children of different races (so limited was her exposure to the world, at this point, that she was not aware that people came in different colors). A voice spoke to her: "These are the children God gives you. I am Teresa, and I will look after your congregation."

Eventually, with other young women attracted by her mission and energy, she did found a new congregation. The Sisters of St. Joseph of Cluny, as they were known, took their name from an abandoned monastery in Cluny, purchased by her father to serve as their motherhouse. At first the Sisters operated schools for the poor, at the same time struggling with their own real poverty. But Nanette's dream came to fulfillment when she was invited to establish a mission on the island of Bourbon, a French colony off the coast of Madagascar. Before long this led to other missions in other poor colonies, including Guadaloupe, Senegal, and Martinique. The dedication of the Sisters and their willingness to serve in the most difficult circumstances won widespread respect. King Louis-Philippe, intending, no doubt, to pay her a high compliment, observed, "Madame Javouhey is a great man!"

In 1828 Mother Javouhey was invited to establish a mission in the district of Mana in French Guiana. This desolate region, with its notoriously cruel climate, was chiefly known for the penal colony on Devil's Island. The French government, anxious to encourage colonization and development, thought the presence of nuns would have a civilizing influence. These hopes were well placed. So successful were Mother Javouhey's efforts that she was asked to undertake a more ambitious project.

France was in the process of emancipating slaves in its colonies. In Guiana, however, the government felt it prudent to establish some transitional program to prepare the slaves for their emancipation.

Mother Javouhey organized a community of six hundred former slaves. The settlement prospered — so much so that it provoked the bitter jealousy of neighboring white farmers, who sent slanderous reports back to France. These critics had an ally in the local bishop, who also resented Mother Javouhey's independence, and who seemed exceptionally eager to believe the worst about her. His anger reached the point where he formally excommunicated her. The Sisters learned of this only when the priest at Mass passed over their mother superior's open mouth, refusing to give her communion. For two painful years she was thus deprived of the sacraments.

This was not her first ordeal with petty hierarchs, nor would it be her last. For over fifteen years her local bishop in Autun, France, waged a systematic campaign, trying by every means, fair and foul, to wrest personal control of her congregation. He believed that he, by rights, should be the congregation's superior general. Thus, he claimed the power to rewrite the Sisters' constitution, putting himself in control of their finances, making all decisions about their mission work, and even forbidding Mother Javouhey to leave the diocese without his permission. When she resisted these prohibitions, which had no legal basis, he threatened to dissolve her congregation. The chaplain he had appointed to the congregation was heard instructing novices that obedience to Mother Javouhey might imperil their immortal souls.

In the end delivery from these torments came through the intervention of a new and sympathetic archbishop of Paris, whose authority

trumped the powers of the bishop of Autun. He invited the congregation to move to Paris and pledged his complete support for its mission
and independence.

By the end of her life, Mother Javouhey was regarded not simply as a
holy servant of God but as a national hero. As she lay close to death she
received news that Bishop d'Héricourt, her old nemesis, had died. "So
he's gone in ahead of me, that good bishop," she reflected. "Well, that
is correct; that is how it should be. A bishop should always enter first."
But then she urged her Sisters to pray for his soul. "We ought to think
of His Lordship as one of our benefactors," she said. "God made use of
him to try us when as a rule we were hearing around us nothing but
praise. That was necessary, for since our congregation was succeeding
so well we might have thought we were something if we hadn't had
these pains and contradictions."

Mother Javouhey died on July 15, 1851. She was beatified in 1950.

See: Glen D. Kittler, *The Woman God Loved* (Garden City, N.Y.: Hanover House,
1959); Kathleen Jones, *Women Saints: Lives of Faith and Courage* (Maryknoll, N.Y.:
Orbis Books, 1999).

Bd. Jeanne Jugan
Founder of the Little Sisters of the Poor
(1792–1879)

*"Go and find Jesus when your patience and strength give out and you feel
alone and helpless. He is waiting for you in the chapel. Say to him, 'Jesus,
you know exactly what is going on. You are all I have, and you know all.
Come to my help.' And then go and don't worry about how you are going
to manage. That you have told God about it is enough. He has a good
memory."*

Jeanne Jugan was born to a poor family in Brittany in 1792. She spent
most of her life in menial service. Poor as she was, however, she believed that God intended her for some larger purpose. In 1837, along
with an older woman and a teenage girl, she rented an attic apartment in the town of Saint-Servan. The three women formed an informal
community of prayer, supporting themselves by spinning and doing
laundry while devoting their free time to catechizing children and
assisting the poor.

It was a time of grave social upheaval. Crop failures meant widespread famine. Even provincial towns were crowded with homeless beggars. It was in this atmosphere that Jeanne conceived of her mission. In 1839, when she was forty-seven, she quit her other jobs and took to begging on behalf of the homeless old women of the town. Operating out of her own apartment she organized a hospice to care for these abandoned women. The young curate of the town, Father Le Pailleur, agreed to serve as her spiritual director.

Jeanne proved particularly talented as an organizer and fund-raiser, and her efforts were soon rewarded with generous support. Within a couple of years she had purchased a new building to house her charitable work. She was even recognized by the French Academy, which granted her a sizeable award. A number of women had joined her, and in 1843 they formed a religious association. Along with vows of poverty, chastity, and obedience, Jeanne added a fourth vow of hospitality. They called themselves Little Sisters of the Poor and elected Jeanne as their superior.

At this point, however, the story takes a bizarre turn. Father Le Pailleur, evidently jealous of Jeanne's success and scornful of her common origins, imposed his authority over the group and appointed one of Jeanne's associates as superior general. Jeanne remarked that he had stolen her work, but she nevertheless acquiesced without further protest.

By 1852, when the community received papal approbation, there were five hundred Sisters in the congregation working in thirty-six houses for the aged poor. Father Le Pailleur was by this time in complete control as superior general. Jeanne had for some years been permitted to continue her successful work as a fund-raiser and public representative of the community. But now he decreed that she must "remain in a hidden life behind the walls of the motherhouse," supervising the manual work of the postulants. She spent the last twenty-seven years of her life in this obscure fashion.

Father Le Pailleur, in the meantime, rose to new heights of self-aggrandizement. He rewrote the history of the congregation to show that he was the true founder, with Jeanne having served simply as one of his early helpers. Jeanne, at this point better known within her congregation simply as Sister Mary of the Cross, was beloved among generations of postulants for her wisdom and loving encouragement. But none of them suspected that this humble and elderly Sister was the true founder of their congregation.

Jeanne lived to see Pope Leo XIII approve the constitutions for the Little Sisters in 1879. By that time they numbered twenty-four hundred. Jeanne died that same year on August 30.

Jeanne Jugan gave little importance to recognition. The success of her mission and the service of the poor were all that mattered. Nevertheless, the true story of her role as founder was eventually recovered. She was beatified by Pope John Paul II in 1982.

See: Boniface Hanley, O.F.M., *With Minds of Their Own* (Notre Dame, Ind.: Ave Maria Press, 1991).

Florence Nightingale
Healer (1820–1910)

"I never pray for anything temporal . . . but when each morning comes, I kneel down before the Rising Sun, & only say, Behold the handmaid of the Lord—give me this day my work to do—no, not my work, but thine."

Florence Nightingale was born into the highest circles of English society—the kind of world where gentlemen did not work, except perhaps to dabble in politics, and the ambition of every sensible young woman was to enter into an excellent marriage. Her family circulated among their several estates, and whenever this became boring they toured the Continent. Florence, who was especially clever, witty, and attractive, had every prospect of making a brilliant match — except that such a life struck her as worse than death.

From an early age she felt a keen sense that God was calling her for some special purpose. When she was only sixteen she recorded this experience: "On February 7th, 1837, God spoke to me and called me to His service." What form this service should take was not at all clear. Ever since she was six she had felt an inexplicable attraction to nursing. Over time this calling assumed an increasingly imperative form. But it was unthinkable for a woman of her class to work in a hospital. Hospitals were vile, dirty places, and the women who worked in them were often recruited from the most disreputable classes. When Florence expressed an interest in nursing her father strictly forbade it. "It was as if," she said, "I had wanted to be a kitchen maid."

Meanwhile there were avid suitors. One in particular she found quite agreeable. Weighing her options, she considered that such a marriage would satisfy her intellectual and passionate nature. But her "moral and active nature" would remain unfulfilled. "I could not satisfy this nature by spending a life with him in making society and arranging domestic things," she reflected. "To be nailed to a continuation and exaggeration of my present life" — the life her parents had chosen for her — "without the hope of another would be intolerable to me.... Never to be able to seize the chance of forming for myself a true and rich life would seem to be like suicide." Marriage, she decided, would not be for her.

At the same time she could not put out of her mind "the great desire to devote myself to the sick and sorrowful." In between parties and "arranging domestic things" she spent her spare time studying government reports on hospital administration and every book she could find on medicine and disease. After some years of this she had acquired an impressive education and a set of passionate convictions about necessary reforms in the practice of health care. Defying her family's wishes, she spent three months in nursing training in a German hospital. Afterward she managed, through connections, to win an appointment as director of a small London charity hospital in 1853. There she was able to put her ideas into practice. These included the importance of sanitation, sound nutrition, and proper ventilation — principles that at that time were routinely ignored even in the best of hospitals.

No sooner had she found this workshop for her theories than the occasion arose that would change her life forever: the outbreak of the Crimean War, which pitted Britain and France as allies of Turkey against Imperial Russia. It was a particularly brutal campaign. Early press accounts offered shocking descriptions of the suffering of British wounded, who accounted for three-quarters of the fatalities. Again through personal connections in the War Office, Nightingale received support to recruit a contingent of thirty-eight nurses, with her in charge, to join the troops in Turkey.

In 1854 she arrived at the military hospital in Scutari to find conditions absolutely disgraceful. The wards were dank and filthy, with thousands of beds filling the crowded hallways. The hospital was built on top of a reeking sewer and the stench permeated the moldy walls. As there were no bathing or laundry facilities, the wounded soldiers lay in blood-stained blankets. In short, it was a scandal.

Nightingale set her nurses to work restoring order and cleanliness. Out of her own resources she supplied the hospital with soap and

Florence Nightingale

towels, clean linen, and medical supplies. Her efforts were not immediately welcomed. Military commanders complained that she was "spoiling the brutes." Even the understaffed medical authorities resented her presumption and her implicit criticism of their incompetence. But these men found it difficult to resist Nightingale's implacable will.

Before long she was essentially in charge not simply of her own nursing staff, but of the entire British medical service in the war. It was difficult to argue with her results. Under her administration the mortality rate was reduced by over 50 percent.

At the same time her personal kindness and dedication to the wounded soldiers became the stuff of legend. Routinely working twenty hours a day, she spent a good part of this time walking the wards, caring for the wounded and attending to their needs. In their letters home they described her as "the Lady with the Lamp," a ministering angel. As one of them wrote, "What a comfort it was to see her pass even. We lay there by hundreds; but we could kiss her shadow as it fell and lay our heads on the pillow again content." Before long, accounts of her work in the British press had made her a national hero.

She did not return to England until the war was over, at which time she was lauded with honors of every kind, including a special medal from Queen Victoria. But as far as Nightingale was concerned, her work was only beginning. She would continue for the next fifty years to campaign tirelessly for medical reform — beginning with the army, but spreading eventually through civil society. Based on her experiences in the war she wrote voluminous reports on every detail of hospital administration, backing up all her arguments with statistical evidence. She wrote a classic textbook and established the world's first modern school of nursing. By such efforts she was largely responsible for establishing the respectability of the profession.

These accomplishments are all the more impressive in the light of her mysterious seclusion. Following her return from the Crimea Nightingale suffered from ailments that for the next fifty years confined her to her bed or couch. She rarely left her house. And yet from this secluded perch, aided by a "cabinet" of secretaries and highly placed agents, she exercised enormous and far-reaching influence. If she had been a man she might well have attained the highest office in the land. But as a woman she had to wield a more indirect form of power. Though her name often evoked a sentimental image of the Lady of the Lamp, there is no question that her accomplishments were the product of a steel will that would tolerate no opposition. Whenever she was told "But we can't," her reply was invariably, "But we must." She lived to the age of ninety, dying on August 13, 1910.

See: Cecil Woodham-Smith, *Florence Nightingale* (New York: McGraw Hill, 1951); Lytton Strachey, *Eminent Victorians* (New York: Penguin Books, 1948 [1918]).

Harriet Tubman
Abolitionist (1820?–1913)

> *"Go down Moses,*
> *Way down in Egypt land.*
> *Tell ole Pharaoh,*
> *Let my people Go!"*
> —Negro Spiritual

Harriet Tubman was born into slavery on a plantation in Maryland, sometime around 1820. The exact date is unknown, since the birth of slaves was not recorded. As she grew up, she experienced the typical cruelties of slave life, the beatings, insults, and daily indignities. Like other slaves she became skilled in the art of passive resistance — working slowly, breaking tools, adopting a false mask of simple-minded contentment — while struggling to maintain an inner conviction that she was indeed worth more than a thing. But Tubman was not content merely to survive with her inner dignity intact. She was convinced that God intended her to be free.

It is one of the miracles of Christian history that African slaves, having received a false gospel from their "Christian" slavemasters, nevertheless heard in the biblical story a message of life and liberation. The slavemasters' catechism stressed the virtue of obedience and counseled slaves to be content with their lot. But the slaves heard a different message. The God of the Bible was the God who led Moses and the Hebrew slaves out of bondage in Egypt, who inspired the prophets, and who was incarnate in Jesus Christ. This was not the god of the slavemasters, but the God of the oppressed.

It was with this God that Harriet Tubman enjoyed a special relationship. From the time she was a child she was subject to deep trances in which she heard the voice of the Lord. In one of these visionary experiences in 1849 she saw "a line, and on the other side of that line were green fields, and lovely flowers, and beautiful white ladies, who stretched out their arms to me over the line, but I couldn't reach them

176   *Harriet Tubman*

no how. I always fell before I got to the line." When she awoke she took this vision as a signal for her to begin her escape.

Though small in stature, Tubman was a strong woman. She had spurned the housework coveted by most slaves in favor of backbreaking field work. She had trained herself over the years to move quietly, to be at home in nature, and to find her way in the dark. All these skills now came into play as she made her break. Traveling by night, following the North Star, she passed through swamps and forests, sleeping by day in the shelter of caves or hidden in a leafy treetop.

When she finally crossed into the free state of Pennsylvania, she looked at her hands "to see if I was the same person. There was such a glory over everything; the sun came like gold through the trees and over the fields, and I felt like I was in heaven." But at once she was seized by a sense of wider mission. "I had crossed the line. I was FREE; but there was no one to welcome me to the land of freedom. I was a stranger in a strange land; and my home, after all, was down in Maryland.... But I was free and THEY should be free. I would make a home in the North and bring them there, God helping me."

And so, having made her perilous way to freedom, Tubman chose to return to the South to assist in the escape of others still in bondage. Over the next twelve years she returned a total of nineteen times to "Pharaoh's Land," in the process rescuing at least three hundred slaves, including her parents. These trips were fraught with danger at every step. It was one thing to travel alone, but quite another to move twenty or thirty people, including children, across hundreds of miles of open country. She was aided over time by a well-organized network of safehouses and supporters, the so-called Underground Railroad. After passage of the Fugitive Slave Act in 1850 it was no longer sufficient to bring slaves to the North. Her trips extended all the way to Canada.

Though armed bounty hunters roamed the countryside, Tubman never lost a single one of her charges. A fantastic price was put on her head and wanted posters were widely circulated. Among whites she was one of the most hated figures in the South. But among slaves she was known as "Moses."

During the Civil War Tubman worked for the Union Army, first as a nurse, then as a scout and spy. She made numerous trips behind Confederate lines. More than once, her cunning and her unassuming appearance saved her from detection. The "Moses" of the wanted posters was imagined to be a person — probably even a man — of remarkable features, certainly not a scrawny, gap-toothed old woman.

After the war Tubman retired to a small house in Auburn, New York. She was worn out and penniless, but still she devoted herself to providing shelter and care to poor blacks. She supported herself by selling vegetables from her garden. In 1869 a white admirer published *Scenes of the Life of Harriet Tubman* as a means of earning her some money. But she was used to poverty, and so she quickly dispersed her income to those in greater need. When the book was published, Frederick Douglass, the great abolitionist and himself a former slave, wrote to her:

> Most that I have done and suffered in the service of our cause has been in public, and I have received much encouragement at every step of the way. You, on the other hand, have labored in a private way. . . . I have had the applause of the crowd . . . while the most that you have done has been witnessed by a few trembling, scared, and foot-sore bondsmen and women, whom you have led out of the house of bondage, and whose heartfelt "God Bless You" has been your only reward.

Tubman lived into her nineties and died peacefully on March 10, 1913.

See: Sarah H. Bradford, *Harriet Tubman: The Moses of Her People* (Gloucester, Mass.: Peter Smith, 1981).

St. Frances Xavier Cabrini
Founder, Missionary Sisters of the Sacred Heart (1850–1917)

"Money we have not, but from our faith will spring forth miracles."

Frances Xavier Cabrini, the tenth of her parents' eleven children, was born on June 15, 1850, in a small village south of Milan. She trained as a schoolteacher, but dreamed of becoming a missionary in China. Two religious congregations turned down her applications, apparently because she seemed too frail for the rigors of convent life.

Instead, with the support of her parish priest, she assumed responsibility for a Catholic orphanage for girls. There, by the strength of her character, she persuaded several of the women staff to join her in founding a new missionary order. Her plan did not find much initial support among the clergy, who believed that mission work was inappropriate for women. But eventually her persistence won out and her order, the Missionary Sisters of the Sacred Heart, was officially authorized.

St. Frances Xavier Cabrini

Still, the exact mission of the congregation remained in doubt. Frances dreamed of bringing the gospel to China. But her chief patron, the bishop of Piacenza, urged her to consider the United States, where masses of poor Italian emigrants were crowding the cities with no one to tend to their welfare. In an audience with Pope Leo XIII Mother Cabrini put her dilemma in the pontiff's hands. "My daughter," he instructed her, "your field awaits you not in the East but in the West." And so in 1889 it was to America that Mother Cabrini and her six initial companions sailed.

The Sisters had been told that Bishop Corrigan of New York had an orphanage awaiting them. When they arrived in New York, however, they were surprised to find no one there to meet them. A letter from Bishop Corrigan, advising them not to come after all, had apparently missed them in transit. There was no orphanage, he said; it was priests he wanted, not nuns. When they finally gained an audience with the bishop, he urged them to get back on their boat and return to Italy. But Mother Cabrini was adamant: "Excellence, in all humbleness I must say, in America I stay."

Stay she did. Mother Cabrini and her Sisters got to work immediately, finding innumerable means of caring for their fellow Italian immigrants, who numbered fifty thousand in New York alone. The Sisters taught their children, cared for their physical and spiritual needs, and offered the solace of their loving devotion. And their ministry prospered. Schools and orphanages sprang up across the country, as more of Mother Cabrini's Sisters arrived from Italy to join the work.

Mother Cabrini herself traveled across the country, and then to Central and South America, establishing communities in Nicaragua, Argentina, and Brazil. After an epidemic broke out in New York, she was asked to take over a hospital. For the first time she balked before a task that seemed too large. But she changed her mind after a dream in which she saw the Blessed Mother nursing the sick. When she asked why Mary was doing such work, she was told it was because she, Mother Cabrini, had refused to work on Mary's behalf. What followed was the founding of New York's distinguished Columbus Hospital.

Mother Cabrini never mastered the English language and her small stature was unimposing, to say the least. But her indomitable will, her inexhaustible energy, and her willingness to face any challenge made her an irresistible force. In an audience with the pope in 1889, he told her to "hurry all over the earth if possible, in order to take the holy name of Jesus everywhere." By the time her order was finally ratified in Rome, its numbers had increased to over a thousand Sisters in eight countries. She personally established more than fifty foundations.

Mother Cabrini died on December 22, 1917. Her canonization by Pope Pius XII (who named her "patroness of immigrants") followed in 1946. Having become a naturalized American citizen in 1907, she enjoyed the distinction of being the "first citizen saint" of the United States.

See: Pietro Di Donato, *Immigrant Saint: The Life of Mother Cabrini* (New York: McGraw Hill, 1960); Kathleen Jones, *Women Saints* (Maryknoll, N.Y.: Orbis Books, 1999).

Rose Hawthorne
Founder of the Servants of Relief for
Incurable Cancer (1851–1926)

"I tried to acquire a fondness for the very poor, and I finally came to like them very much if they were rather good. But I was not satisfied with liking them; I wanted to love all the poor whom I met."

Rose Hawthorne was born on May 20, 1851. She was the third and favorite child of Nathaniel Hawthorne, the great American writer and author of *The Scarlet Letter.* Her father died when Rose was thirteen, and her mother's death followed only a few years later. Bereft with this loss, Rose accepted the marriage proposal of George Lathrop, a young American writer she had met in Europe. They were married in 1871, soon after her twentieth birthday. They had one son, who died at the age of four. This sorrow was compounded by the gradual deterioration of her marriage, largely as a result of Lathrop's alcoholism. For a time a common attraction to Catholicism held promise of restoring the marriage. In 1891 they were both received into the Catholic Church. But two years later they formally separated.

Rose at this time was in her forties. Her life had been spent in devotion to her husband and in the frivolous obligations of what was called "society." Now finding herself alone in New York City with no family responsibilities, she felt that she was called to some more heroic expression of her faith.

She had become aware of the terrible plight of the impoverished victims of cancer, a disease for which there was little available treatment. Once diagnosed, such cases were not permitted to remain in New York hospitals. Those without family or other means were banished to die in bleak isolation on Blackwell's Island. Rose became convinced that her vocation was to provide an alternative to this fate.

Immediately she took a nursing course and then found lodging in the squalid immigrant quarter of the Lower East Side. At first she set about visiting cancer patients in their homes. But eventually she began inviting them into her own apartment, where she offered them loving care and companionship until they died. For support she relied on contributions from friends, for she adamantly refused any payment or gift in exchange for her services. For a woman of refined taste and fastidious habits, it was not an easy or natural adjustment to this new life. Day after day she spent washing the cancerous sores and changing the dressings and bedclothes of her impoverished guests. But rather than simply providing nursing care, Rose was determined to extend friendship and respect, to convey a sense of dignity to those who had become outcasts. Inspired by the example of St. Vincent de Paul she borrowed his motto to describe her mission: "I am for God and the poor."

After the death of George Lathrop, Rose believed she ought to formalize her vocation by entering religious life. In 1900 she and a companion in her work, Alice Huber, were received into the Dominican order. Six years later her own Dominican congregation, the Servants of Relief for Incurable Cancer, was formally established, and she became known as Mother Alphonsa.

She died at the age of seventy-five on July 9, 1926, at the motherhouse of her congregation in Hawthorne, New York. The work of her congregation continues today in a number of homes around the country. According to the strict rule she established, no money is accepted from patients, their families, or even from the state.

This trust in providence later inspired Dorothy Day, who was reading the biography of Rose Hawthorne when she decided to launch the *Catholic Worker*. Hawthorne, Day observed, had not waited for official authorization or financial backing before beginning her charitable mission, working out of her tenement apartment and trusting that if it were God's work, money and support would follow.

So the influence of Rose Hawthorne has extended in many directions. The modern hospice movement was begun without reference to her example, but she may fairly be credited with pioneering this new attitude toward "death and dying." In her ministry she affirmed the sanctity of life, even in its most distressing guise, even in its final moments.

See: Diana Culbertson, O.P., ed., *Rose Hawthorne Lathrop: Selected Writings* (New York: Paulist, 1993); Katherine Burton, *Sorrow Built a Bridge: A Daughter of Hawthorne* (New York: Longman, Green, 1937).

St. Maria Skobtsova
Orthodox Nun and Martyr (1891–1945)

"I am your message, Lord. Throw me like a blazing torch into the night, that all may see and understand what it means to be a disciple."

The story of Mother Maria Skobtsova is like a tale in three acts, each with its own drama and each revealing different dimensions of her extraordinary personality. In the first act, she was born Lisa Pilenko into a prosperous aristocratic family in Russia. In this life she was a distinguished poet and a committed political activist who married twice, first to a Bolshevik whom she eventually divorced, later to an anti-Bolshevik, from whom she was later separated. During the revolutionary upheaval, she served as mayor of her hometown, in the process risking persecution from both the Left and the Right. In 1923, with her three young children she joined the throng of refugees uprooted by revolution and civil war and made her way to Paris. Soon after her arrival, her youngest daughter, Nastia, died of meningitis. The impact of this loss initiated a profound conversion. She emerged from her mourning with a determination to seek "a more authentic and purified life." She felt she saw a "new road before me and a new meaning in life, ... to be a mother for all, for all who need maternal care, assistance, or protection."

In Paris she became deeply immersed in social work among the destitute Russian refugees. She sought them out in prisons, hospitals, mental asylums, and in the back streets of the slums. Increasingly she emphasized the religious dimension of this work, the insight that "each person is the very icon of God incarnate in the world." With this recognition came the need "to accept this awesome revelation of God unconditionally, to venerate the image of God" in her brothers and sisters.

She was encouraged by her bishop to become a nun, but she would take this step only on the assurance that she would be free to develop a new type of monasticism, engaged in the world and marked by the "complete absence of even the subtlest barrier which might separate the heart from the world and its wounds."

In 1932 she made her monastic profession and became Mother Maria Skobtsova, thus beginning the "second act" in her drama. Instead of confining herself to a monastic enclosure, she took a lease on a house in Paris, large enough to include a chapel, a soup kitchen, and a shelter for destitute refugees. Her "cell" was a cot in the basement beside the boiler. As she wrote, "At the Last Judgment I shall not be asked whether I was successful in my ascetic exercises, nor how many bows and prostrations I made. Instead I shall be asked, Did I feed the hungry, clothe the naked, visit the sick and the prisoners."

Her house became a center not only for the works of mercy but for the renewal of Orthodoxy. While her kitchen was crowded with the down and out, her drawing room was the scene of spirited discussions among the leading emigré intellectuals of Paris. Out of these discussions a new movement was born, Orthodox Action, committed to realizing the social implications of the gospel. As Mother Maria explained, "The meaning of the liturgy must be translated into life. It is why Christ came into the world and why he gave us our liturgy."

The third and shortest act of Mother Maria's life began with the German occupation of Paris in 1940. In the context of Nazi racism, her commitment to seek out and revere each person as the icon of God assumed a deliberately subversive meaning. Aside from her usual work of hospitality, she was aided by her chaplain, Father Dimitri Klepinin, in rescuing Jews and other political refugees. These efforts, linked to the organized Resistance, continued until they were arrested by the Gestapo in 1943. Father Dimitri and Maria's son Yuri died in Buchenwald. Maria was sent to Ravensbruck concentration camp, where she managed to live for almost two years under conditions of indescribable cruelty and horror. Though stripped of her religious habit, she remained the nurturing mother, strengthening the faith and courage of her fellow prisoners and helping to keep alive the flame of humanity in the face of every calculated assault.

In becoming a nun Maria had said, "I think service to the world is simply the giving of one's own soul in order to save others." Now in her hunger, illness, and exposure to the elements, she found the ultimate destination of her vocation. In light of the redemptive suffering of Christ she found a meaning to her own suffering. As she wrote in a message smuggled out of the camp, "My state at present is such that I completely accept suffering in the knowledge that this is how things ought to be for me, and if I am to die I see in this a blessing from on high."

As she hovered close to death, she composed a final mute expression of her spirituality. With a needle and thread, purchased at the price of her precious bread ration, she embroidered an icon of Mary holding the infant Jesus, the child already bearing the wounds of the cross. On the eve of Easter, March 31, 1945, days before the liberation of the camp by Russian troops, Mother Maria perished in the gas chamber of Ravensbruck.

In 2003 she was canonized by the Russian Orthodox Church.

See: S. Stratton Smith, *The Rebel Nun* (Springfield, Ill.: Templegate, 1965); Sergei Hackel, *Pearl of Great Price: The Life of Mother Maria Skobtsova* (Crestwood, N.Y.: St. Vladimir's Seminary Press, 1981); *Mother Maria Skobtsova: Essential Writings* (Maryknoll, N.Y.: Orbis Books, 2003).

Caryll Houselander
Mystic (1901–1954)

"We cannot see Christ in His glory, but we can see Him and touch Him in man's sufferings."

Caryll Houselander did not fit the usual image of a saint or mystic. She was a chain-smoker, known for her salty language and her taste for gin. It was difficult to judge her pretty or plain, as she liked to cover her face with a white chalky substance that, in the words of a friend, gave her "the tragic look one associates with clowns and great comedians." She was reclusive and undoubtedly eccentric. Yet she was drawn like a magnet to those whom others found impossible or repulsive — neurotics, sinners, lonely hearts, and otherwise miserable people who bore the wounds of Christ.

She was born in Bath, England, on October 29, 1901. Her childhood was marked by unhappiness, due largely to the strife between her ill-matched parents. They separated when she was nine, and Caryll was sent to a French convent school. It was there that she had the first of several mystical visions that would shape her distinctive vocation: to awaken others to the presence of Christ in the world.

Among the French nuns in her convent school was one Sister from Bavaria, whose isolation and loneliness were undoubtedly intensified by the anti-German sentiment of the day. One day Caryll came upon the nun quietly weeping, an expression of inconsolable grief on her face. As she looked at her she "saw" that the nun was wearing a crown of thorns.

Despite this early experience, she went through years of alienation from the church. Her next mystical vision came as she was walking down the street one day and happened to look up at the sky. She saw what appeared to be a "gigantic and living Russian icon" of Christ the King crucified, his face sharp with grief over the sufferings of the world. Immediately afterward she noticed posters announcing the assassination of the Russian Tsar and his family. She recognized in these pictures the face of her vision, "but without its glory." In that moment she felt a premonition of the terrible things that were to come to the world.

Around this time, she fell in love with a mysterious Russian-born British agent, Sidney Reilly (the so-called "Ace of Spies"), whose exploits have been celebrated in books and films. Houselander was apparently "torn in shreds" by her feelings for Reilly, though they were not reciprocated. He eventually married another woman and went on to die as a prisoner in Russia. Houselander remembered him always, with sorrow and gratitude: "Because I loved that man," she wrote, "I have loved many other people, animals, and things."

The end of this affair — along with another, even more powerful vision — helped to bring her back to the church. One evening, during rush hour, she stood in a crowded underground train. As she looked at the people on the train, "quite suddenly I saw with my mind, but as vividly as a wonderful picture, Christ in them all. But I saw more than that; not only was Christ in every one of them, living in them, dying in them, rejoicing in them, sorrowing in them — but because He was in them, and because they were here, the whole world was here too, here in this underground train. . . . I came out into the street and walked for a long time in the crowds. It was the same here, on every side, in every passerby, everywhere — Christ." Her vision lasted with intensity for several days and altered her life completely. She was left with an intense understanding of the ongoing mystery of the Incarnation: "He is in everyone — there can be no outcasts." In this light, "ordinary life became sacramental."

A talented artist, Houselander supported herself with wood carving and decorating churches. Later she began writing poetry and children's books. All the while her most intense energies went into her contacts and relationships with other people. She did not preach about Christ.

Rather, she listened; she offered friendship — especially to those who had no friends; she sought to awaken others to a sense of their own divine spark. Her empathy and understanding at times seemed preternatural. Like many of the great spiritual directors, she seemed to have a gift for reading souls. After years of ministry to the mentally ill, a number of psychiatrists began sending her patients for what they called "social therapy." As one of them described it, "She loved them back to life."

Houselander had a particular compassion for sinners, those "whose soul seems to be dead, because it is Christ, who is the life of the soul, who is dead in them; they are His tombs, and Christ in the tomb is potentially the risen Christ."

And yet, for all the intensity of her spiritual vision, she was, in the words of her friend and publisher, Maisie Ward, "one of the most amusing people I ever knew." She enjoyed off-color jokes and delighted her friends with her abilities as a mimic. There was an energy and vitality in her that made people feel glad to be alive. "I am obsessed by the spirit of this age," she wrote. "With all its faults I love it and believe in it. I believe that it is the most serious duty I have, to see, to *recognize* Christ in it and to go on, never to go back."

With the outbreak of World War II Houselander's mission took on a more urgent and public form. In her book *This War Is the Passion*, written amid the nightly terror of bombs falling over London, she offered a message of consolation to those struggling with their faith. Christ too had suffered through anguish and terror, and he was present now in the sufferings of the world. "We have to stretch Christ in us, then, to fit the size of this war, the cross overshadowing the whole world.... The arms of Christ stretched on the cross are the widest reach there is, the only one that encircles the whole world."

Gradually her vocation as a writer was taking over. She produced fifteen books in a dozen years. "I am a drain pipe," she wrote. "God wants to pour words through me." As her writing brought her attention, it also brought increasing demands on her time. She never turned anyone away, even as the pain of cancer gradually sapped her energies. After considerable suffering, she died on October 12, 1954, at the age of fifty-two.

Writing to a friend, she had noted, "It is amazing to think that in heaven, when everything is understood we shall keep on saying to one another, 'How astonishing that we should ever have doubted the mercy in it all.' 'Who *on earth* would have guessed what was *really* happening?' "

See: Maisie Ward, *Caryll Houselander: That Divine Eccentric* (New York: Sheed and Ward, 1962); *Caryll Houselander: Essential Writings,* selected with commentary by Wendy Wright (Maryknoll, N.Y.: Orbis Books, 2005).

Satoko Kitahara
"The Mary of Ants Town" (1929–1958)

"I feel my path to Heaven will be a long and painful one. I do not intend to work just for my own eternal salvation, closing my eyes to the people around me. No, I want to offer God many beautiful sacrifices so that I may help others avoid the pains of hell and reach him in heaven. If my sufferings can help achieve that, what a joy!"

Satoko Kitahara was raised in an affluent Tokyo suburb. Her father was a professor, a position of considerable status. Though her family was sheltered from the effects of the worldwide Depression, like all Japanese they suffered during World War II. After Satoko's father was drafted into the army, she and her brother went to work in an aircraft factory. Conditions were so difficult that by the end of the war her brother had died, while Satoko collapsed with tuberculosis. She survived the firebombing of Tokyo, which killed tens of thousands and left thirteen million people homeless. In the aftermath of her country's defeat, the subsequent occupation, and the disillusioning revelations of war crimes and militarist lies, she suffered a profound crisis of meaning.

Her younger sister had enrolled in a Catholic school run by Mercedarian nuns. One day Satoko sought out one of these nuns and asked her opinion about the meaning of life. "Why not find out what Christians think about that?" the nun answered. So began Satoko's study of the Bible and the Catholic faith, which concluded, to her family's dismay, with her decision to be baptized. From then on, Satoko wrote, "I experienced a desire amounting almost to a necessity to 'serve,' which seemed to be a natural accompaniment to being a follower of Christ." She even wondered about becoming a nun, though the recurrence of her tuberculosis precluded that option.

Around this time she read an article about a shantytown of homeless squatters who supported themselves by collecting recyclable scrap and rubbish. They called themselves "Ants Town." Two men were behind this enterprise: Ozawa-san, "the Boss," an ex-con and entrepreneur who had conceived the idea of employing homeless ragpickers; and Tooru Matsui, a writer and ex-attorney, who was known as the Professor. Matsui had formed this band of ragpickers into a community, coming up with the name Ants Town, because "ants work hard, anywhere at all, and gain strength from community." Recently they had been joined by a simple Polish Franciscan, Brother Zeno, who had lent the enterprise his spiritual authority — along with his gift for attracting publicity.

After reading about Ants Town, Satoko decided to go and see for herself. She was shocked to see such destitution less than a mile from her home. "I had lived in the pampered, educated ignorance of an oversophisticated world," she reflected. Most Japanese tended to scorn the ragpickers as criminal misfits. But Satoko found them to be hardworking families with children, people whose homes had been destroyed by air raids and had been left behind in Japan's postwar boom. She was immediately attracted by the idea of helping them.

Brother Zeno invited her to organize a Christmas show for the children. From this beginning, Satoko became increasingly committed to the people of Ants Town. She offered lessons to the children, told them stories, and organized excursions. At night she would return to her comfortable home, where her mother would inspect her for lice and carefully sterilize her clothes. Matsui, the Professor, was a cynical critic of Christianity. He saw it as a Western religion, lacking in sensitivity to Japanese cultural values. One night he boldly challenged Satoko: "Thousands of years of what your religion calls charity have made no difference to the poverty of the world. Yes, rich young ladies like you and nuns in fine robes get bored and take a stroll through the slums, scattering a few leftovers. That's the extent of Christian charity! . . . You in your fine two-story house, you wouldn't have a clue about the misery of people who have to live in destitution 365 days a year!"

His words left her speechless. It seemed as if Christ himself had spoken to her through this unbeliever. As a parting shot, Matsui had told her to look up 2 Corinthians 8:9. There she found the words, "For you know the grace of our Lord Jesus Christ, that though he was rich, yet for your sake he became poor, so that by his poverty you might become rich."

It was a moment of revelation. Previously she had pitied the people of Ants Town. Now she wanted to become one of them. "I had thought

Satoko Kitahara

I was a great Christian because I condescended to dole out some free time. There was only one way to help those ragpicker children: become a ragpicker like them."

The next day she joined some children who begged door to door and burrowed through trash cans. By the end of the day she had collected a hundred yen's worth of hemp. The Professor, impressed, rewarded her with her own rubbish cart. Afterward, she began arriving each day at 5 a.m. to join the ragpickers on their rounds. After work she would help bathe the children and help them with their homework. Her work caught the attention of newspaper reporters. They called her Mary of Ants Town.

Satoko's recurring tuberculosis forced her to leave her work at Ants Town for six months. Upon recovering she told her family that God was calling her to live in Ants Town, regardless of the consequences. To her surprise, however, the Boss and the Professor opposed this move, fearing that the harsh conditions would kill her. To disguise their true motives, they pretended to dismiss her harshly, claiming her services were no longer needed. Though deeply hurt, Satoko entrusted herself to the will of God. But as her condition steadily deteriorated her doctor suggested that she should be allowed to follow her heart's desire. She would probably die in Ants Town, but at least she would die happy. The Boss and the Professor readily agreed. In fact, so moved were they by Satoko's faith and her devotion to the poor that they both asked to be baptized.

Meanwhile the city was making plans to evict the ragpickers. Satoko said that if they attempted this she would sit in front of city hall fasting and praying until they relented or she died. One of the city officials was so touched by her witness that he personally arranged for an alternative site under financial terms that the ragpickers could afford. The Boss and the Professor credited this victory to Satoko's prayers. Now, they said, it was time to pray for Satoko's recovery. She refused to hear of this. From her adamancy they concluded that Satoko had offered her life for the people of Ants Town. The next day she slipped into a coma and died at the age of twenty-nine.

See: Paul Glynn, *The Smile of a Ragpicker* (Hunters Hill, Australia: Marist Fathers Books, 1992); Boniface Hanley, O.F.M., *With Minds of Their Own* (Notre Dame, Ind.: Ave Maria Press, 1991).

Maura O'Halloran
Christian Zen Monk (1955–1982)

*"Suddenly I understood that we must take care of things
just because they exist."*

In a Buddhist monastery in northern Japan there is a statue of a young
Irish-American woman whose memory is revered by many pilgrims.
How a Catholic woman came to be honored as a Buddhist saint is an
interesting story of "interreligious dialogue." But it also says something
about the convergent paths of holiness and their capacity to meet in a
spirit of compassionate awareness.

Maura O'Halloran was born in Boston, the daughter of an Irish father
and American mother. When she was four the family moved to Ireland,
where she was educated in convent schools and later graduated from
Trinity College, Dublin. Her father died when she was fourteen, and
she played a large role in the upbringing of her four younger siblings.

From a young age, Maura displayed a deep awareness of human
suffering. After college she spent time working in soup kitchens and
traveled widely in Latin America. Her concern for social justice was
accompanied by a serious attraction to the spiritual life. After experi-
menting for some years with various methods of prayer and meditation,
she decided to explore the wisdom of the East.

In 1979 she flew to Japan and applied for admission to a traditional
Buddhist monastery in Tokyo. Many Catholics, and even Jesuit priests,
have undergone training in Zen meditation in Japan, finding no inher-
ent conflict between their Christian faith and the principles of Zen. But
at the time of Maura's arrival there were few Western women who had
been accepted into the very male world of a Zen monastery. Maura was
admitted, and so she embarked on the rigorous training of a monk.

Her journals offer an unusual record of her experience, which included sustained periods of meditation, arduous manual labor, and an
ascetic discipline of mind and body. Under the guidance of her Roshi
(master), she struggled to solve her assigned *koans*, the famous Zen
riddles designed to free the mind of dualistic illusions and lead the
novice on the path to enlightenment. In the cold of winter she joined
the other monks on an annual begging expedition in the North. With
her shaved head and monk's robe, wearing only straw sandals in the
snow and sleet, she would join the other monks as they passed through

the streets, ringing a bell and holding out their bowls for alms and donations of food.

After six months of intensive training, Maura experienced an ecstatic breakthrough. While being interrogated by her Roshi she was suddenly overcome by tears and laughter. "It is enlightenment!" her Roshi cried. Afterward, when she went outside, she was overcome with a feeling of compassion for everything in existence.

This was not the end of her training. In the months that followed she concentrated more energy than ever on her meditation and her self-discipline. By the next year her Roshi made her an extraordinary offer. If she would agree to marry a fellow monk, he would entrust his temple to her. Torn between the desire to obey her Roshi and a conviction that this was not where she was intended to remain, she experienced a strange physical collapse. Her Roshi at this point accepted her plan to leave the monastery at the conclusion of her training. Some months later, Maura reflected on her vocation:

> I'm twenty-six and I feel as If I've lived my life. Strange sensation, almost as if I'm close to death. Any desires, ambitions, hopes I may have had have either been fulfilled or spontaneously dissipated. I'm totally content. Of course I want to get deeper, see clearer, but even if I could only have this paltry, shallow awakening, I'd be quite satisfied.... So in a sense I feel I've died. For myself there is nothing else to strive after, nothing more to make my life worthwhile or to justify it. At twenty-six, a living corpse and such a life!... If I have another fifty or sixty years (who knows?) of time, I want to live it for other people. What else is there to do with it?... So I must go deeper and deeper and work hard, no longer for me, but for everyone I can help.

As this reflection makes clear, Maura did not consider enlightenment something to be grasped for herself alone. Rather, she wished to empty herself to serve others in the way of compassion. This was Maura's wish. But it was not her karma. Instead, after leaving the monastery on her way back to Ireland, she was killed in a bus accident in Thailand on October 22, 1982. She was twenty-seven.

In a letter of condolence to her mother her Roshi wrote,

> She had achieved what took the Shakuson [Shakyamuni Buddha] eighty years in twenty-seven years. She was able to graduate Dogen's thousand-day training. Then she left this life immediately

to start the salvation of the masses in the next life! Has anyone known such a courageously hard working Buddha as Maura? I cannot possibly express my astonishment.

Through a memoir published by her mother in a Catholic journal and the later publication of her journals, Maura's story has earned a devoted following among Christians as well as Buddhists. Her short road to holiness in a Zen monastery has been compared to the compressed career of Therese of Lisieux, the French nun who set out as a child to become a saint. Both young women, having accomplished their spiritual business in this world, promptly departed. It is certain that Maura would have identified with the words of Therese, who said she hoped to spend her heaven doing good on earth.

See: Pure Heart, Enlightened Mind: The Zen Journals and Letters of Maura "Soshin" O'Halloran (Boston: Charles E. Tuttle, 1994); Ruth L. O'Halloran, "In Twenty-Seven Short Years," Commonweal (February 28, 1992).

Corrie Ten Boom
Rescuer and Witness (1892–1983)

"It is not on our forgiveness any more than on our goodness that the world's healing hinges. But on His. When He tells us to love our enemies, He gives, along with the command, the love itself."

Corrie Ten Boom lived with her older sister, Betsie, and their widowed father, Caspar, in the rooms above a clock repair shop in the town of Haarlem, Holland. The Ten Booms were devout Christians who measured their quiet lives by the plain values of the gospel. With the outbreak of World War II and the Nazi occupation of Holland, that simple faith was put to a terrible test.

For all the Dutch people the occupation meant hardship and privation. But for one people, the Jews, it had a more ominous meaning. Restrictions on Jewish liberty came gradually, like a tightening noose, beginning with signs in shop windows: "JEWS WILL NOT BE SERVED." But by 1942 it was plain enough where this campaign was headed. Despite the dangers, Corrie felt compelled to do something. A silent prayer was forming in her heart: "Lord, Jesus, I offer myself for Your people. In any way. Any place. Any time."

The opportunity came quickly. One night, just before curfew, a woman carrying a suitcase knocked on the door. She introduced herself as a Jew. Someone had told her that the Ten Booms might help her. Immediately Corrie invited her in. Two nights later an elderly couple arrived in a similar fashion. In this unplanned manner the Ten Booms' home became a refuge for Jews and anyone in need.

This was no business for amateurs. Before long Corrie had made connections with members of the underground, who provided stolen ration cards and constructed an ingenious hiding space in one of the upstairs bedrooms. And so they carried on with their double lives. It was difficult to know whom to trust. When they let their pastor in on their secret and asked if he could help rescue a Jewish woman and her child, he reacted with horror. "Definitely not," he said. "We could lose our lives for this Jewish child." Caspar Ten Boom held the child close and replied, "I would consider that the greatest honor that could come to my family."

Inevitably, their luck ran out. One day the Gestapo arrived and searched their home from top to bottom. The Jews were hidden safely in their hideaway. But Corrie, Betsie, and Caspar were taken away. It was the last the daughters would see of their father, who died ten days after his arrest.

Corrie spent four months in solitary confinement. Despite her terrible anguish, she found consolation in a smuggled Bible and the thought, which came slowly, that all of this — the war, the suffering, her own desolation — could be "part of the pattern first revealed in the Gospels. Hadn't Jesus been defeated as utterly and inarguably as our little group and our small plans had been?" And with this thought came another: "If the Gospels were truly the pattern of God's activity, then defeat was only the beginning." In this light, who could guess what victory might be achieved, even in a lonely prison cell?

She was eventually reunited with Betsie, but only to be loaded onto a crowded train for transport to a concentration camp. It was in this next phase of their journey that Corrie came to measure her sister's spiritual depth. After enduring their introduction to the cruelties of the camp, Corrie cried out, "Betsie, how long will it take?" Her sister made a surprising reply: "Perhaps a long, long time, perhaps many years, but what better way could there be to spend our lives?" Corrie stared at her in disbelief. What was she talking about? "These young women," Betsie explained. "That girl back at the bunkers, Corrie. If people can be taught to hate, they can be taught to love! We must find the way, you and I, no matter how long it takes."

At this, Corrie wondered, "not for the first time, what sort of a person she was, this sister of mine...what kind of road she followed while I trudged beside her on the all-too-solid earth."

But this was not the end of their journey. Eventually they arrived at Ravensbruck, the notorious concentration camp in Germany. They survived the first terror when a careless guard neglected to confiscate their precious Bible. Though she had read the Bible every day of her life, now Corrie found that the text "was simply a description of the way things were — of hell and heaven, of how men act and how God acts." She had read before about Christ's arrest and torture. "Now such happenings had faces and voices."

Desperately Corrie wondered how they could live in such a place. Betsie found her answer in the words of scripture: "Comfort the frightened, help the weak, be patient with everyone. See that none of you repays evil for evil, but always seek to do good to one another and to all." There was the answer! "We can start right now to thank God for every single thing about this new barracks!" — for being assigned together; for the gift of God's word; for the presence of so many people desperate for some kindness.

The camp held thirty-five thousand women of all nationalities. By day they performed heavy labor, always under the threatening whip of the guards who lashed out with unprovoked fury. In their barracks at night, Betsie and Corrie would conduct prayer services for any who were interested. But Betsie was steadily weakening. There came a time when she could not present herself for inspection. As she lay on a stretcher waiting to be removed to the hospital barracks, she whispered to Corrie, "We must tell people what we have learned here. We must tell them that there is no pit so deep that he is not deeper still. They will listen to us, Corrie, because we have been there."

Betsie died the next day. When Corrie saw her body she was amazed by her beautiful expression: "The care lines, the grief lines, the deep hollows of hunger and disease were simply gone. This was the Betsie of heaven, bursting with joy and health." Walking away, she reflected, "Now what tied me to Betsie was the hope of heaven."

Two days later Corrie received a miraculous certificate of discharge. For no good reason, apparently a mistake, she was being released. Half dead herself, she struggled to make her way back to Holland, where she waited out the last months of the war. When she entered her old house in Haarlem she felt the strong spirit of Betsie, reminding her of their mission, "We must tell them what we learned...."

And so she found a new voice. "If this was God's new work for me, then He would provide the courage and the words. Through the streets and suburbs of Haarlem I bumped on my bicycle rims, bringing the message that joy runs deeper than despair."

Corrie Ten Boom lived on for nearly forty years, traveling to more than sixty countries to bear witness to God's love. She died on her ninety-first birthday, April 15, 1983.

See: Corrie Ten Boom, with John and Elizabeth Sherrill, *The Hiding Place* (Grand Rapids, Mich.: Chosen Books, 1971).

Bd. (Mother) Teresa of Calcutta
Founder of the Missionaries of Charity (1910–1997)

"To show great love for God and our neighbor we need not do great things. It is how much love we put in the doing that makes our offering something beautiful for God."

On September 10, 1946, the woman who would become Mother Teresa was traveling on a train to Darjeeling, a hill station in the Himalayas. At the time she was simply Sister Agnes, a thirty-six-year-old Loreto Sister of Albanian extraction, who had spent the past twenty years teaching in her order's schools in India. Though she was a devoted nun, beloved by her mostly middle-class students, there was nothing to suggest that she would one day be regarded as one of the most compelling Christian witnesses of the twentieth century. But on this day she received "a call within a call." God, she suddenly felt, wanted something more from her: "He wanted me to be poor with the poor and to love him in the distressing disguise of the poorest of the poor."

So, with the permission of her congregation, she left her convent. In place of her traditional religious habit she donned a simple white sari with blue border and went out to seek Jesus in the desperate byways of Calcutta. Eventually she was joined by others — including many of her former students. They became the Missionaries of Charity. And she became Mother Teresa.

With time Mother Teresa would establish centers of service around the globe for the sick, the homeless, the unwanted. But she was particularly identified with her home for the dying in Calcutta. There, destitute and dying men and women, gathered off the streets of the city, were welcomed to receive loving care and respect until they died. Those who had lived like "animals in the gutter" were enabled, in Mother Teresa's home, to "die like angels" — knowing that they were truly valued and loved as precious children of God.

It was not Mother Teresa's way to change social structures. "We are not social workers," she said, but "contemplatives in the heart of the world. For we are touching the body of Christ twenty-four hours a day." It was this mystical insight, which she obviously lived, that made Mother Teresa such a widely inspiring figure. She did not simply practice charity; she embodied it.

God has identified himself with the hungry, the sick, the naked, the homeless; hunger, not only for bread, but for love, for care, to be somebody to someone; nakedness, not of clothing only, but nakedness of that compassion that very few people give to the unknown; homelessness, not only just for a shelter made of stone, but that homelessness that comes from having no one to call your own.

For many years Mother Teresa toiled in obscurity. But eventually she was "discovered" by the world. She became the subject of documentary films and biographies; she received honorary degrees from prestigious universities and countless honors, including the Nobel Peace Prize for 1979. Widely regarded as a "living saint," she nevertheless remained remarkably unburdened by such adulation. Nor did she have any exalted sense of her own vocation. "We can do no great things," she said, "only small things with great love." Often when people begged to join her in her "wonderful work" in Calcutta she would respond gently but firmly: "Find your own Calcutta!" As she explained,

Don't search for God in far lands — he is not there. He is close to you, he is with you. Just keep the lamp burning and you will always see him. Watch and pray. Keep kindling the lamp and you will see his love and you will see how sweet is the Lord you love.

In later life Mother Teresa traveled widely around the world. In the affluent West she had no trouble finding poverty — both the material kind and a no less destructive impoverishment of the spirit. The answer in both cases was love, a love that would begin with persons and ultimately transform the world. But before we try to love the entire world, we should start by trying to love one other person — someone apparently unlovable, unwanted, or rejected. "You can save only one at a time. We can love only one at a time." That, she believed, is what we were put on earth to do: "Something beautiful for God." Mother Teresa died on September 5, 1997.

She was beatified with unusual speed in 2003.

See: Eileen Egan, *Such a Vision of the Street* (New York: Doubleday, 1985); *Mother Teresa: Essential Writings*, ed. Jean Maalouf (Maryknoll, N.Y.: Orbis Books, 2001).

BLESSED ARE
THE PURE OF HEART

A philosopher • a mystical abbess • a religious prophet • a visionary • a witness of the Holocaust • a missionary • a novelist • a teenage martyr • a dying mother

Holy women have typically been commended for their purity — a virtue commonly reduced to sexual continence. This understanding is reinforced by the list of martyrs, from St. Agnes to St. Maria Goretti, who died while defending their "virginity." But purity of heart is not ultimately the same as chastity. According to Kierkegaard's famous phrase, it is "to will one thing."

The pure-hearted are notable for their focus and concentration. Their energies are not dissipated. In the world, but not of it, they do not allow their hearts to be ensnared by unworthy objects. Nothing distracts them from pursuing the one goal worthy of their full devotion. Their reward? "They shall see God."

St. Thecla of Iconium
Evangelist (first century)

"In the name of Jesus I baptize myself on my last day."

The story of St. Thecla is preserved in *The Acts of Paul and Thecla*, a second-century text that enjoyed wide popularity in the early church. Many church fathers, including Augustine and Ambrose, wrote approvingly of Thecla, while others, such as Jerome and Tertullian, dismissed her legend as a fraud. For centuries the church tried to distinguish between the edifying aspects of Thecla's story (her heroic faith, her valiant defense of virginity) and the more subversive aspects of her witness: the claim, for example, that she served as a co-apostle with St. Paul, preaching and engaging in active ministry. For centuries she was celebrated in the Eastern church as a "protomartyr among women and equal with the Apostles." In the West, however, hers was one of the names removed from the calendar of the saints following Vatican II.

According to her *Acts,* Thecla was a beautiful young woman whose life was transformed when she heard St. Paul preaching in the street outside her window. Transfixed by his words, she would not depart from the window, either to eat or sleep, "till with exceeding joy she was subdued by the doctrines of faith." Her mother was alarmed by this behavior — the more so when, under the influence of Paul's preaching, Thecla announced her intention to break off her engagement and embrace a life of chastity. This news brought "a universal mourning in the family," but the reverberations extended to the wider social order.

Thecla's fiancé Thamyris took action, denouncing Paul to the governor as a menace to society and causing him to be locked up. Oblivious to the potential for scandal, Thecla bribed Paul's jailor in order to spend the night sitting at his feet, listening to his words of Christ and kissing his chains. When her family found her the next day, their anger was even more vehement, her own mother leading the outcry: "Let the creature be burnt for refusing Thamyris, that all women may learn from her to avoid such practices."

Thecla was stripped and tied to a stake and surrounded by kindling. In the jeering crowd Thecla thought she saw the "Lord Jesus in the likeness of Paul," come to comfort her. But as she fixed her eyes on him she saw him ascend into heaven. The fire was set and Thecla would surely have perished had not a miraculous downpour quenched the flames.

Set loose, Thecla was soon reunited with Paul, and together they embarked on a mission to Antioch. But there, once again, she was forced to rebuff the unwelcome attentions of another suitor, this time a "person of great power" named Alexander. Humiliated by rejection, he too denounced Thecla to the governor, who this time condemned her to be thrown among wild animals. Her first ordeal, with a hungry lioness, ended happily when the beast merely licked her feet and then bravely defended her from other ravenous creatures.

At this point, Thecla observed a pit of water and decided that this — "her last day" — presented a fitting occasion for her baptism. Despite the warning cries of the crowd — for the water was filled with dangerous "she-calves" — Thecla threw herself into the water and baptized herself in the name of Christ. Upon her survival of all these ordeals even the governor was moved to ask, "Who *are* you?"

"I am a servant of the living God," Thecla replied, "and as to my state, I am a believer on Jesus Christ his Son, in whom God is well pleased.... He alone is the way to eternal salvation and the foundation of eternal life. He is a refuge to those who are in distress, a support to the afflicted, a hope and defense to those who are hopeless."

Impressed by her fortitude, the governor returned her clothes and released her, thus inspiring thunderous cheers from many women in the crowd. "There is but one God," they cried, "who is the God of Thecla!"

None was more surprised than Paul to see her alive — the more so when she greeted him with news of her unconventional baptism. "He who assists you in preaching has assisted me to baptize," she proclaimed. Now recognizing her as a fellow apostle, Paul commissioned her to preach the gospel. And so Thecla returned to her hometown and other towns, and "enlightened many in the knowledge of Christ." Wherever she went, according to her chronicler, "a bright cloud conducted her in her journey."

Little is recorded of Thecla's further adventures. After some time, however, she reportedly retired to a cave, where she spent many years in prayer. Eventually her reputation drew other women to her side and in this monastic community she instructed them "in the oracles of God."

The story draws to an abrupt close with an account of her mysterious "translation by the Lord." This occurred after many years in her cave, during which time she had acquired a wide reputation for her miraculous healing powers. This ministry cut into the profits of local doctors, who decided, by way of retaliation, to incite some "rakish fellows" to go and "debauch this virgin." When they came to Thecla's cave and tried to lay hands on her, she prayed to God for protection. In reply she heard a voice from heaven, saying, "Fear not, Thecla, my faithful servant, for I am with thee. Look and see the place which is opened for thee: there thy eternal abode shall be; there thou shalt receive the beatific vision." Immediately a rock opened up in the cave. Thecla passed inside the rock, which instantly closed behind her, leaving the astonished men holding only a piece of her veil.

"Thus ends her life," concludes her chronicler. But her story would live on, frequently cited by other women as a precedent for their call to equality and active ministry in the church. Those scholars who disavowed her story as a mere "wives' tale" found themselves holding only a piece of her veil. She was out of their reach, enclosed in holy mystery, where no man could touch her.

See: Acts of Paul and Thecla.

St. Agnes
Virgin and Martyr (d. 304?)

"You may stain your sword with my blood,
but you will never be able to profane my body, consecrated to Christ."

It is said that Agnes was born to a rich and noble family of Rome and that at a young age her beauty attracted the interest of many prosperous suitors. She rebuffed them all, insisting that she had consecrated her virginity to her true spouse, Jesus Christ. Her suitors denounced her as a Christian, and she was brought before a magistrate. He in turn tried various forms of persuasion, ranging from mild entreaty to the display of instruments of torture. But nothing would compel her to offer incense to the gods. When she remained adamant, the governor had her condemned to a house of prostitution, where every man might have free use of her. It was found, however, that she exuded such a powerful aura of purity that no one could lay a finger on her. Infuriated by this young woman's defiance, the judge then ordered her to be beheaded. Agnes greeted the sentence joyfully and, according to St. Ambrose, "went to the place of her execution more cheerfully than others go to their wedding." At the time of her death she was thirteen years old.

The fact that the first recorded account of St. Agnes appeared over a hundred years after her death has prompted doubts about the historicity of her "acts," if not the actual existence of this servant of God. Nevertheless she has been one of the most popular of Christian saints. In the past her memory undoubtedly served a tendency to idealize the virgin state. This was reinforced by the appellation "virgin," attached by the church to Agnes and other unmarried women saints. There is no corresponding word to recognize married women saints (except widow), nor is there any corresponding interest in the marital — or sexual — status of male saints. (We know, for instance, that St. Augustine was no virgin.)

In the story of Agnes, however, the opposition is not between sex and virginity. The conflict is between a young woman's power in Christ to define her own identity versus a patriarchal culture's claim to identify her in terms of her sexuality. According to the view shared by her "suitors" and the state, if she would not be one man's wife, she might as well be every man's whore. Failing these options, she might as well be dead. Agnes did not *choose* death. She *chose* not to worship the gods of her culture. The God she worshiped set an altogether different value on her body, her identity, and her human worth. Espoused to Christ, she was beyond the power of any man to "have his way with her." "Virgin" in this case is another way of saying Free Woman.

St. Catherine of Alexandria
Martyr (date unknown)

"Come my beloved, my spouse, behold the door of heaven is opened to thee; and to those that shall celebrate the memory of thy passion with devout minds I promise the protection of heaven!"

In the aftermath of Vatican II a reform of the calendar led the church to disavow a number of popular but, in all likelihood, nonexistent saints. St. Catherine of Alexandria, one of the most popular of all saints, was among these demobilized from active service. Though her cult had flourished since at least the tenth century, there was little to connect her to her supposed adventures in Roman times, and it was reluctantly determined that no such person ever existed.

Nevertheless, for centuries her "remains" attracted pilgrims to a monastery on Mt. Sinai. What is more, hers was one of the heavenly voices that supposedly spoke to St. Joan of Arc, thus empowering the peasant maid to defy every authority of her age. For refusing to disavow her voices Joan went to the stake, and for the same holy disobedience she was later canonized. It is a case that brings to mind Karl Barth's famous dictum, when asked by a student whether he really believed a snake spoke to Eve in the Garden: "The important thing is not whether or not a snake could talk; the important thing is what he said."

According to what the editors of *Butler's Lives* call "her completely worthless *acta*," St. Catherine was supposed to be the daughter of a patrician family in Alexandria, Egypt, sometime in the Roman era. Through her study of philosophy she became convinced of the truth of Christianity and converted to the illicit faith. When she sought to convert the emperor himself, he had her examined by fifty of the leading philosophers of the court. Unable to refute her arguments, they were all in fact persuaded to convert. (Consequently, they were all also burned to death.) The emperor was so impressed by Catherine's beauty, if not her brilliance, that he tried to induce her to be his consort. This offer she declined, preferring instead to be imprisoned and tortured. While in prison, however, she successfully converted the emperor's wife, her jailer, and two hundred of the imperial guards. All these too were consequently slain. Enraged, the emperor condemned her to be tortured on a spiked wheel (hence the "catherine wheel" that is her famous emblem). But the machine miraculously broke apart and killed many onlookers. At this point, and before she could perform any more mischief, the exasperated emperor had this dangerous woman put to the sword.

In removing Catherine of Alexandria from the canon of saints, the church has indicated that the minimal requirement for the legitimate cult of a saint is that such a person actually existed. But it is not this minimal requirement that has strengthened the faith and inspired the imitation of subsequent generations. More important, in many cases, is the meaning that Christians find in the stories of the saints, in short, what they "say" to us.

St. Catherine of Alexandria, a saint who never was, served for centuries as "the patroness of maidens and women students, of philosophers, preachers and apologists, of wheelwrights, millers and others" (*Butler's Lives*). She may continue to represent the subversive power of women's wisdom, a voice which many would like to silence lest it subvert the whole world with its irrefutable logic. So Catherine continues

St. Catherine of Alexandria

to inspire and illuminate us with her edifying story, like the light emanating from a distant star that no longer exists.

See: *The Golden Legend of Jacobus de Voragine* (London: Longman, Green, 1941).

St. Hilda of Whitby
Abbess (610–680)

"All that knew her called her Mother."
—St. Bede

St. Hilda was one of the great lights of the early Anglo-Saxon church. According to Bede, whose *History* is the principal source for her life, she was the great niece of St. Edwin, king of Northumbria. With the rest of her family she was baptized by St. Paulinus when she was thirteen. Says Bede, "She spent thirty-three years most nobly in secular occupations" before deciding to "serve God alone." Hilda spent time in a number of monasteries in East Anglia before returning home to found a new monastery at Whitby. This would remain her home for the rest of her life, and under her leadership it would become an important center for the spread and consolidation of the Christian faith in England.

Whitby was a double monastery — that is, one comprising both men and women who lived separately but gathered together to chant the office. In the tradition of Celtic monasticism, in which Hilda was formed, it was not unusual for a woman to preside over such a mixed community. Hilda set a standard for holiness, wisdom, and scholarship, promoting through her example "the observance of righteousness, mercy, purity, and other virtues, but especially in peace and charity." Bede observes that in her monastery "no one there was rich or poor, for everything was held in common, and none possessed any personal property."

Hilda also served as a spiritual director, serving not only her monastic children but the wider community. "So great was her prudence that not only ordinary folk, but kings and princes used to come and ask her advice in their difficulties." Five of her monks went on to become bishops. She was also influential in encouraging the gifts of St. Caedmon, the cowherd and poet who became a monk of Whitby.

As a reflection of the prestige of Whitby, the monastery was chosen as the site for the important church synod of 664. The synod was called, ostensibly, to resolve disagreements about the correct day for observing

Easter. But this issue was symptomatic of deeper tensions between those favoring the Roman model of authority, rooted in the episcopal hierarchy, and those inclined to the more monastic model characteristic of the Celtic church. Hilda favored the latter, but the synod decided otherwise.

Hilda's last years were spent in painful illness. She never retired from her office nor did she ever fail to give thanks to God. By her own example she instructed her flock "to serve God rightly when in health, and to render thanks to him faithfully when in trouble or bodily weakness." Her last counsel to her community was to "maintain the gospel peace among yourselves and with others." She died on November 17, 680, and her feast is observed on that date.

See: Bede, *A History of the English Church and People* (Baltimore: Penguin, 1955).

St. Christina of Markyate
Maiden of Christ (1097–1161)

"I am free to love Christ above all."

Christina was the daughter of a noble Anglo-Saxon family in Huntingdonshire, England. As a child she accompanied her parents on a pilgrimage to the Abbey of St. Alban, where she found herself immediately attracted by the atmosphere of piety and prayer. Without telling anyone she used her fingernail to draw a cross on the doorway as "a secret sign that she had placed her affection there." She followed this gesture at Mass the next day by offering herself to God in perpetual virginity. Unfortunately, Christina's desires were at odds with her parents' plans. The chronicle of her subsequent struggles — both physical and spiritual — to pursue her vocation involves an extraordinary cast of characters: bishops, noblemen, merchants, abbots, and holy hermits. The effort of one young woman to claim her own spiritual identity seems to have shaken her society to its roots.

Christina's story has many shocking turns, beginning with her escape from the lecherous advances of a visiting bishop. Frustrated in his own illicit desires, the bishop proposed that a young nobleman named Burthred would be a worthy suitor. Her parents embraced this suggestion with enthusiasm. They believed their assent to the betrothal was sufficient to nullify any objections by their daughter. But Christina remained immovable in the face of all efforts to win her consent, whether

St. Christina of Markyate

by bribery, flattery, or naked threats. Finally, her resistance exhausted, Christina accepted the betrothal. But her basic attitude remained unchanged. She would never consummate the marriage, she insisted, being in her mind already consecrated to Christ.

Fed up with Christina's scruples, her parents encouraged Burthred to gain access to her chamber and take their daughter by force. Christina successfully talked him out of it, though this left him open to the ridicule of his friends. The next night they all planned to invade her chamber en masse. Once again Christina escaped, but only by hiding behind a tapestry on her bedroom wall.

The next stop was an ecclesiastical court. Christina's father admitted that he had forced her betrothal against her will, but argued nevertheless that to disregard his authority now would make him "the laughing stock of everyone we know." It would turn the social order on its head. After hearing his arguments, the assembled church canons chastised Christina for her willfulness and folly. Marriage, they reminded her, was a holy sacrament — not to mention the holy duty of honoring her parents. Christina defended herself by her own recourse to scripture, standing finally behind the sanctity of her primary vow to Christ. When they accused her of simply holding out for a wealthier husband, she replied, "Certainly a wealthier one. For who is richer than Christ?"

The conflict dragged on. The canons referred the case to the bishop, who initially surprised the plaintiffs by defending Christina. But after further consideration — and a sizeable bribe — he reversed his decision and handed her back to Burthred. Still Christina refused to submit. And now her parents were beside themselves. Her mother took the lead in her persecution. She employed spells and potions to excite Christina's lust. On one occasion she pulled out her daughter's hair and beat her savagely, and then presented her before a party of gaping revelers; "she swore that she would not care who deflowered her daughter provided that someone did."

Eventually, Christina made a daring escape, disguising herself as a man and riding off on horseback. While her family scoured the countryside, promising to kill anyone who aided her, she found help from a network of local monks and hermits. She was finally passed along to a hermit named Roger, who provided a horribly cramped space — no more than a hole in the ground — in a corner of his cell. For four years she crouched there, emerging only at night to relieve herself outdoors.

In time these trials came to a surprising end. Impelled by a vision of the Mother of God, Burthred proclaimed his willingness to release

Christina from her marriage vows and begged her pardon for all she had suffered. The marriage was formally annulled. So ended this stage of Christina's life — the dramatic battle for her vocation.

But Christina's spiritual adventures were far from over. In her years as a solitary hermit she was often tempted by doubts and evil apparitions. At one point, for example, she feared that God had abandoned her. But then one day while praying, she was "caught up from earth to heaven" and heard a divine message: "Don't be afraid of these horrible temptations, for the key of your heart is in my safe keeping, and I myself watch over your mind and the whole of your body. No one can enter unless I allow them to." Afterward she never again suffered any doubt.

Christina's story was recorded by an anonymous monk of St. Alban's, the abbey to which she remained closely affiliated. Little is known of her later life. Evidently she acquired a wide reputation for wisdom and holiness. She accepted consecration as a nun and became the abbess of a convent in Markyate. Famous for her visions and healing powers, she was sought out by abbots, bishops, and even kings for her counsel. She died in 1161.

See: The Life of Christina of Markyate, trans. with an introduction by Monica Furlong (Berkhamsted: Arthur James, 1997).

St. Hildegard of Bingen
Abbess and Visionary (1098–1179)

"In the year 1141 . . . a fiery light, flashing intensely, came from the open vault of heaven and poured through my whole brain. Like a flame that is hot without burning, it kindled all my heart and all my breast, just as the sun warms anything on which its rays fall. And suddenly I could understand what such books as the Psalter, the Gospel and the other Catholic volumes both of the Old and New Testament actually set forth."

St. Hildegard was by any standard one of the remarkable figures of her age: abbess and founder of a Benedictine religious community; author and theologian; prophet and preacher; musician and composer; poet and artist; doctor and pharmacist. She had visions in which the word of God — both in scripture and in the book of nature — was revealed to her. Yet for eight hundred years she remained in relative obscurity. Only in recent decades has she emerged into the light, partly thanks to contemporary interest in the role of women in history. But

St. Hildegard of Bingen

increasingly Hildegard is honored not only as an outstanding historical figure but as a visionary whose ecological and holistic spirituality
speaks prophetically to our time.

Hildegard was born in 1098 in the German province of Rheinhessen,
the tenth child of noble parents. When she was eight she was given to
the care of a holy anchoress, Bd. Jutta, who lived in a cottage attached
to a nearby Benedictine abbey. Jutta raised the child and educated her
until the age of eighteen, when Hildegard put on the habit of a Benedictine nun. By this time a monastic community had gathered about Jutta.
When the old woman died in 1136 Hildegard became prioress.

Up to this point it seems that Hildegard was an unexceptional nun.
Only to Jutta had she confided the secret of the visions which, as she
later wrote, she had enjoyed since the age of three. "These visions which
I saw I beheld neither in sleep nor dreaming nor in madness nor with
my bodily eyes or ears, nor in hidden places; but I saw them in full
view and according to God's will, when I was wakeful and alert, with
the eyes of the spirit and the inward ears."

After she became prioress her visions pressed upon her with greater
urgency until she eventually described them to her confessor. She was
bidden to write them down, and the text was presented to the archbishop of Mainz. He in turn read them and had them examined by a
team of theologians who certified their orthodoxy. Henceforth she was
provided with a monk as secretary and with his help she began her
major work, *Scivias* (Know the Ways), which occupied her efforts over
the next ten years. Eventually Pope Eugenius III himself read her book
and authorized her to continue to write.

Her *Scivias* is the record of a series of visions concerning the relation between God, humanity, and the cosmos. With extraordinary
symbolic paintings that accompany the text, Hildegard presents a picture of human beings and the cosmos as emanations from God's love,
"living sparks" or "rays of his splendor, just as the rays of the sun
proceed from the sun itself." She shows the effects of sin in ruptur-
ing creation, and the drama of redemption that ultimately restores the
world to its intended state, purified of its infirmities and reconciled
with the divine energy of its origins.

About this time Hildegard received a divine call to move her community to a new site on the Rupertsberg, a hill above the Rhine,
near Bingen. This involved an ordeal with the monks and the town of
her original foundation, who depended on the traffic of pilgrims and
thus adamantly opposed her plan. But after she became deathly ill —

a frequent occurrence when Hildegard's will was crossed — she had her way.

Between 1152 and 1162 Hildegard made numerous preaching tours through the Rhineland. Her authority as a holy preacher was widely recognized, and her reputation extended far beyond her native Germany. She corresponded with kings, popes, and other figures of note, sharing her spiritual insights but also freely dispensing criticism where she felt it was needed. Besides her religious writings, she wrote extensively on medicine and physiology. She avidly studied the use of medicinal herbs and seems to have anticipated the principles of homeopathy. In addition she composed religious music of haunting beauty and originality; music, she wrote, was a symbol of the harmony that Satan disturbed.

There are many elements of Hildegard's visions that speak to our ecological age. She had a wide understanding of the cosmos as a whole and of the human place in it. Human beings, she wrote, are the universe in microcosm, made of the same elements that constitute the world. But within the great cosmos human beings are the thinking heart, called to be co-creators with God in shaping the world. Through human sin the entire world was fractured and fell out of harmony with the Creator. But this sin does not erase the original goodness and blessing of creation. Through Christ — first fruits of a new creation — the cosmos and human beings find their way back to their original destiny. Constantly Hildegard refers to God as "Living Light," and she employs a remarkable word — "greenness" (*viriditas*) — to describe the animating energy or grace of God that shines forth in all living things. For this holistic vision Hildegard has been particularly celebrated by proponents of "creation spirituality."

Toward the end of her life Hildegard ran afoul of local church authorities after she allowed a young man who had been excommunicated to be buried in the monastery cemetery. She was ordered to have the body disinterred. This Hildegard refused, insisting that before dying the youth had been reconciled with the church and received the sacraments. Nevertheless, the bishop had the convent placed under an interdict, forbidding the celebration or reception of the Eucharist. It was a terrible sanction, and Hildegard protested bitterly. Eventually the interdict was lifted, but she lived on only a few months longer. She died on September 17, 1179.

See: Hildegard of Bingen: Mystical Writings, ed. Fiona Bowie and Oliver Davis (New York: Crossroad, 1995); Hildegard of Bingen, *Illuminations,* with commentary by Matthew Fox (Santa Fe, N.Mex.: Bear, 1985).

Beatrice of Nazareth
Mystic (1200–1268)

"As a fish swims the length and breadth of the sea and rests in its depths, as a bird flies through the air, so the Soul feels her mind completely unrestrained in the height, width, and depth of Love."

Beatrice was the last of six children born to a prosperous family in Tienan, near Brussels. An exceptionally clever child, she is reported to have memorized all 150 Psalms by the age of five. A year later her mother was dead, and Beatrice was sent away from home to study with a community of Beguines. At the age of ten she was entrusted as a child oblate to a Cistercian convent in Bloemendaal. Thus, virtually all her life was spent in the company of religious women.

Beatrice felt well-suited to monastic life. At the age of fifteen she was "clothed in white garments, the garments of joy, that is, the novice's habit." Shortly thereafter she was sent to another abbey to "learn the art of writing manuscripts." For the next twenty years Beatrice kept a journal describing her spiritual experiences. Although this original text was lost, it apparently served as the primary source of a biography, composed in Latin after her death by an anonymous cleric.

Beatrice's first mystical experience occurred on Christmas day in 1217. While singing the evening prayers with the other nuns she found her heart ascending with Christ "right up to the Father's presence." She received a vision of the Holy Trinity, seen "not with bodily but with intellectual eyes, with eyes not of the flesh but of the mind." While enjoying the company of "this array of supercelestial powers who gazed ceaselessly on the supreme Godhead," she was suddenly returned "to her outer senses," recalled "from heavenly delights to the miseries of the human condition" by the prodding of another nun, who had supposed her to be merely dozing.

Beatrice continued to experience supernatural visitations. She responded at times with tears, at other times with a "madness in her heart" that made her laugh for joy. Her reputation for wisdom and holiness extended beyond her community, though she shrank from special attention, thinking herself "so much more vile."

In 1235 Beatrice moved to a new Cistercian monastery known as Nazareth, one of several endowed by her father. It was probably at Nazareth that she composed a short mystical treatise, "Seven Manners of Love," the Dutch manuscript of which was discovered only in 1925.

Her text offers a description of the ways by which the devout Soul ascends to God, whom Beatrice names simply Love. Since it is by love that we proceed to Love, there is an essential identity in the spiritual life between our path and our destination.

Like other contemporary mystics, Beatrice drew on the language of Eros to describe this experience. The seven "manners" begin with a "fierce longing"; this may be followed by "pain and misery," for the soul "wants what she cannot have." At higher levels the soul experiences "great delight," followed by a reckless and overpowering passion, wherein the soul feels "Love raging within, like devouring fire, drawing everything inside it and consuming whatever it can destroy."

In the final stage, the soul is "raised into the eternity of Love simply by the Love of eternity itself." It becomes "one with the invulnerable wisdom of the silent heights. [It] plunges into the deep abyss of the Deity, who is everything in everything that exists, indestructible, above everything, everlasting, almighty, all-embracing, and who is the supreme force within everything that exists."

Beatrice served as prioress of Nazareth for over thirty years until her death in 1268.

See: Bernard McGinn, *The Flowering of Mysticism* (New York: Crossroad, 1998).

Hadewijch of Brabant
Beguine Mystic (thirteenth century)

"Make haste to virtue in veritable Love; and take care that God be honored by you and by all those whom you can help, with effort, with self-sacrifice, with counsel, and with all that you can do unremittingly."

Almost nothing is known of the life of Hadewijch, a Flemish mystic who lived sometime in the middle of the thirteenth century. Although a prolific author, she inspired no contemporary biography; all that is known of her story must be inferred from her letters and other extant writings. She was apparently a Beguine. This fascinating movement, which flourished in the Low Countries in the thirteenth and fourteenth centuries, attracted women to a new form of community-based religious life, distinct from the alternatives of marriage or traditional enclosure. The Beguines stressed the value of prayer, the works of mercy, simplicity of life, and an affective spirituality focused on the humanity of Jesus. It seems that Hadewijch may have occupied a position of leadership in one such community.

Hadewijch's teachings are contained in letters of spiritual counsel, a great body of poetry, and a series of recorded "visions." The visions describe a number of revelations in which she was afforded particular insights into spiritual realities: "Once on Pentecost Sunday I received the Holy Spirit in such a manner that I understood all the will of Love in all . . . "; "After one Easter Sunday I had gone to God; and he embraced me in my interior senses and took me away in spirit."

The central theme of Hadewijch's writings is Love, a word that dominates nearly every page. Indeed she has been described as a "love-mystic." Everywhere she turned, whether in creation, in community, or in her inner depths, she encountered the love of God. No subject failed to ignite her passion: "Once I heard a sermon in which St. Augustine was spoken of. No sooner had I heard it than I became inwardly so on fire that it seemed to me everyone on earth must be set ablaze by the flame I felt within me. Love is all!" Insofar as she responded to this reality with love she felt herself plunged into the most profound communion with God.

Hadewijch's love was not a warm inner glow; it was fire, passion, burning desire, the agony and ecstasy of courtly romance. At the conclusion of one of her visions she remarked, "Then I returned into myself, and I understood all I have just said; and I remained to gaze fixedly upon my delightful sweet Love."

Hadewijch's letters, apparently addressed to various of her spiritual daughters, reflect a receptive and nurturing personality. Her spiritual discourse is interspersed with expressions of personal affection, and exhortations to virtue, simplicity, and faithfulness: "O sweet dear child, be wise in God!" As a spiritual director Hadewijch did not place much stress on prayer, fasting, or external discipline. Instead, her emphasis was on love as the essential key to the knowledge and service of God: "Do everything with reliance on Love. . . . Let us live in sweet love. Live for God; let his life be yours, and let yours be ours."

The sweetness of Hadewijch's spiritual discourse gives no evidence of the pressures and criticism that surrounded the Beguine movement. At some point Hadewijch was evicted from her community; under what circumstances we cannot know. Her last letters reflect the pain of this experience, but also the enduring power of her faith:

O sweet child, your sadness, dejection, and grief give me pain! And this I entreat you urgently, and exhort you, and counsel you, and command you as a mother commands her dear child, whom she loves for the supreme honor and sweetest dignity of Love, to cast away from all alien grief, and to grieve for my sake as little as you can. What happens to me, whether I am wandering in the country or put in prison — however it turns out, it is the work of Love.

"Wandering in the country or put in prison"? Exactly what peril Hadewijch faced is unknown, but these and worse fates befell other Beguine mystics. Whatever her fate, there was no circumstance that could separate Hadewijch from her love of God.

In love I have experienced all these attributes, and I have acted with justice toward these persons, however much they have failed me. But if I possess this in love with my eternal being, I do not possess it yet in fruition of Love in my own being. And I remain a human being, who must suffer to the death with Christ in Love; for whoever lives in veritable Love will suffer opprobrium from all aliens, until Love comes to herself, and until she is full-grown within us in virtues, whereby Love becomes one with men.

And so Hadewijch vanished from history, leaving behind her love poems, a handful of letters, and a final exhortation: "Farewell and live a beautiful life."

See: *Hadewijch: The Complete Works*, Classics of Western Spirituality (New York: Paulist, 1980).

St. Gertrude the Great
Mystic (1253–1302)

"Inscribe with your precious blood, most merciful Lord, your wounds on my heart, that I may read in them both your sufferings and your love."

Of the birth and background of St. Gertrude there is no record. When she was five she was given to the nuns of the monastery at Helfta in Saxony, and within the walls of that enclosure she remained for the rest of her life. This monastery was one of the great religious communities of its time, distinguished by women of great learning as well as a number of famous mystics. One of them, St. Mechtild (d. 1298), was put in charge of the girl and oversaw her education and upbringing. Their relationship remained particularly intimate.

When she came of age Gertrude was professed as a nun. The religious life was all she had ever known. Nevertheless she truly owned her vocation only at the age of twenty-five. The turning point came one evening as she was preparing for bed. Suddenly she experienced a vision of Christ in the form of a young man. He spoke to her and said, "Fear not. I will save and deliver you." The figure was bathed in a dazzling light that emanated from his five wounds. He went on to say, "You have licked the dust with my enemies and sucked honey from thorns. Now come back to me, and my divine delights shall be as wine to you."

For the rest of her life Gertrude enjoyed frequent mystical revelations, often couched in dialogues with Christ, her Beloved Spouse. Believing these revelations were not for her own sake alone she forced herself to record them in a book, *The Herald of Divine Love,* a work combining great theological sophistication with mystical ardor. Nearly all the themes of Catholic theology are treated in her book, though the principal theme is God's love for his creatures. Gertrude had a special devotion to the Sacred Heart of Jesus, the point where human and divine love are most intimately joined.

Gertrude was often in poor health. Once when she was too sick to attend a sermon, the Lord spoke to her: "Would you like me to preach to you, my dearest?" When she assented, "the Lord made her lean against his heart, with the heart of her soul close to his divine heart. When her soul had sweetly rested there awhile, she heard in the Lord's heart two wondrous and very sweet pulsations." He told her that the first pulse was for the salvation of sinners, the second for the salvation of the just.

Gertrude served her community as a spiritual director and was frequently called upon to lead the community in prayer. When another of Helfta's mystics asked the Lord what he most liked about Gertrude, he answered: "Her freedom of heart." She died on November 17, 1302. Her feast day is observed on November 16.

See: Gertrude of Helfta: The Herald of Divine Love, ed. Margaret Winkworth, Classics of Western Spirituality (New York: Paulist, 1993).

Bd. Kateri Tekakwitha
"Lily of the Mohawks" (1656–1680)

"Who may tell me what is most pleasing to God that I may do it?"

Blessed Kateri was born in 1656 near present-day Auriesville, New York — the same place, and among the same people, where St. Isaac Jogues and other Jesuit missionaries had suffered martyrdom ten years before. The lingering ambivalence toward the Christian "Blackrobes" ran through her own family. While her mother, a captured Algonquin, was herself a Christian, her father, a Mohawk chief, viewed the new religion and its foreign emissaries with deep suspicion. Both parents died in an outbreak of smallpox when Kateri was only four. Her own scarred face showed the marks of the disease, which had also darkened her vision, causing her to stumble in bright sunlight. As a result her people called her Tekakwitha — "the one who walks groping her way."

She grew up like other girls of her village. But something about Kateri set her apart. She resisted the role that was expected of her — to become a wife and mother of her own family. Her memory of her own mother's faith was doubtless limited. Yet when a Jesuit missionary, Father Jacques de Lamberville, arrived in her village in 1674, she eagerly sought his company and surprised him by requesting baptism. Two years later her wish was granted. She was given the baptismal name of Kateri — a Mohawk version of Katherine.

Kateri's conversion provoked great resentment among her family and tribal community. Their scorn steadily escalated to the point where Father de Lamberville feared for her survival. Finally he urged her to flee. Under cover of darkness, and with the help of two fellow converts, she set off from her village by foot and made a trip of two hundred miles to Sault Sainte Marie, a Christian mission near Montreal. There, on Christmas Day, 1677, she made her first communion.

Free at last to practice her faith, Kateri was exhilarated. Still, she had to grope her way in a world that supplied no clear models. She attended daily Mass, spent much of her time in prayer, and otherwise occupied herself by serving the aged and infirm. Yet even the seasoned missionaries were astonished and somewhat perplexed by her devotional zeal and her extreme asceticism. They urged her in the direction of a Christian marriage, yet she continued to resist that option. Instead, she proposed founding a convent, an idea that was quickly dismissed as there was no basis, at the time, to suppose that Native Christians were suited for religious life. Nevertheless, in 1679 Kateri made a public vow of chastity.

That was as far as she could go with her dream of life as a religious. The next spring she fell gravely ill. After uttering the words, "Jesus, I love you," she died on April 17, 1680, at the age of twenty-three. Many witnesses testified that upon her death all marks of the pox disappeared from her face.

In 1980 Kateri Tekakwitha was beatified by Pope John Paul II, becoming the first Native American to be recognized as a saint.

See: Marie Cecilia Buerhle, *Kateri of the Mohawks* (Milwaukee: Bruce Publishing Company, 1954); "Kateri Tekakwitha: Icon of Otherness," in Joan Chittister, *A Passion for Life* (Maryknoll, N.Y.: Orbis Books, 1996).

Mother Ann Lee
Shaker (1736–1784)

"Clean your room well, for good spirits will not live where there is dirt. There is no dirt in heaven."

The Shakers are remembered today largely for their handiwork — baskets, boxes, and furniture of surpassing simplicity and beauty. This mysterious, Spirit-filled sect flourished in a number of American communities in the nineteenth century. With their elaborate rule of life, their unadorned simplicity, their celibacy, their approach to work as a form of worship, and their commitment to peace, the Shakers resembled a type of monasticism — though of an extreme Protestant variety. By their way of life and mode of worship the Shakers believed themselves to be living in the presence of Christ, in a restored state of Edenic innocence. As Thomas Merton, the modern Trappist monk, memorably wrote, "The peculiar grace of a Shaker chair is due to the fact that it was made by someone capable of believing that an angel might come and sit on it."

The seeds of the movement lay in a group of religious dissenters in Lancashire, England, who in the 1750s came to be known as "shaking Quakers." The name came from their tendency to sway and tremble as they meditated. "Affected under the power of God," they were "occasionally exercised in singing, shouting, or walking the floor... or swiftly passing and repassing each other, like clouds agitated by a mighty wind."

A young woman named Ann Lee joined their company in 1758, and soon she took a leading role. Ann came from a poor family and received no education before going to work in a textile mill. After joining the "shakers" she married a blacksmith and bore four children, all of whom died in infancy. With this great loss she entered a deep spiritual crisis, which eventually resulted in a dramatic conversion: "My soul broke forth to God, which I felt as sensibly as ever a woman did a child, when she was delivered of it." Reborn into the spiritual kingdom, she denounced all worldliness and set out to proclaim her vision.

Her preaching provoked violent opposition. She was charged with fanaticism, heresy, and blasphemy. She was beaten and even stoned by angry crowds. Throughout this persecution, she wrote, "I felt surrounded with the presence of God, and my soul was filled with love."

With other Shakers she was repeatedly arrested for disrupting the Sabbath by standing in church and giving testimony. In prison, one day, she beheld "the grand vision of the very transgression of the first man and woman in the Garden of Eden, the cause wherein all mankind was lost and separated from God." She claimed that Christ had appeared to her, commissioning her to preach the gospel of the stainless life. "I was converse with Christ!" she said, "I felt him present with me, as sensibly as I felt my hands together!"

When she got out of prison she discovered that her fellow Shakers had had the same experience. This convinced them that they were truly living in a new age of Christ's spirit. Ann Lee, who took the title of Mother Lee, felt a special union with Christ. "He is my head and my husband," she proclaimed, "and I have no other! I have walked, hand in hand with him in Heaven. . . . Feel the blood of Christ running through my soul and body, washing me; Him do I acknowledge, as my head and Lord."

Mother Lee moved her flock to America in 1774. A testimonial by one of her followers at that time described her thus: "Her countenance was mild and expressive, but grave and solemn. Her glance was keen and penetrating; her countenance inspired confidence and respect; and by many of the world, who saw her, without prejudice, she was called beautiful."

She was also called many other things: harlot, drunkard, and even witch. The Shakers' hope to find a more hospitable welcome in their new country was not immediately rewarded. For their practice of confession and their commitment to celibacy they were accused of being Catholics. After the outbreak of the Revolutionary War, because of their refusal to bear arms, they were accused of being traitors. Their form of life and worship was easily misunderstood and gave rise to wild rumors. Mother Lee's belief in the radical equality of the sexes — she referred to God as Father and Mother — won enemies on every side.

Nevertheless, after some years Mother Lee won her first American converts. As one of them said, "Her whole soul was always engaged in the work of God; and the spirit of God seemed to breathe in all her words and action." Shaker communities began to take root in New York and elsewhere, their members united in joyous belief that they were creating an earthly paradise. "Put your hands to work, and give your hearts to God," Mother Lee proclaimed. "Every breath is continual prayer to God."

Still, persecution continued to hound her ministry. One night a Shaker meeting where she was preaching was broken up by a group of zealous Christian neighbors. After enduring a beating Mother Lee was tied by her heels behind a wagon and dragged over an icy road for several miles. She never recovered from this ordeal and died at her community at Niskeyuna, New York, on September 8, 1784.

She did not live to see the full flowering of the Shakers in the mid-nineteenth century, nor their steady, inevitable decline. According to a later Shaker: "Every cycle has its prophets — as guiding stars; and they are the burning candles of the Lord to light the spiritual temple on earth, for the time being. When they have done their work, they will pass away; but the candlesticks will remain and other lights will be placed in them."

See: Edward Andrews, *The People Called Shakers* (New York: Oxford, 1953); Thomas Merton, *Seeking Paradise: The Spirit of the Shakers* (Maryknoll, N.Y.: Orbis Books, 2003).

St. Bernadette Soubirous
Visionary of Lourdes (1844–1879)

"O Jesus, keep me under the standard of your cross. Let me not just look at you crucified but have you living in my heart."

In traditional stories of the saints it is common to remark on the many ways, even as children, that they stood out among their neighbors. But even the most zealous admirers of St. Bernadette, try as they might, could find little to distinguish her. She was good, honest, and devout;

on this much everyone agrees. Otherwise she was quite ordinary. She considered herself of no importance, simply a poor vehicle of God's grace, who was content to withdraw into obscurity once her mission was complete.

Bernadette Soubirous was born in Lourdes, a small town on the northern slopes of the Pyrenees, in 1844. The eldest of six children, she lived in a basement hovel with the rest of her family. She was sickly, suffering from asthma, and once barely surviving an outbreak of cholera. She could not read. Her teachers considered her dull. And yet she would soon be at the center of a series of events that would turn her world upside down.

On a cold morning in February 1858 when she was fourteen, Bernadette and two other children were gathering firewood near a remote cave beside the river Gave de Pau. As she passed by the grotto she heard an odd rustling. Looking up she saw a beautiful young woman, "no bigger than myself," barefoot, clad in a white and blue outfit, and holding a rosary. At this sight Bernadette dropped to her knees and reached into her pocket for her own rosary. The other children, who saw nothing, mocked her pious display.

When she reported this experience, her parents were deeply suspicious and at first forbade her to return. But when they relented she was joined by other children and eventually by enormous crowds of curious neighbors who had heard of the alleged apparition. Over a period of two months Bernadette encountered and conversed with the Lady on eighteen occasions. Some of the messages were personal to Bernadette: "I do not promise to make you happy in this life, but in the next," the Lady said. In other cases she seemed to address herself to a wider audience: "Pray for poor sinners! Pray for the world so troubled!" When asked to identify herself, the Lady answered, "I am the Immaculate Conception" (a dogma defined only in 1854 concerning the Virgin Mary's preservation from original sin). It was an odd expression; Bernadette herself confessed that she had no idea what it meant.

In one of the final encounters, the Lady instructed Bernadette to drink from the waters in the cave. This was puzzling, since there was no visible source of water. But when Bernadette scratched in the ground she unearthed a growing stream. Muddy at first, the water became clear. Before long it was a gushing spring, which continues to the present day to produce twenty-seven thousand gallons a week.

St. Bernadette Soubirous

By the time these visions concluded they had become a cause of extreme confusion, consternation, and excitement among local townspeople, church officials, and civil authorities. Far from rushing to embrace these events as a miracle, church officials were initially reserved. Bernadette was subjected to grueling interviews as a series of priests and ecclesiastical authorities cross-examined her concerning every detail of her visions. At times they seemed frustrated that God should have vouchsafed such favors to an illiterate peasant girl and not to someone better schooled in Mariology. How likely was it that the Blessed Mother had spoken in the regional patois and not in proper French? If this was indeed the Blessed Mother, the wife of St. Joseph, how could Bernadette maintain that she wore no wedding ring? To these and similar queries, Bernadette could only affirm what she had seen, and from this she never deviated.

As if it wasn't hard enough to endure the scrutiny of skeptics, the adulation of the pious was even more difficult. In short order Bernadette became a celebrity. People doted on her and vied to receive her blessing. She was mortified. In part to escape this attention, she eagerly sought the refuge of religious life. Encouraged by her parish priest, she entered an order of nursing Sisters and was sent far from home to a convent in Nevers. There, upon taking her vows, she became simply Sister Marie Bernard.

But this was not the end of her trials. Her superior enjoyed the attention occasioned by the presence of such a spiritual celebrity. She would frequently summon Bernadette to the parlor to recite the details of her visions before important visitors. And yet she treated Bernadette with extreme severity, justifying her harshness as a "safeguard of her humility."

Bernadette's health, never robust, began to deteriorate. As tuberculosis entered her bones, she suffered terrible pain. Yet she never complained or sought special treatment. On her deathbed, she was visited again by bishops, who asked her to describe once more the Lady's veil — its length, its width, its folds. "Can I remember all that?" Bernadette asked. "If they want to know let them make her reappear."

By this time Lourdes had become the most popular pilgrimage site in Europe, its cult embraced by the church. Tens of thousands of visitors arrived each year, drawn in part by reports of the miraculous cures associated with the waters of the grotto. But Bernadette was never among the pilgrims. She did not return to Lourdes, even when a minor basilica was consecrated in 1876 before a crowd of a hundred thousand people.

"Our Lady used me," she said. "They have put me back in my corner. I am happy to stop there."

Bernadette died on April 16, 1879, at the age of thirty-five. She was canonized in 1933.

See: Margaret Gray Blanton, *The Miracle of Bernadette* (Englewood Cliffs, N.J.: Prentice-Hall, 1958).

St. Maria Goretti
Martyr (1890–1902)

"No, it's a sin. God does not want it!"

Maria Goretti was the third of five children born in 1890 to a poor Italian tenant farmer and his wife. Her father died of malaria when she was ten, leaving her mother to support the family. They shared a dwelling with another family, the Serenellis, whose eighteen-year-old son, Alessandro, regularly made sexual advances toward young Maria. One day, when she was not quite twelve, he confronted her alone in their cottage and tried to rape her. When she put up resistance he repeatedly stabbed her. She died the next day from her wounds, though not before receiving the Eucharist and expressing forgiveness for her assailant (she hoped to see him in heaven, she said).

Alessandro was sentenced to thirty years in prison. Some time into his sentence, he had a dream in which Maria appeared to him, again conveying her forgiveness and appealing to him for conversion. He awoke a changed man. Upon his release from prison he immediately went to Maria's mother and begged her forgiveness.

In the meantime, Maria's story had spread far beyond her small village. She was regularly invoked as a symbol of purity and Christian virtue. Thousands of people remembered her in their prayers, and many miracles were credited to her name. She was canonized in 1950 by Pope Pius XII before a record crowd that included her mother and siblings, and, more remarkably, the man who had murdered her.

The canonization of Maria Goretti was unusual in several respects. Unlike traditional martyrs, she had not died in "defense of the faith," but in defense of Christian virtue. In supporting her cause, it appeared that the church intended her story as a challenge to the contemporary culture of sexual permissiveness. Addressing the crowd gathered for her canonization, the pope excoriated the press, cinema, and the fashion industry for their corruption of sexual morality. Generations of Catholic children — particularly girls — were imprinted with the example of the child martyr Maria, and advised to heed her message.

But what was that message? If Maria Goretti had survived her rape and then expressed the same astonishing charity toward her assailant, would she have been similarly honored by her family and her church?

The story of Maria Goretti shares in the ambiguous legacy of all those ancient stories of "virgin martyrs" such as St. Agnes, St. Barbara, and St. Lucy, who suffered death in the name of Christ rather than allow themselves to be defined or defiled by a patriarchal culture. Typically, in these stories, a young woman who refuses to submit to marriage is threatened with gang rape or sexual humiliation, before meeting a violent end. But it does further violence to the memory of these women to reduce their witness to a sermon on the virtues of modest dress or the perils of premarital sex.

Like her foresisters, the peasant girl Maria Goretti, with no one to protect her, clung fiercely, with a warrior spirit, to her own identity and sense of honor. Yet her stand was based on more than simple self-protection. She bore witness to a redemptive power large enough to embrace the salvation of her assailant and to transcend all the cruel circumstances of their lives.

As Kathleen Norris has written, "Sometimes it takes a death to make us see the obvious. Sometimes it is a fierce little girl who is hard to kill, who gives witness to a mystery beyond our understanding and control. And in the wild center of that young girl's heart, we glimpse a love stronger than death, a love that shames us all."

See: Kathleen Norris, "The Virgin Martyrs: Between 'Point Vierge' and the 'Usual Spring,'" in A Tremor of Bliss: Contemporary Writers on the Saints, ed. Paul Elie (New York: Harcourt Brace & Company, 1994); Kathleen Norris, "Maria Goretti," in Martyrs, ed. Susan Bergman (Maryknoll, N.Y.: Orbis Books, 1996).

Etty Hillesum
Mystic of the Holocaust (1914–1943)

"God is not accountable to us, but we are to Him. I know what may lie in wait for us.... And yet I find life beautiful and meaningful."

Little is known of the external life of Etty Hillesum, a young Jewish woman who lived in Amsterdam during the Nazi occupation and who died as one of the millions of victims of the Holocaust. This obscurity is in contrast with her well-documented internal life. From the day when Dutch Jews were ordered to wear a yellow star up to the day she boarded a cattle car bound for Poland, Etty consecrated herself to an ambitious task. In the face of her impending death, she endeavored to bear witness to the inviolable power of love and to reconcile her keen sensitivity to human suffering with her appreciation for the beauty and meaning of existence. For the last two years of her life Etty kept a meticulous diary, recording her daily experiences and the unfolding of her interior response. Published four decades after her death, this book was quickly recognized as one of the great moral documents of our time.

Etty maintained a clear sense of solidarity with the Jewish people. But her personal reflection was nourished by an eclectic range of sources, including Rilke, the Bible, St. Augustine, and Dostoevsky. When a friend exclaimed indignantly that her attitude on the love of enemies sounded like Christianity, she responded, "Yes, Christianity, why ever not?" But in fact she had little interest in organized religion of any kind. In a time when everything was being swept away, when "the whole world is becoming a giant concentration camp," she felt one must hold fast to what endures — the encounter with God at the depths of one's own soul and in other people.

There is an earthy and embodied dimension to Etty Hillesum's spirituality. She described her romantic adventures with no more reticence than she reserved for descriptions of her prayer. For Etty, everything — the physical and the spiritual without distinction — was related to her passionate openness to life, which was ultimately openness to God.

In the meantime her life was unfolding within the tightening noose of German occupation. Etty's effervescence might seem to resemble a type of manic denial. The fact is, however, that she seems to have discerned the logic of events with uncommon objectivity. In this light, her determination to affirm the goodness and beauty of existence becomes nothing short of miraculous. Her entry for July 3, 1942, reads:

> I must admit a new insight in my life and find a place for it: what is at stake is our impending destruction and annihilation.... They are out to destroy us completely, we must accept that and go on from there.... Very well then.... I accept it.... I work and continue to live with the same conviction and I find life meaningful.... I wish I could live for a long time so that one day I may know how

Etty Hillesum

to explain it, and if I am not granted that wish, well, then somebody else will perhaps do it, carry on from where my life has been cut short. And that is why I must try to live a good and faithful life to my last breath; so that those who come after me do not have to start all over again.

For Etty, this affirmation of the value and meaning of life in the face of overwhelming evidence to the contrary became her guiding principle. In the midst of suffering and injustice, she believed, the effort to preserve in one's heart a spirit of love and forgiveness was the greatest task that any person could perform. This, she felt, was her vocation.

With increasing regularity, Etty described her compulsion to drop to her knees in prayer. Toward the end of her journals, God had become the explicit partner of her internal dialogue:

God take me by Your hand, I shall follow You faithfully, and not resist too much, I shall evade none of the tempests life has in store for me, I shall try to face it all as best I can....I shall try to spread some of my warmth, of my genuine love for others, wherever I go. ...I sometimes imagine that I long for the seclusion of a nunnery. But I know that I must seek You amongst people, out in the world. And that is what I shall do....I vow to live my life out there to the full.

Etty worked for a while as a typist for the Jewish Council, a job that delayed her deportation to the transit camp at Westbork. Eventually she renounced this privilege and volunteered to accompany her fellow Jews to the camp. She did not wish to be spared the suffering of the masses. In fact, she felt a deep calling to be present at the heart of the suffering, to become "the thinking heart of the concentration camp."

Her sense of a call to solidarity with those who suffer became the specific form of her religious vocation. But it was not a vocation to suffering as such. It was a vocation to redeem the suffering of humanity from within, by safeguarding "that little piece of You, God, in ourselves."

I know that a new and kinder day will come. I would so much like to live on, if only to express all the love I carry within me. And there is only one way of preparing the new age, by living it even now in our hearts.

On September 7, 1943, Etty and her family were placed on a transport train to Poland. From a window of the train she tossed out a card that read, "We have left the camp singing." She died in Auschwitz on November 30. She was twenty-nine.

See: An Interrupted Life: The Diaries of Etty Hillesum, 1941–1943 (New York: Pantheon, 1983).

Mollie Rogers
Founder of the Maryknoll Sisters (1882–1955)

"There is nothing more astonishing than life, just as it is, nothing more miraculous than growth and change and development, just as revealed to us. And as happens so often when we stop to regard God's work, there is nothing to do but wonder and thank Him, realizing how little we planned, how little we achieved, and yet how much has been done."

Mollie Rogers dated the beginning of her vocation to a summer evening at Smith College when a crowd of her fellow students rushed outdoors singing "Onward Christian Soldiers." They had just signed the Student Volunteer pledge to go to China as Protestant missionaries. Mollie shared their exhilaration, mixed with a certain regret that there was no similar Catholic mission group that she could support. She made her way to the parish church and there, "before Jesus in the tabernacle, I measured my faith and the expression of it by the sight I had just witnessed. From that moment I had work to do, little or great, God alone knew."

There was no immediate issue from this resolution. But several years later in 1905 Mollie, now an instructor at Smith, sought out Father James Anthony Walsh, local director of the Society for the Propagation of the Faith in Boston. He immediately enlisted her help with *Field Afar,* a new journal aimed at stimulating mission awareness in the U.S. church.

Walsh, an Irish-American priest in his thirties, was at the time collaborating with Father Thomas Price from North Carolina on a plan to establish an American foreign mission society. Their objective: the great expanse of China. It is hard today to appreciate the magnitude of this vision. Until 1908 the United States was itself designated as a mission territory. America was still in the midst of a massive influx of European immigrants, and a good number of the Catholic priests serving in the country were themselves foreign born. Overseas mission at the time was considered a Protestant enterprise, while the Catholic Church had its hands full dealing with more pressing needs at home. Nevertheless in 1911 Walsh and Price won support from the American bishops to establish a mission seminary. This was the origin of the Catholic Foreign Mission Society of America, soon to be known as Maryknoll.

Mollie was one of a small group of women who volunteered to join the priests in Ossining, New York, to help with the launching of this project. Their work was mostly confined to secretarial work on *Field Afar*. But as the Society took shape Mollie became more and more convinced that the women had a wider role to play than as mere helpers to the priests. Why, she asked, shouldn't women also serve as overseas missionaries? She won over Walsh and Price to her project. They perceived the advantage of women missioners who could more easily relate to the women of China. But to pursue this plan it was necessary that they form a religious congregation. Mollie had felt no special call to become a nun, but if that is what it took to become a missioner she was game.

This plan encountered resistance from Vatican officials who doubted that women were suited to the rugged demands of mission. The congregation that Rogers envisioned also represented a departure from the conventional model of religious life. She wished her Sisters to live amid the people — not cooped up in monastic enclosures, but able to move freely about to bear witness to the gospel. Despite reservations, the Vatican in 1920 granted approval. A year later Mollie Rogers and twenty-one other women made their formal religious vows as Maryknoll Sisters of St. Dominic.

The Sisters were helped in their early formation by members of other religious congregations. But Mollie Rogers, or Mother Mary Joseph as she was now known, found it difficult to adjust to the discipline and spirituality of these nuns, rooted in the traditions of the old world. Rogers was interested instead in adapting religious life to the needs of mission. Refusing "to be hampered by an over-regimented and parceled-out prayer life," she fought hard to impress on the congregation the importance of flexibility and individuality. Describing the ideal Maryknoll Sister, she said,

I would have her distinguished by Christ-like charity, a limpid simplicity of soul, heroic generosity, selflessness, unfailing loyalty, prudent zeal, gracious courtesy, an adaptable disposition, solid piety, and the saving grace of a kindly humor.

The first mission of the Maryknoll Sisters was among Japanese immigrants on the West Coast. But soon Rogers's dream was fulfilled when the first Maryknoll Sisters were sent to China. Again, as she had hoped, the Sisters branched out beyond the work of support for the priests or traditional works of charity. In China, and eventually elsewhere, Maryknoll Sisters went out into the countryside to befriend the poor and to engage in the direct work of evangelization. Other missions followed in Korea, the Philippines, and eventually throughout the world.

Rogers followed the work of her Sisters with maternal pride and made several trips overseas to survey their progress. But it was not her vocation to join them. Instead she remained at the motherhouse directing the congregation until she retired from office in 1950. At the time of her death on October 9, 1955, there were eleven hundred Maryknoll Sisters serving worldwide.

In years to come the Maryknoll Sisters would achieve a heroic image for their exploits in the jungles of Africa and Latin America, and for their sufferings during World War II and under communist persecution in China. Later still, beginning in the 1960s, their commitment to social justice and their "option for the poor" would entail a different type of heroism. But as the congregation grew and evolved over time the Sisters continued to draw inspiration from the vision and personality of Mollie Rogers, who once wrote, "Love, work, prayer, and suffering will sustain us in the future as they have in the past. All who are here now, all who will come after us, will have no other tools than these with which to build."

See: Penny Lernoux (with Arthur Jones and Robert Ellsberg), *Hearts on Fire: The Story of the Maryknoll Sisters* (Maryknoll, N.Y.: Orbis Books, 1993).

Raïssa Maritain
Poet and Contemplative (1883–1960)

"It is an error to isolate oneself from men.... If God does not call one to solitude, one must live with God in the multitude, make him known there and make him loved."

The life of Raïssa Maritain was inextricably intertwined with that of her husband, Jacques, the renowned Catholic philosopher. In their long life together they were united not only by bonds of matrimony but by "holy friendship," a union in which God remained an intimate third partner.

Raïssa and Jacques met as students at the Sorbonne. Raïssa had been born in Russia. Her parents, Orthodox Jews, had moved to France to seek better educational opportunities for their gifted daughters. Raïssa had advanced so quickly in her studies, despite having to learn a new language, that she was admitted to the university at the age of sixteen.

She met Jacques Maritain when he solicited her signature on a petition protesting the treatment of socialist students in tsarist Russia. The attraction between them was immediate, and they were soon inseparable. They were married in 1904. Raïssa and Jacques shared a passion for poetry, art, and social justice. But they soon found another bond — a common obsession with the question of truth and a need to discover the meaning of life. Though neither had much religious training, they found it intolerable to imagine that existence might be absurd. They made a vow that if they had not, within a year, found an answer to their quest they would end their lives.

Soon after this they began to attend the lectures of the philosopher Henri Bergson, from whom they acquired a "sense of the Absolute." They were led in turn to the novelist Léon Bloy. He was not only a devout Catholic but a prophet, whose writings celebrated God's predilection for the poor, while excoriating the sins of bourgeois Christianity. From their friendship with Bloy the Maritains were introduced to the world of Catholicism but also to Holy Scripture. Raïssa was particularly moved by Bloy's writings on the Jews, chosen by God for a special role in the history of salvation. Within a year of their first meeting with Bloy the Maritains were baptized in 1906. Bloy was their godfather.

Having found their way to the church, Raïssa and Jacques ever after conceived of their lives in religious terms. They took vows as Oblates of St. Benedict and soon after made a vow of perpetual celibacy. Despite this private commitment, they felt strongly that they were not meant for monastic life, but were called to live out their faith in the midst of the intellectual and artistic circles in which they were immersed.

In the first volume of her memoirs, *We Have Been Friends Together,* Raïssa described the early years of their marriage almost entirely in terms of their relationships with such figures as Bloy, the artist Georges Rouault, and the poet Charles Péguy. Throughout their life together the Maritains' salon was the center of an extraordinary Catholic intellectual revival. Jacques became the most eminent Catholic philosopher of the twentieth century. Raïssa was also recognized through the publication of several volumes of poetry and prose. But otherwise she remained more in the background, the intimate collaborator in her husband's work. He later said that her aid and inspiration had penetrated everything he wrote: "Every good thing comes from God. But as an intermediary on earth everything good has come to me from her."

Raïssa died on November 4, 1960. It was only then that Jacques discovered her private journals and so realized the depth of spirituality that had remained hidden even from him. Later published, the journals reflected Raïssa's intense life of prayer and her understanding of her vocation as a contemplative "on the roads of the world." Indeed, on the basis of these writings, Thomas Merton called her "perhaps one of the great contemplatives of our time."

In one of her entries she had written: "I have the feeling that what is asked of us is to live in the whirlwind, without keeping back any of our substance, without keeping back anything for ourselves, neither rest nor friendships nor health nor leisure — to pray incessantly... in fact to let ourselves pitch and toss in the waves of the divine will till the day when it will say: 'That's enough.'"

See: Raïssa Maritain, *Raïssa's Journal* (Albany, N.Y.: Magi, 1974); *We Have Been Friends Together* (London: Longman, Green, 1942).

Flannery O'Connor
Novelist (1925–1964)

"The Catholic writer... will feel life from the standpoint of the central Christian mystery: that it has, for all its horror, been found by God to be worth dying for."

"There won't be any biographies of me," predicted Flannery O'Connor (and a good thing, too, was the implication), "because... lives spent between the house and the chicken yard do not make exciting copy." Lacking in excitement, her short life was nevertheless marked by its own human drama. Among other things, she left behind a small output of novels and stories that assured her place among the very greatest of American writers. In her lifetime, discerning critics perceived the importance of religious themes in her work. But only with the posthumous publication of her letters in *The Habit of Being* did it become clear how much the shape of her art owed to her Catholic faith. What is more, the letters revealed just how much her personal circumstances, her sharp intelligence, and her deeply held faith had combined to forge a prophetic vision of extraordinary depth.

Flannery O'Connor

Early in life O'Connor was diagnosed as suffering from lupus, an incurable, debilitating disease that sapped her energy and confined her to her mother's dairy farm in Milledgeville, Georgia. There she wrote as her strength permitted — two hours in the morning — and tended the menagerie of ducks, swans, and peacocks with which she surrounded herself. She disliked sentimentality and piety and reacted strongly against the temptation of critics to drag her medical history into consideration of her writing. And yet her illness imposed on her a discipline and sense of priorities that she managed to turn to the advantage of her art. From Teilhard de Chardin she borrowed the phrase "passive diminishment" to describe a quality she admired: the serene acceptance of whatever affliction or loss no effort can change. "I have enough energy to write with and as that is all I have any business doing anyhow, I can with one eye squinted take it all as a blessing. What you have to measure out, you come to observe closer."

In her imposed confinement, she poured much energy into correspondence. Many of her letters dealt with her faith and the religious dimension of her stories. To one correspondent she wrote,

I write the way I do because (not though) I am a Catholic. This is a fact and nothing covers it like the bald statement. However, I am a Catholic peculiarly possessed of the modern consciousness.... To possess this *within* the Church is to bear a burden, the necessary burden for the conscious Catholic. It's to feel the contemporary situation at the ultimate level.

For O'Connor the Catholic doctrines of creation, fall, and redemption were the lens through which she viewed the world. But as an artist she also valued the vivid sacramental dimension of Catholicism — the notion that grace is always mediated through nature, and mystery through manners. "I feel that if I were not a Catholic I would have no reason to write, no reason to see, no reason ever to feel horrified or even to enjoy anything." She frankly acknowledged her orthodoxy and baffled her more secular-minded friends by confessing to find in dogma a source of liberation ("it preserves mystery for the human mind").

The church, she believed, was the only thing likely to make the world endurable. She could believe this and still acknowledge the church's own sins — they were all the more painful to her. "The only thing that makes the Church endurable is that it is somehow the Body of Christ and that on this we are fed."

O'Connor saw clearly the crisis of faith in a "religionless age" — a time when it is so much easier not to believe, when "nihilism is the gas we breathe." Often, she stressed the cost of faith:

> I think there is no suffering greater than what is caused by the doubts of those who want to believe. I know what torment this is, but I can only see it, in myself anyway, as the process by which faith is deepened. What people don't realize is how much religion costs. They think faith is a big electric blanket, when of course it is the cross.

Unlike most other "Catholic writers," O'Connor avoided Catholic settings in her stories. Most of her characters are a strange assortment of backwoods fanatics, secular-minded intellectuals, and self-described "good country people." Her stories are set on that contested territory where God and the devil have it out. The endings are often violent, even apocalyptic; her characters are pruned and emptied of their illusions and even their "virtues" before they can face the truth. Yet even in the darkest of her stories there is a dimension of mystery and innocence and possibility. It is the dimension of grace that heals, though first it cuts with the sword of Christ.

"All my stories," she wrote, "are about the action of grace on a character who is not very willing to support it." To the modern reader, inclined to believe that grace and faith are "twin idiocies," the point of view in her stories might seem grim and cynical. But O'Connor believed her stories were ultimately hopeful — in the same sense in which she believed that purgatory was the most hopeful doctrine of the church.

Flannery O'Connor died of lupus on August 3, 1964, at the age of thirty-nine. In her last year she completed several of her greatest stories, all written more or less *in extremis*. She had, as her friend Sally Fitzgerald observed, attained her personal form in art as well as in life. She would have been happy to be remembered for her stories. Posthumously, however, she has achieved an unexpected reputation as a Christian apologist. She was able to make the life of faith seem reasonable and attractive without losing a sense of ambiguity. She combined detachment with a sense of the preciousness of life. She faced the horrors of history without losing sight of the resurrection. Thus, in her highly personal and modest way she exemplified the virtue and responsibility of hope.

See: Flannery O'Connor, *The Habit of Being*, ed. Sally Fitzgerald (New York: Farrar, Straus & Giroux, 1979); *Flannery O'Connor: Essential Writings*, ed. Robert Ellsberg (Maryknoll, N.Y.: Orbis Books, 2003).

Cassie Bernall
Witness of Columbine (1981–1999)

"P.S. Honestly, I want to live completely for God. It's hard and scary, but totally worth it."
— From a note written by Cassie the night before she died

On the morning of April 20, 1999, two teenage boys from Columbine High School in Denver, Colorado, driven by some nihilistic impulse, entered their school with an arsenal of guns and bombs. In the ensuing rampage they killed thirteen of their fellow students and teachers and wounded many more, before eventually turning their guns on themselves. What had provoked this cruelty? In the following days and weeks there was much speculation about this dark mystery. But there were other mysteries.

One of them concerned Cassie Bernall, a seventeen-year-old junior, who was among the victims on that bloody day. Students fleeing for shelter under tables in the library clearly heard the exchange between Cassie and her killers. "Do you believe in God?" one of the boys had asked. A student recalls: "She paused, like she didn't know what she was going to answer, and then she said yes. She must have been scared, but her voice didn't sound shaky. It was strong. Then they asked her why, though they didn't give her a chance to respond. They just blew her away."

As this story circulated around the globe, many were left to wonder what could prepare a young girl, confronted in a decisive moment with the ultimate test, to bear such witness to the faith within her. To her friends and family Cassie's response was perfectly in character. But while honoring her courage, they were reluctant to turn her into a stereotypical saint or martyr. In a touching and honest memoir, her mother described the remarkable journey that had led to her final testimony.

There had been a time, only a few years earlier, when Cassie had traveled a road not far removed from that of her killers. Her dark and sullen moods might have passed for typical adolescent rebellion, except that her parents came across a cache of letters exchanged with her best friend. In the girls' violent fantasies of killing their parents and taking their own lives, her parents discovered how little they really knew about their daughter. After confronting Cassie about their discovery, they took drastic action. They moved to a new neighborhood, enrolled her in a different school, and tightly monitored her activities — all the while contending with her anger, resentment, and ongoing deceptions.

Cassie was a hard case, and it was not at all clear that she could be rescued. But in time something began to change. She consented to attend a weekend youth retreat with a girl she had befriended. The talks that weekend in 1997 had to do with overcoming the temptations of evil and breaking with selfishness. As Cassie listened her heart was somehow opened. Approaching the altar during one worship service, she wept in remorse for her life. Afterward, the friend who had invited her remarked on the difference: "There was something new about her." Her mother noticed the difference when Cassie greeted her with an uncharacteristic hug and said, "Mom, I've changed. I've totally changed. I know you are not going to believe it, but I'll prove it to you."

Her parents were understandably skeptical. And in fact she did not become overnight a perfect, happily adjusted teenager. She still had her moods. She still worried and complained that her parents didn't understand; she still had her moments of oblivious, teenage selfishness. But something had indeed changed.

She herself regarded that date, March 8, 1997, as a second birthday, the day she opened her life up to God. Many of her friends and even her family did not know at the time just how deeply she had been affected. She didn't go about in a pious cloud, preaching about Jesus. The change showed itself in her hopefulness and generosity, her openness to life. After her death her pastor spoke about Cassie's daily "dying to self." He acknowledged that that might sound morbid and dramatic. But, as he put it, "It's not a negative thing, but a way of freeing yourself to live life more fully. The world looks at Cassie's 'yes' of April 20, but we need to look at the daily 'yes' she said day after day, month after month, before giving that final answer."

She became actively involved with a church youth group — participating avidly in Bible study, worship, and service activities. But she also liked activities outside of church — snowboarding, photography, and hanging out with her friends. As one of them said, "People can call Cassie a martyr, but they're off track if they think she was this righteous, holy person, and that all she did was read her Bible. Because she wasn't like that. She was just as real as anybody." Noting all the publicity about her story, her friend continued, "I think she'd be flipping out. She's probably in heaven rolling her eyes at it all and going oh-my-gosh, because she'd want to tell everyone who admires her so much that she wasn't really so different from anybody else."

Cassie Bernall

Like any other teenager, Cassie experienced doubt and depression. Like anyone, she was uncertain of the road she walked. "I wonder what God is going to do with my life," she wrote. "Like my purpose. Some people become missionaries and things, but what about me? What does God have in store for me? Where do my talents and gifts lie? For now, I'll just take it day by day. I'm confident that I'll know someday. Maybe I'll look back at my life and think, 'Oh, so that was it!' Isn't it amazing, this plan we're a part of?"

On the last morning of her life she was running behind. She had stayed up late the night before, trying to finish homework. She ran down the stairs in her black velvet Doc Martens, grabbed her backpack, shouted a last goodbye to her mother, and dashed out the door. She did not know that she was rushing to the final appointment of her short life.

"Do you believe in God?" Perhaps a different answer would not have altered her fate. But for many people desperate to find some glimmer of grace in this senseless tragedy, it made all the difference that she said "Yes."

See: Misty Bernall, *She Said Yes: The Unlikely Martyrdom of Cassie Bernall* (Farmington, Pa.: Plough Publishing House, 1999).

Daria Donnelly
Laywoman (1959–2004)

"My getting sick increased my attention to the everyday heroism of refugees, the depressed, the arthritic, the mourning, the lonely, all those who know how good it is simply to get through a day."

The first sign of something wrong came when she broke a vertebra, just months after giving birth to her daughter. Daria Donnelly was forty-two, the mother of two young children, Leo and Josie, when she received the diagnosis of multiple myeloma, a rare, typically fatal blood cancer that weakens the immune system and eats away at the bones. Like anyone under such circumstances, Daria felt the terrible injustice of this news. But she proved to be unusually prepared — by faith and discipline — to face her ordeal. She was determined to make each remaining day a witness to life, and to make this her legacy to those she loved.

Daria grew up in Pittsburgh in a large, loving, and devoutly Catholic family. Photographs from her early childhood capture the paradoxical combination of gravity and levity that forever marked her personality. Even by the standards of her Irish-Catholic roots, she took her faith seriously. After studying religion at Wesleyan College she worked in a Catholic Worker house in Rochester and then traveled to Jerusalem to study Jewish-Christian relations. In this light it was not entirely surprising that she would later marry a Jewish lawyer, Steve Weissburg. In their home both traditions would hold equal honor.

Daria earned a doctorate in English, writing her dissertation on the poetry of Emily Dickinson. She taught for some years at Boston University and then retired to a more inward life at home in Cambridge with her baby son, Leo. Eventually she was hired as an editor at *Commonweal*, the liberal Catholic journal, where she took special delight in writing a semiannual review of children's literature. She was an insightful and empathetic editor who, as one of her friends put it, respected language "that was adequate to the world as she knew it (and she knew it at its very best and worst)."

She applied the same care and precision to all aspects of her life, particularly to friendship. As a result, scores of otherwise unconnected people would later describe her as their best friend. In part, this reflected her capacity for focus and generosity. She was a keen listener and gave everything in return.

Daria engaged in many quiet ministries: volunteering in her son's school, befriending the elderly, and welcoming the company of the odd and friendless. But like her favorite poet, Emily Dickinson, she was a natural contemplative, a discerning observer of life and its dramas. She read the world as if it were a poem, sometimes lovely and sometimes sad, but pointing to some meaning that could not be expressed in any other way.

The news of her illness, so soon after Josie's birth, hit like a thunderclap. Her friends were devastated. But Daria accommodated herself to her circumstances with a calm, unselfish, and benevolent balance that more than ever became the mark of her personality. Graciously she accepted the support of her friends and neighbors as she adjusted to the narrowing constraints on her existence. Her title at *Commonweal* was revised to "Editor-at-Large." "I love the title," she wrote. "It makes me seem out and about, maybe even hard to find. A flattering fiction, as, in truth, I do a good imitation of Emily Dickinson. Stay put. Travel by other means."

She endured the devastating rigors of two stem-cell replacements — the sickness, the weakness, the vulnerability to every germ and jolt. She took it all in, both the bitterness and the sweetness of life.

She remained intimately connected to the life of the church, even as it was rocked by scandal. As often as she could she received communion from a eucharistic minister. Asked later whether she had received the sacrament of the sick, her pastor commented that she had personally used up half the year's supply of holy oil. Yet there was nothing sentimental or parochial about her faith; it was simply the ground she walked on, the air she breathed. As her pastor noted, "She was to her core a woman of symbol, of story, of sacrament. She reached in the deepest Catholic sense toward the loving, nourishing, reconciling grace of God through the ordinary, commonplace things of God's created universe."

She warmly encouraged this present collection of "gal saints" and urged the author to include examples of ordinary women, especially mothers, and those who knew the spiritual challenge of finding God amid the chaos and distractions of family life. Of a previous book on saints, she wrote in her characteristic zany e-mail style: "Your book was full of insight and sharp people but where are the kids? That's not your fault: does our church ever give the high five to saintly parents??? The noise the joy the distraction: Nouwen, Merton, the modern prophets, they don't have kids, and as result they can't sort all the noise of culture: and their diagnosis is limited. . . . Saints use it all. Anyway it depresses me that there seems to be so little recognition of the saint mother saint father. . . . I'm overtuned to the kids I am sure, but since the sickle man came calling here I am like thy will be done, hell no I won't go, kids need their mothers."

Her initial prognosis was a matter of months, yet she lived on for nearly three years, grateful for each extra day to be with Steve, to watch their children grow, to add to their store of memories and their reservoir of love. She continued to read the Bible, the newspaper, and her beloved poets. But meanwhile every part of her body seemed steadily to give out. "Oh man, what next?" she wrote, after another downturn. "I feel like I might wake up without legs or something."

She was prepared for death, but never resigned. In another e-mail: "I was embarrassed last year to discover how obsessed the Gospels are with healing: it's the focus: and the healings are literal. I went to hip schools which discounted miracles or explained them away as Jesus' way of letting us know he was God. Dumb, huh? There is nothing hip about healing, only essential."

Only weeks before her death, she wrote to a young child about her care for a rescued horse: "The only thing that matters is showing love and compassion in the time that is given us. Your love for Leroy has altered the universe."

After her long ordeal, the end came suddenly on September 21, 2004. She had taken time to plan her funeral, including long prayers of thanks for all the friends, family, and caregivers who had accompanied her with such faithfulness. The prayers ended with the final words: "May Josie, Leo, and Steven be well; may they be free from suffering; may Josie, Leo, and Steven be filled with loving kindness; may they be happy."

Who can measure the significance of such a life? Daria Donnelly's brand of "ordinary" holiness, set amid "the noise the joy the distraction" of family life, expressed in daily (hourly, minute-by-minute) acts of faith and compassion, tested by intolerable suffering, bearing witness through all circumstances in the promise of the gospel, leaves no great monument in the world. But, as George Eliot wrote of her heroine in *Middlemarch*, "The effect of her being on those around her was incalculably diffusive, for the growing good of the world is partly dependent on unhistoric acts, and that things are not so ill with you and me as they might have been is half owing to the number who lived faithfully a hidden life."

Daria Donnelly

BLESSED ARE
THE PEACEMAKERS

A queen • a reformer • an artist • a martyr of the "White Rose" • a pacifist • a pilgrim • a journalist • a theologian

In the early centuries of the church the word "peacemaker" might well have served as a synonym for Christian. In that era followers of Jesus were distinguished by their refusal to kill or to study war. Many paid a heavy price for this commitment. That would change after Christianity became the official religion of the Roman empire. Nevertheless (especially among monastic orders) the memory of Christ's admonitions lived on, if only as a "counsel of perfection." Several women saints, including Catherine of Siena and Elizabeth of Portugal, were particularly renowned for their role as peacemakers.

It was only in the twentieth century, however, that Christians on a wide scale began to recover the vocation of peacemaking — not just as a code of personal conduct but as a social imperative. Not by coincidence this was also the century that witnessed the rise of organized violence on a global scale, for the first time threatening the survival of all life on earth. In this era Christ's blessing of the peacemakers took on a special resonance and urgency — not just as the concern of certain exceptional figures, but as a mission entrusted to the entire church.

According to Christ, those who accept this mission receive a new identity and name: "They shall be called children of God."

St. Catherine of Siena
Doctor of the Church (1347–1380)

"All the way to heaven is heaven, because He said, 'I am the way.'"

St. Catherine of Siena was one of the greatest saints of a tumultuous era. While the Black Death wreaked its devastation, mercenary armies roamed the countryside, waging protracted warfare on behalf of their client-cities. Avoiding the chaos and dangers of Rome, the papacy had decamped to a palace in Avignon, France, leaving administration of the church in the hands of corrupt and high-handed legates. This was the world into which Catherine was born. Like other great mystics, she enjoyed an intimate relationship with Christ. This was certified by a dazzling array of miraculous signs, which even in her lifetime made her something of a celebrity. What was distinctive about the holiness of Catherine was the way she mediated through her own heart the burning love of Christ and the needs of her time.

The daughter of a prosperous wool dyer, she was the twenty-fourth of twenty-five children. Her parents had hopes that Catherine would serve the family well by making an advantageous marriage. But she adamantly resisted this plan, insisting that she was called to betrothal with Christ. As a sign, she cut off her beautiful golden hair. Her family retaliated by treating her as a servant. But with Christ's help she constructed within herself "a secret cell" to which she happily retreated from her daily drudgery. In the end her father was won over. All it took was the sight of a dove hovering over Catherine's head as she knelt in prayer. Afterward he consented to her vocation, noting that Christ would not make such a bad son-in-law.

Rather than enter a formal religious order, Catherine put on the habit of a Dominican tertiary. "My cell," she said, "will not be one of stone or wood, but of self-knowledge." In what did this self-knowledge consist? She received the answer in a vision of Christ: "Know, daughter, that I am He who is, and thou art that which is not." From this simple formula, Catherine would develop her whole understanding of the spiritual life and her vocation.

For three years she remained enclosed in her room. During much of this period she was besieged by doubts, demonic visions, and taunting voices, until she finally banished them with laughter. Immediately Christ appeared to her. "And where were *you* when all this was happening?" she asked, reproachfully. "I was in your heart," came the reply.

After this, according to her biographer, she received daily visitations by Christ, sometimes in the company of Mary Magdalene and other saints. The climax of this period came during Shrove Tuesday 1367, while all the town celebrated and Catherine remained praying in her room. In a mystical betrothal Christ appeared to her and placed a ring on her finger, visible only to herself.

This was the signal for Catherine to begin the second great phase of her career. She emerged from her room, rejoined her family, and set about serving her neighbors. Again, the move was prompted by the command of Jesus: "The service you cannot do me you must render your neighbors." The next several years found her nursing the sick, distributing alms to the poor, and ministering to prisoners and plague victims. Through miraculous healings and her air of spiritual authority, she began to attract disciples — the so-called Caterinata — including both men and women, even friars and priests. Affectionately, they called her Mamma.

In 1374 there came another turning point. After praying for a long time in an ecstatic state, Catherine appeared for a matter of hours to have died. Afterward she described an excruciating experience of union with God: "My heart could bear it no longer, and the love became as strong as death; then the heart broke in two." Now Christ commanded her to return to the world "for the good of souls." But it was the wider world and the universal church that claimed her attention. She commenced her role as a public figure, dictating hundreds of letters to the pope, monarchs, and other persons of note, counseling them on the performance of their duties. She also wrote her great work, *The Dialogue*, describing the contents of her mystical conversations with Christ.

For some years Catherine had served as a local peacemaker, mediating between feuding families in Siena. Now she took up a more difficult challenge: mediating in an armed conflict between the city of Florence and the Avignon-based papacy. With her retinue of followers, she traveled across Italy to meet with the contending parties. Everywhere she went she was greeted by enthusiastic crowds. Finally she journeyed all the way to Avignon to meet personally with Pope Gregory XI. While honoring the pope as her "sweet Christ on earth," she was blunt and uncompromising in her insistence that he return to Rome. The court in Avignon, she claimed, stank of sin. The pope's place was beside the bones of the martyrs.

The mission was a surprising success. Affected by her appeal, the pope did in fact return to Rome. But the victory was not all that

Catherine had hoped for. Soon after his return, Gregory died. He was succeeded, disastrously, by Urban VI, a pope who exemplified the expression "to be driven mad by power." Before long the college of cardinals, regretting their decision, elected a second pope. But having failed first to persuade Urban to abdicate, the church was now saddled with two rival, and soon-to-be warring, pontiffs, a scandalous condition that would last for several decades.

Catherine remained adamantly loyal to the unworthy Urban, judging that for all his faults he had been duly consecrated. But she could not help feeling that the wound in the body of Christ could be healed only by tremendous sacrifice. After praying that she might atone for the sins of the church, she experienced her final vision. It seemed as if the church, like a mighty ship, was placed on her back. She collapsed to the ground in terrible pain and paralysis. After several weeks she died on April 29, 1380, at the age of thirty-three. Upon her death the marks of the stigmata and her "wedding band" were clearly visible on her body. In 1970 St. Catherine was named a Doctor of the Church.

See: Catherine of Siena, *The Dialogue*, Classics of Western Spirituality (New York: Paulist, 1980); Carol Lee Flinders, *Enduring Grace* (San Francisco: HarperSan-Francisco, 1993).

St. Elizabeth of Portugal
Queen (1271–1336)

"Do not forget that when sovereigns are at war they can no longer busy themselves with their administration; justice is not distributed; no care is taken of the people; and this alone is your sovereign charge, this the main point of your duty as kings."

Like her great-aunt St. Elizabeth of Hungary, St. Elizabeth of Portugal was a royal daughter, betrothed as a child to a foreign prince for reasons of state. The daughter of the king of Aragon, she was born in 1271. At twelve she was married to King Denis of Portugal, a profligate man, who tolerated his wife's piety while making no secret of his own infidelities. Elizabeth bore two children, a son and a daughter. Her son, Alonso, would later come close to open rebellion against his neglectful father. For her role in effecting a reconciliation between father and son

St. Elizabeth of Portugal

Elizabeth became popularly known as "the Peacemaker." But her talents as a peacemaker were exercised on an even greater level when she personally prevented a war between Portugal and Castile.

Elizabeth lived up to the public responsibilities of her office as queen. But the greater part of her time was spent in prayer and a variety of charitable projects. She established hospitals, orphanages, and religious houses throughout the kingdom, as well as halfway homes for "fallen women."

When her husband fell seriously ill in 1324, she devotedly nursed him until his death the following year. After making a pilgrimage to Compostela she put on the habit of a Franciscan tertiary and lived in the monastery of Coimbra that she had helped to found. She lived there for eleven years in poverty and prayer, emerging occasionally to intercede between rival monarchs, most of whom were relatives, either by blood or marriage. Even as she lived she was credited with numerous miracles, and she was popularly revered by the people of Portugal.

She died in 1336 and was canonized three centuries later by Pope Urban VIII, who named her the Patroness of Peace.

See: Vincent McNabb, O.P., "St. Elizabeth of Portugal," in *Saints Are Not Sad,* ed. F. J. Sheed (New York: Sheed & Ward, 1949).

Ida B. Wells
Reformer (1862–1931)

"We submit all to the sober judgment of the Nation, confident that, in this cause, as well as all others, 'Truth is mighty and will prevail.' "

Ida B. Wells was born into slavery in Holy Springs, Mississippi, in 1862, just months before the signing of the Emancipation Proclamation. Her parents and three siblings died in an outbreak of yellow fever when she was sixteen. To support her younger sisters and brothers she passed herself off as eighteen and got a job as a teacher. Her struggle against racial injustice began in 1884 when a train conductor tried to evict her from her first-class seat to make room for a white man. She did not go quietly: "The conductor tried to drag me out of my seat, but the moment he caught hold of my arm I fastened my teeth in the back of his hand." Reinforcements eventually removed her from the train. Even so she continued to fight back. Wells hired an attorney and successfully sued the railroad. Although the company won on appeal with the state

Supreme Court, Wells's courageous stand made her a national figure — at least among that part of the nation that knew firsthand the sting of racism. On the strength of this reputation she became the editor of a black newspaper in Memphis called *The Free Speech*. In 1892, when three black men were lynched in Memphis, Wells had occasion to test the power of that brave title.

As it happened, Wells knew the lynching victims well — she was godmother to the daughter of one of the men. Their murder galvanized Wells to action and supplied the focus of her subsequent career. In a stream of editorials and investigative articles she shone the light of truth on one of the darkest corners of American life.

Lynching was the ultimate form of white terrorism. Its victims might be seized from their homes, accosted on the street, or dragged from jail. Taunts and beatings would escalate to horrible mutilation, burning, or public hanging, often conducted before a cheering audience. Though relatively rare in slavery times (when a black life had an actual dollar value), the incidence of lynching had steadily increased since the time of Reconstruction, from 52 in 1882 to more than 250 in 1892. The pretext was often some alleged "outrage" against Southern (white) womanhood.

Wells conducted exhaustive research and documented the actual reasons behind most lynchings: failure to show proper deference to whites, registering to vote, "talking back," complaining about working conditions, or having the bad luck to be caught by a mob already on its way to another lynching. Whether performed by Klansman in the dead of night, or in broad daylight before festive crowds, lynching was a powerful sign addressed to all black Americans — a reminder that the underlying code of slavery lived on, even if the forms had changed.

Wells was out of town when her first editorial appeared. This was fortunate. An outraged mob stormed the newspaper office, destroyed the presses, and left the warning that she would be lynched herself if she ever returned. In the words of an editorial in one of the competing city newspapers: "The fact that a black scoundrel is allowed to live and utter such loathsome and repulsive calumnies is a volume of evidence as to the wonderful patience of Southern whites. But we have had enough of it."

As a result of these threats Wells became a "journalist in exile." Though she settled in Chicago she did not abandon the struggle. Every time a lynching occurred she would, at great personal risk, travel to the site to interview witnesses and gather facts. She would not let the nation ignore these atrocities as simply a crude example of Southern mores. She lectured throughout the country as well as in England. She lobbied in Washington, challenged churches and religious organizations to speak out, and published her stories in papers throughout the land.

Ida B. Wells did not bring an end to lynching in America; in the year after her death in 1931 there were twenty-eight recorded lynchings. But her courageous witness lit a torch that inspired subsequent generations of black women to carry on the struggle for dignity and freedom. She embodied the principles of "true leadership" that she described in a lecture in 1891: "The main requisites of such leadership are first, devotion to principle, or courage of conviction. No great reform in the world's history has ever been successful or far-reaching in its influence without an earnest, steadfast devotion which so takes hold of its leaders that they willingly brave the world's censure — aye, even death itself in its defense."

See: Lynne Olson, *Freedom's Daughters: The Unsung Heroines of the Civil Rights Movement from 1830 to 1970* (New York: Scribner, 2001).

Jane Addams
Social Reformer and Nobel Laureate (1860–1935)

"The things which make men alike are finer and better than the things which keep them apart, and ... these basic likenesses, if they are properly accentuated, easily transcend the less essential differences."

Jane Addams was born in 1860 in the town of Cedarville, Illinois. Although she came from a wealthy family with no particular interest in social work, her study of the Bible implanted in her a desire to serve the poor. Her personal mission took shape after a trip to England in 1888 when she visited Toynbee Hall, a "settlement house" in a poor slum of London. Upon returning home she established a similar enterprise in Chicago — Hull House — which remained her home for the rest of her life. Hull House became the model for a network of similar settlement houses in urban slums. Aside from offering basic services — kindergarten, adult education, medical care, food, and shelter — the aim of Hull House was to promote community and self-respect among the immigrant poor. It was a haven for those cast aside by the tide of industrial "progress."

Although she was baptized in the Presbyterian Church, Addams remained aloof from organized religion. Yet she saw her work in Hull House and in social reform as consonant with the great humanitarian spirit that animated the early Christian movement, and that now sought to embody itself "not in a sect but in society itself." While churches tended to promote "personal virtue," the time had come, she believed, to promote the exercise of "social virtue" in the service of humanity.

Addams was a central figure in most of the progressive movements of her day. She fought for child-labor laws, women's rights, and housing reform, and against political corruption. She was a founder of the American Civil Liberties Union and the National Association for the Advancement of Colored People. Her work among immigrants and the destitute won her wide praise and admiration. One editorial described her as "a great professor without a university chair, a guiding woman in a man-made world, a brooding spirit of the mother hovering with gentle sympathy over the troubled sea of poverty, of weakness, of arrogance, of pride, of hate, of force."

But her strong pacifist stand during World War I quickly turned the tide of public opinion against her. Teddy Roosevelt, whom she had previously regarded as a friend, called her "the most dangerous woman in America"; she was denounced in editorials and headlines as a "Red" and a traitor. It was one thing to help the poor; it was another thing to draw connections between the violence of poverty and the system of militarism.

After the war Addams helped found the Women's International League for Peace and Freedom, serving as its president for the rest of her life. Though she no longer commanded the widespread admiration of her fellow citizens, her efforts continued to be recognized abroad. In 1931 she was awarded the Nobel Prize for Peace.

She died on May 21, 1935.

See: James Weber Linn, *Jane Addams* (New York: D. Appleton-Century, 1935); Jane Addams, *Twenty Years at Hull-House* (New York: Macmillan, 1934).

Sophie Scholl and Companions
Martyrs of the White Rose (d. 1943)

"We will not be silent. We are your bad conscience."

In the summer and fall of 1942 the citizens of Munich were astonished by a series of leaflets that began to circulate throughout the city.

Slipped into mailboxes by unknown hands, left in empty bus stops or on park benches, the leaflets contained a sweeping indictment of the Nazi regime and enjoined readers to work for the defeat of their own nation. At a time when the merest hint of private dissent was a treasonable offense, the audacity of this open call to resistance threw the Gestapo into a rage.

Contrary to the suspicions of the authorities, the authors of these leaflets, who called themselves simply "The White Rose," were not members of any sophisticated organization. They were in fact a few dozen university students who had been inspired by Christian faith and the uncorrupted idealism of youth to challenge the edifice of tyranny. At the center of the group were a brother and sister, Hans and Sophie Scholl, only twenty-four and twenty-one years old. Hans was a medical student who had served on the Russian front. Sophie studied philosophy. Discerning with uncommon clarity the depth of Nazi depravity, they had decided to wage a spiritual war against the system, armed with no other weapons than courage, the power of truth, and an illegal duplicating machine. Their strategy was simple. At the very least they hoped to shatter the illusion of unanimous consent and to defy the Nazis' claim to omnipotence. Beyond that, they dared hope that by proclaiming the truth they might break the spell in which all Germany was enthralled and inspire those with doubts to move toward active resistance.

Sophie and her brother were devout Christians. They believed that the struggle against Hitler was a battle for the soul of Germany, and thus a duty for all Christians. As one of their leaflets read, "Everywhere and at all times of greatest trial men have appeared, prophets and saints who cherished their freedom, who preached the One God and who with His help brought the people to a reversal of their downward course. Man is free, to be sure, but without the true God he is defenseless against the principle of evil.... We must attack evil where it is strongest, and it is strongest in the power of Hitler.... We will not be silent. We are your bad conscience. The White Rose will not leave you in peace."

Emboldened by the furor caused by their leaflets, members of the White Rose began to make other dangerous gestures, such as writing "Down with Hitler" on street signs and the walls of buildings. It was perhaps inevitable that the circle of amateurs would be discovered. The end began on February 18, 1943, when Hans and Sophie were caught distributing leaflets outside a lecture hall in the university. Under arrest and realizing that their fates were sealed, they proceeded to confess to all the actions of the White Rose, thus hoping to spare other conspirators from discovery. Despite their efforts, however, the Gestapo quickly rounded up the rest of the circle, both in Munich and in Hamburg, where an allied cell had formed.

Hans and Sophie Scholl along with their fellow conspirator Christoph Probst, a twenty-three-year-old medical student, were quickly convicted of treason and sentenced to death. All witnesses attest to the extraordinary poise with which Hans and Sophie met their fate. Their bravery was based not just on a confidence in the verdict of history, but on a deep faith that the executioner's block was the entryway to freedom and eternal life. They were beheaded on February 22, 1943.

See: Inge Scholl, *The White Rose: Munich 1942–43* (Middletown, Conn.: Wesleyan University Press, 1983).

Käthe Kollwitz
Artist (1867–1945)

"One day, a new idea will arise and there will be an end to all wars. I die convinced of this. It will need much hard work, but it will be achieved."

Käthe Kollwitz, one of the great artists of the twentieth century, was an avowed socialist and pacifist. In her artistic vision these words were not mere ideological labels. They represented a moral and spiritual affirmation of the preciousness of human life and a spirit of resistance to all the idols of death.

She was born in Konigsburg in East Prussia in 1867, the daughter of a minister. She lived most of her life in Berlin, where she married Karl Kollwitz, a doctor who practiced medicine in a working-class section of the city. She drew on his patients as models for many of her drawings and lithographs. Few other artists have been so committed to representing the private struggles and suffering of the poor. Her depictions of hunger, unemployment, domestic violence, and the oppressive burden of despair are among the most poignant images in all of twentieth-century art.

Kollwitz was particularly sensitive to the experience of women, especially the aspects of maternal love. Many of her drawings depict mothers delighting in the presence of their children. But she also depicted a mother's fierce determination to protect her young, and the corresponding potential for devastating loss. Kollwitz herself was no stranger to such loss. In World War I her youngest son, Peter, was killed at the front. His death struck "like a thunderbolt," for a long time crippling her ability to work. "Peter," she wrote, "was seed for the planting that should not have been ground." Eventually she transformed her grief into a passionate commitment to peace and the struggle against all the causes of war.

She had sympathized with the communist revolution in Russia as well as the parallel revolutionary struggles in Germany. In a powerful sequence of engravings she celebrated the doomed Peasants' Revolt of the sixteenth century and its mythic embodiment in the peasant mother, Black Anna. But with the death of her son her commitment to socialism became intertwined with a resolute pacifism.

After the war she was commissioned to design a war memorial at the Soldiers Cemetery near Dixmuiden. She worked on the statue for many years. When it was finally unveiled in 1932, it revealed a scene entitled "Mourning Parents," its figures plainly modeled after herself and her husband, Karl. It remains a devastating image of sorrow over the waste of life.

In the years to come Kollwitz continued to put her art at the service of her conscience and her spiritual vision. With the rise of the Nazis, however, her work was banned and could not be publicly shown. She managed to remain in Berlin throughout the Nazi era and the devastation of the war. Her husband died in 1940. Two years later, her grandson, another Peter, was killed in action.

Still, driven by her sense of personal responsibility, she continued to draw as long as health permitted. As she wrote, "Culture arises only when the individual fulfills his cycle of obligations. If everyone recognizes and fulfills his cycle of obligations, genuineness emerges. The culture of a whole nation can in the final analysis be built upon nothing else."

In April 1945 her granddaughter asked her if she was a pacifist. "Yes," she answered, "if you understand by pacifism more than just antiwar. It is a new idea — that of the brotherhood of man."

She died on April 22, a few days before the Armistice.

See: Renate Hinz, ed., *Käthe Kollwitz: Graphics, Posters, Drawings* (New York: Pantheon, 1981); Mina C. Klein and H. Arthur Klein, *Käthe Kollwitz: Life in Art* (New York: Schocken, 1975).

Muriel Lester
"Ambassador of Reconciliation" (1884–1968)

"The job of the peacemaker is to stop war, to purify the world, to get it saved from poverty and riches, to heal the sick, to comfort the sad, to wake up those who have not yet found God, to create joy and beauty wherever you go, to find God in everything and in everyone."

Muriel Lester was born in an upper-class family in Leytonstone, England. Like other members of her class, she seldom had occasion to wonder how the "other half" lived. But an event in early childhood opened a window to a life of service among the poor and neglected. Whenever her family took a train to the West End of London she noticed that her fellow first-class passengers would tightly close up the windows of their carriage and cover their noses "to protect ourselves from the foul smell that pervaded the whole atmosphere of Bow," a particularly wretched neighborhood in the East End. One time she glanced out the window at "the rabbit-warren of unsavory dwelling houses ... sordid and leaking." "Do people live there?" she asked. "Oh yes," her nanny answered. "Plenty of people live down there, but you needn't worry about them. They don't mind it. They're not like you. They enjoy it."

These words never left her. Years later, after finishing with school, she found opportunities to visit the East End, to get to know the kind of people who lived there, and to discover that they were, in fact, just like herself — though thinner, paler, and destined in most cases to live a short life of worry and want. She determined to leave her privileged life behind and devote herself to befriending the poor of Bow, to do what she could to share their lives and enlarge their hopes.

With her sister Doris, she established a community center called Kingsley Hall, named after their deceased brother. Among its many services were a children's center, a center for adult education, and a social club — a teetotaling alternative to the pubs, where working families could find good cheer and companionship. A program of informal Bible study led eventually to Sunday-evening worship services. The Hall began to take on an increasingly religious spirit, and, much to her surprise, Lester found herself "turning into a parson." Though rooted in the spirit of the Gospels, the community was independent of any denomination. It was simply a "fellowship, based on the attempt to practice the presence of God."

From her early reading of Tolstoy, Lester had come to believe that the gospel was incompatible with any kind of violence. "Once your eyes have been opened to pacifism, you can't shut them again. Once you see it, you can't unsee it. You may bitterly regret the fact that you happen to be one of the tiny minority of the human race who have caught this angle of vision, but you can't help it." From reading Tolstoy, she said, she had become aware of "the peculiar importance of doing Jesus Christ the honor of taking Him seriously, of thinking out His teaching in terms of daily life, and then acting on it even if ordered by police, prelates, and princes to do the opposite."

The outbreak of World War I provided a test for her pacifist convictions. In public meetings she denounced the war, comparing it to "cannibalism, chattel slavery, blood-feuds, and dueling. . . . an insult to God and man. . . . a daily crucifixion of Christ." It was a wildly unpopular stand, but she was not alone. With other like-minded pacifists she helped found the Fellowship of Reconciliation, and later the International FOR, an international organization of religious pacifists.

Lester was a tireless promoter of her causes — whether for the poor, the rights of women, the message of peace, or the cause of Indian independence. She even took to speaking on soapboxes in Hyde Park, an experience that refined her cool nerve and clever wit. But for all her frenetic activity, Lester maintained a discipline of contemplative prayer. The necessity of this practice became clear, early in her career, when she found herself on the verge of physical and mental collapse. She felt she had become "unhitched from the source of strength and serenity." The solution was "to realize that with every breath I drew I was actually breathing in the spirit of God." Learning to let go, to yield herself to the "rhythmic flow of the Eternal Spirit," she found a reserve of enormous strength and peace.

This discipline of prayer, Lester found, was something anyone could practice in the midst of daily life, "while you dress, bathe, brush your hair, walk, or work or sit in the bus." In meeting a newcomer she made it a practice to ask, "Now I wonder what of God I am going to find in this person?" Such questions transformed every day into a spiritual adventure.

In 1926 Lester made the first of many trips to India, where she met and began a lifelong friendship with Mohandas Gandhi. Later, when Gandhi traveled to London to take part in a Round Table conference with the British government, he passed up the hospitality of the Crown to accept Lester's invitation to reside for three months at Kingsley Hall. The poor of London, he said, were more like the people he was used to. Lester campaigned vigorously for Gandhi's cause. Later, after being named an "Ambassador at Large" for the IFOR, she ranged ever farther in her journeys around the globe. In the 1930s she investigated the brutality of Japanese occupation in China and went on, courageously, to tell Japanese audiences about the atrocities being committed in their name. From there she went to America to confront scrap metal merchants who were supplying Japan with the raw materials for its munitions. She was in the United States when World War II broke out. During a trip through Latin America she learned that Kingsley Hall had been bombed in the London Blitz. Still she continued to speak out publicly about the effects on Europe of the food blockade. As a result she was detained by British authorities in Trinidad and held for ten weeks in an internment camp. When public outcry forced her release and allowed her return to England, she was briefly jailed and then deprived of her passport.

The problem, as she said, was that she "refused to pronounce a moratorium on the Sermon on the Mount for the duration of the war." Difficult as it was to practice the way of nonviolence in the spirit of Jesus or Gandhi, the alternative, she believed, was simply inconsistent with the plain message of the gospel. "We should stop praying the Lord's Prayer," she wrote, "until we can see that 'Our Father' means that we are tied to the same living tether not only with our fellow countrymen but with everybody on the planet."

Muriel Lester continued her traveling, writing, and public speaking into her eighties. She died on February 11, 1968.

See: Richard Deats, ed., *Ambassador of Reconciliation: A Muriel Lester Reader* (Philadelphia: New Society Publishers, 1991).

Dorothy Day
Co-Founder of the Catholic Worker (1897–1980)

"Whatever I had read as a child about the saints had thrilled me. I could see the nobility of giving one's life for the sick, the maimed, the leper.... But there was another question in my mind. Why was so much done in remedying the evil instead of avoiding it in the first place?... Where were the saints to try to change the social order, not just to minister to the slaves, but to do away with slavery?"

When Dorothy Day died in 1980 at the age of eighty-three it was observed that she was "the most influential, interesting, and significant figure" in the history of American Catholicism. This was an extraordinary statement on behalf of someone who occupied no official position in the church — indeed, someone whose ideas were almost universally rejected throughout most of her life. The Catholic Worker, a lay movement she founded in 1933 and oversaw for nearly fifty years, was an effort to show that the radical gospel commandment of love could be lived. She understood this challenge not just in the personal form of charity (the works of mercy) but in a political form as well, confronting and resisting the social forces which gave rise to such a need for charity. She represented a new type of political holiness — a way of serving Christ not only through prayer and sacrifice but through solidarity with the poor and in struggle along the path of justice and peace.

As a result some people called her a communist. She was shot at, jailed, and investigated repeatedly by the F.B.I. She was not seriously disturbed by criticism. "The servant is not greater than his master," she liked to quote. On the other hand there were many who liked to call her saint. That was another matter. "When they call you a saint," she often said, "it means basically that you're not to be taken seriously." She regarded it as way of dismissing her challenge: "Dorothy can do that; she's a saint!" The implication was that hard decisions must have come easily for her. Actually, no one knew as well as she how dearly she had paid for her vocation: "Neither revolutions nor faith is won without keen suffering. For me Christ was not to be bought for thirty pieces of silver but with my heart's blood. We buy not cheap in this market."

Day was born in Brooklyn in 1897. Though she was baptized as an Episcopalian, she had little exposure to religion. By the time she was in college she had rejected Christianity in favor of the radical cause. She dropped out of school and worked as a journalist in New York with a variety of radical papers and took part in the popular protests of her day. Her friends were communists, anarchists, and an assortment of New York artists and intellectuals, most of the opinion that religion was the "opium of the people."

A turning point in her life came in 1926 when she was living on Staten Island with a man she deeply loved. She became pregnant, an event that sparked a mysterious conversion. The experience of what she called "natural happiness," combined with a sense of the aimlessness of her Bohemian existence, turned her heart to God. She decided she would have her child baptized as a Roman Catholic, a step she herself followed in 1927. The immediate impact of this was the painful end of her common-law marriage. The man she loved had no use for marriage. But she also suffered from the sense that her conversion represented a betrayal of the cause of the poor. The church, though in many ways the home of the poor, seemed otherwise to identify with the status quo. So she spent some lonely years in the wilderness, raising her child alone, while praying for some way of reconciling her faith and her commitment to social justice.

The answer came in 1932 with a providential meeting. Peter Maurin, an itinerant philosopher and agitator, encouraged her to begin a newspaper that would offer solidarity with the workers and a critique of the social system from the radical perspective of the Gospels. The *Catholic Worker* was launched on May 1, 1933. Like a true prophet, Maurin was concerned not simply to denounce injustice but to announce a new social order, based on the recognition of Christ in one's neighbors. In an effort to practice what they preached, Day converted the office of the Catholic Worker into a "house of hospitality" — the first of many — offering food for the hungry and shelter for the tired masses uprooted by the Depression.

But Day's message did not end with the works of mercy. For her the logic of the Sermon on the Mount also led to an uncompromising commitment to nonviolence. Despite widespread criticism she maintained a pacifist position throughout World War II and later took part in numerous civil disobedience campaigns against the spirit of the Cold War and the peril of nuclear war. Later, in the 1960s, when social protest became almost commonplace, Day's peacemaking witness — rooted in her daily life among the poor and sustained by the discipline of liturgy and prayer — retained a particular credibility and challenge.

The enigma of Dorothy Day was her ability to reconcile her radical social positions (she called herself an anarchist as well as a pacifist) with a traditional and even conservative piety. Her commitment to poverty, obedience, and chastity was as firm as any nun's. But she remained thoroughly immersed in the secular world with all the "precarity" and disorder that came with life among the poor. Her favorite saint was Therese of Lisieux, the young Carmelite nun whose "little way" indicated the path to holiness within all our daily occupations. From Therese Day drew the insight that any act of love might contribute to the balance of love in the world, any suffering endured in love might ease the burden of others; such was the mysterious bond within the body of Christ.

In combining the practice of charity and the call to justice Day represented a type of holiness not easily domesticated, but perhaps of special relevance to our times. She called on the church to recover its identity as an offense and mystery in the eyes of the world. Her life was a living parable, focused on what she called the mystery of the poor: "that they are Jesus, and what you do for them you do to Him." She died on November 29, 1980.

See: Robert Ellsberg, ed., *Dorothy Day: Selected Writings* (Maryknoll, N.Y.: Orbis Books, 1992); Jim Forest, *Love Is the Measure: A Biography of Dorothy Day* (Maryknoll, N.Y.: Orbis Books, 1993); Rosalie Riegle, *Dorothy Day: Portraits by Those Who Knew Her* (Maryknoll, N.Y.: Orbis Books, 2003).

Peace Pilgrim
(?–1981)

"I am a pilgrim, a wanderer. I shall remain a wanderer until mankind has learned the way of peace, walking until I am given shelter and fasting until I am given food."

She called herself Peace Pilgrim. Otherwise she had no interest in describing the particulars of her early life, her age, or even her given name. She walked back and forth across the United States for almost three decades, owning nothing but the clothes she wore: a pair of navy blue slacks and a blue shirt, blue sneakers, and a tunic bearing her chosen name and, on the back in white letters, the simple words, "25,000 Miles on Foot for Peace."

As far as she would reveal, Pilgrim's early years were conventional and uneventful. Like other people she had pursued money and possessions. But at a certain point she realized that this "self-centered" existence did not bring fulfillment. After spending one night wandering in the woods she came to "a complete willingness, without any reservations, to give my life to God and to service." "Please use me!" she prayed to God. "And a great peace came over me."

So began a long, fifteen-year period of preparation for an as-yet undefined mission. Embracing a life of simplicity, she worked as a volunteer with various social service and peace organizations. Apart from weaning herself from material possessions, she also pursued an arduous course of spiritual discipline to adjust to the demands of a "God-centered existence." She was determined to live by what she called "the laws that govern the universe." These included the fact that evil can be overcome only by good; that only good means can attain a good end; that those who do unloving things hurt themselves spiritually.

Among the disciplines she practiced were purification of the body, purification of thought ("I don't eat junk foods and I don't think junk thoughts"), and purification of desire and motive (doing nothing for self-glory or other impure ends). She also practiced various "relinquishments," letting go of the feeling of "separateness," of attachments, and of all negative feelings.

There came a point one morning when she suddenly felt uplifted in a dimension of "timelessness, spacelessness, and lightness." She seemed not to be walking on the earth. "Every flower, every bush, every tree seemed to wear a halo. There was a light emanation around everything, and flecks of gold fell like slanted rain through the air." During this time of illumination she conceived her life mission: she would go on pilgrimage for peace, praying constantly, rousing people from their apathy, and awakening the hearts of all whom she encountered.

Pilgrim set off from Los Angeles on January 1, 1953. The war in Korea was raging. Nuclear arsenals were proliferating around the globe. The McCarthy-era investigations were smelling treason in every corner, raising suspicions that even the word "Peace" was simply a shrewd disguise for subversion.

Peace Pilgrim set off with no publicity and no organizational backing. Carrying nothing but what she could hold in the pockets of her tunic — a toothbrush, a pen, and leaflets to distribute to anyone who asked — she simply walked from town to town, and eventually state to state. She accepted food and hospitality when it was offered. Otherwise she fasted or slept outdoors — under a tree or a bridge, or simply in the nearest field. The bold words on her tunic proclaimed her message and invited conversation with curious passersby. To whomever she met she described her purpose: "My pilgrimage covers the entire peace picture: peace among nations, peace among groups, peace within our environment, peace among individuals, and the very, very important inner peace."

Newspapers and eventually television journalists publicized her travels. She was invited to speak in countless schools, churches, and universities. Sometimes she was arrested as a vagrant. She considered such adventures no distraction from her essential mission. Wherever she went she engaged her listeners as human beings, bearers of the image of God, with whom she eagerly shared her teachings: how to overcome evil with good, falsehood with truth, hatred with love.

By 1964 her pilgrimage had surpassed her original goal of twenty-five thousand miles. After that she ceased counting. But she did not cease walking. Long after her hair had turned silver with age, she maintained her constant pilgrimage, showing no loss of energy or enthusiasm with the passing years. It was not the walking that killed her. She made what she liked to call "the glorious transition to a freer life" on July 7, 1981, when a car in which she was being driven to a speaking engagement was hit in a head-on collision.

"Who am I?" she had written. "It matters not that you know who I am; it is of little importance. This clay garment is one of a penniless pilgrim journeying in the name of peace. It is what you cannot see that is so very important. I am one who is propelled by the power of faith; I bathe in the light of eternal wisdom; I am sustained by the unending energy of the universe; this is who I really am."

See: *Peace Pilgrim: Her Life and Work in Her Own Words,* compiled by some of her friends (Santa Fe, N.Mex.: An Ocean Tree Book, 1982).

Mirabehn
Servant of Peace (1892–1982)

"God's grace . . . runs through life like a thread strung through a row of beads, the two ends of which are finally joined together."

Madeline Slade, the daughter of an English admiral, grew up in comfort and luxury. Her early life revealed no extraordinary qualities. And yet beneath her quiet exterior there burned a hunger for service — a desire to devote herself to someone or something larger than herself. When, as she believed, God had revealed her purpose in life, she gave herself with complete devotion. That purpose, as it turned out (to the dismay of her patriotic family), was to put herself at the service of Mahatma Gandhi, the nonviolent champion of India's independence.

Her path to India was convoluted. It began, curiously enough, with a passion for Ludwig van Beethoven. From the first time she heard Beethoven's music she felt herself come alive as never before. Through his music she experienced a kind of communion with God. This led her in turn to the Swiss writer Romain Rolland. After reading his *Vie de Beethoven* she felt that she had found a kindred spirit. But since Rolland spoke no English, she prepared to meet him with a year of study in Paris. When at last she felt herself worthy, she wrote Rolland and arranged an interview. He proved courteous, if somewhat perplexed by the young woman's intentions. Slade, for her part, felt tongue-tied. But the hand of Providence intervened when Rolland mentioned his most recent book, a biography of Mahatma Gandhi, whom he called "another Christ." Now Slade's purpose was clear. After reading his book she determined: "I was to go to Mahatma Gandhi, who served the cause of oppressed India through fearless truth and nonviolence, a cause which, though focused in India, was for the whole of humanity.... The call was absolute, and that was all that mattered."

If her resolution was impulsive, she was deliberate in her planning. Even before notifying Gandhi, she embarked on another year of preparation, not only earning the cost of her passage, but adopting a vegetarian diet, learning to sit on the floor, mastering the art of spinning, and (on the basis of misinformation) studying the Urdu language. When at last she applied to Gandhi, he warned of the rigors of the climate and hard work, but welcomed her interest. As a final step she had an outfit made from imported Indian handspun cloth and embarked for her new country in 1925.

She arrived during a quiet period in the independence struggle. Gandhi was based in his ashram in Sabarmati, devoting himself to experiments in village uplift. At their first meeting Gandhi said, "You shall be my new daughter." He assigned her to learn Hindustani, to perfect her spinning, and to clean the ashram latrines. She thought she was in heaven.

In time she adjusted to the shortcomings of ashram life. Not everyone shared Gandhi's discipline or convictions, and some of the Mahatma's experiments provoked grumbling. For example, there was his decision to institute a "raw" diet, calculated to save time in cooking; after this induced constipation throughout the ashram, the experiment was deemed a failure. But Slade never wavered in her devotion to Gandhi, whom she, like his other followers, called simply "Bapu" (Father). He in turn gave her a new name, Mirabehn (Sister Mira), after a heroic Indian mystic.

Mirabehn accompanied Gandhi on many of his most critical campaigns. She nursed him during his frequent fasts, waited on him during conferences with his comrades, and traveled to London with him in 1931 when he took part in the historic Round Table discussions with the British government. At times seemingly uncomfortable with her personal devotion, Gandhi put her at a distance, assigning her to work in distant ashrams. On one occasion he wrote her, "You must not cling to me as in this body. The spirit without the body is ever with you.

And that is more than the feeble embodied imprisoned spirit with all the limitations that flesh is heir to." He encouraged her to "grow along your own lines. You must retain your individuality at all costs."

And yet at other times Gandhi expressed his own attachment. "You are on the brain," he wrote to her during one separation. "I look about me and miss you. I open the spinning wheel and miss you. So on and so forth. You have left your home, your people, and all that people prize most, not to serve me personally but to serve the cause I stand for.... Now that you are not with me, my anger turns itself upon me for having given you all those scoldings."

Over time Gandhi recognized Mirabehn as one of his most trusted lieutenants. She advised him on strategy, organized cooperatives, went to jail with other activists, and even, after the outbreak of World War II, helped plan for nonviolent civilian defense against possible Japanese invasion. In 1942 she was arrested with Gandhi and his inner circle and spent much of the war years detained with him in the Aga Khan's palace.

After the war, as the hour of India's independence in 1947 drew near, Gandhi saw his dreams of a unified, peaceful India crumbling in the face of political ambitions and Muslim-Hindu violence. Mirabehn had gone to work in northern India on projects of agricultural reform. She was there when news came on January 31, 1948, that Gandhi had been assassinated by Hindu nationalists. Stunned by the news, she looked up into the heavens, "and, through the boughs of the trees, the stars were shining in peaceful splendor far, far away. They told of Bapu's spirit released and at peace, and as I gazed on them it was as if Bapu was there — yes, there and with me too. It all became one." She declined to return to Delhi for his state funeral. There was no need. "Bapu must be left in peace, and you must stand on your own legs," she told herself.

Mirabehn lived on in India for ten years after Gandhi's death. Though she was intimately acquainted with the first generation of India's ruling party, she avoided politics, choosing instead to work in the remote northern reaches, near the Himalayas, on village development projects, forestry, and animal husbandry. As she later put it, she was in a state of hibernation. Outwardly she engaged in constructive work, but inside the passion had gone out of her life.

Then one day she received in the mail a new book by Romain Rolland. Something long buried within her began to stir: "Yes, it was the spirit of him from whose music I had been separated for over thirty years that I heard and felt, but now with new vision and inspiration."

She became conscious once more "of the realization of my true self." Thus, she felt liberated to begin a new phase of her life, and a return, after a most circuitous route, to her first love. She left India and devoted the next twenty years of her life to studying the work of Beethoven. She died in Vienna on July 20, 1982, at the age of eighty-nine.

See: Mirabehn, *The Spirit's Pilgrimage* (Arlington, Va.: Great Ocean Publishers, 1984).

Penny Lernoux
Journalist (1940–1989)

"You can look at a slum or peasant village... but it is only by entering into that world — by living in it — that you begin to understand what it is like to be powerless, to be like Christ."

In the 1970s Christians around the world become aware of two extraordinary and related stories unfolding in Latin America. One was about the spread of terror and repression wrought by brutal military dictatorships throughout the continent. The other story concerned the transformation of the Latin American church. Traditionally a conservative institution allied with the rich and powerful, the church was being renewed as a prophetic force, a champion of human rights and the cause of the poor. These stories converged in the imprisonment, torture, and martyrdom of countless Christians, guilty only of professing the gospel message of justice and peace.

One woman who helped to tell these stories to the world was Penny Lernoux, an American journalist based in Latin America. Lernoux first went to Latin America in 1962. Though born a Catholic, she had drifted away from the church, disillusioned in part by its conservatism and seeming irrelevance. In the early 1970s, however, she came into contact with priests and missioners who were living out a different model of the church in solidarity with the poor. The encounter renewed her faith at the same time as it affected her mission as a journalist. As she later wrote,

It was through them that I became aware of and entered into another world — not that of the U.S. Embassy or the upper classes, which comprise the confines of most American journalists, but the suffering and hopeful world of the slums and peasant villages.

The experience changed my life, giving me new faith and a commitment as a writer to tell the truth of the poor to the best of my ability.

While other American journalists were covering the repression in Latin America in terms of a war against communism, Lernoux told the story from the standpoint of the poor. Through her writings, especially her landmark history of the suffering church of Latin America, *Cry of the People*, she became a critical link between the churches and peoples of North and South America. It was clear that her writing was rooted in something deeper than professional commitment; her writing was itself an expression of her faith. She became a witness, a voice for the voiceless, a hero to many who depended on her courage in reporting the truth.

In the church of Latin America she had seen the promise of renewal and reform for the world church. In later years she was saddened by Vatican policies aimed at curbing the influence of this church, the silencing and scorn directed at many of its most prophetic ministers and theologians. Her last book, *People of God*, was a study of the struggle between contending models of world Catholicism, "the church of Caesar, powerful and rich, and the church of Christ — living, poor, and spiritually rich."

Penny Lernoux died on October 8, 1989, one month after being diagnosed with cancer. At the time she was working on a history of the Maryknoll Sisters, the repayment of a debt she felt to the Sisters she had known in Latin America and through whom she had regained her faith. In the end the Maryknoll Sisters took her in, giving her a home in their center in Ossining, New York. It was an unexpected turn in her journey, but one that was mysteriously illuminated in the light of faith. Two weeks before her death she wrote,

> I feel like I'm walking down a new path. It's not physical fear or fear of death, because the courageous poor in Latin America have taught me a theology of life that, through solidarity and our common struggle, transcends death. Rather, it is a sense of helplessness — that I who always wanted to be the champion of the poor am just as helpless — that I, too, must hold out my begging bowl; that I must learn — am learning — the ultimate powerlessness of Christ. It is a cleansing experience. So many things seem less important, or not at all, especially the ambitions.

Penny often quoted a saying in the Latin American church, that "we make our path by walking it." For Penny, it was finally a path that led full circle. She was buried in the cemetery of the Maryknoll Sisters.

See: Tom Fox, "Penny Lernoux: Faithful to the Truth," in *Cloud of Witnesses,* ed. Jim Wallis and Joyce Hollyday (Maryknoll, N.Y.: Orbis Books, 2005); Penny Lernoux, *Cry of the People* (New York: Doubleday, 1980).

Eileen Egan
Peacemaker (1912–2000)

"My life has had a single strain: to see Jesus in every human being, to realize that each one is inviolable and sacred in the eyes of God, and then to translate that into everything I do."

Eileen Egan was born in Wales to Irish Catholic parents. Raised on stories of Irish oppression, she was quick to correct anyone who, deceived by her refined accent, mistook her for English. Others might have been misled by her evident piety and simple dress to believe she was a nun. She was in fact a committed laywoman, engaged in the fields of international relief, journalism, and political activism. Yet she brought to all her activities a strong sense of religious vocation. Inspired by her heroes, Dorothy Day, Mother Teresa, and Mahatma Gandhi, she sought to recognize in all people the image of God. It was she, in fact, who first coined the phrase "seamless garment" to refer to an ethic opposing all recourse to war, economic injustice, capital punishment, abortion, or any practice or ideology that undermined the sacredness of life.

Egan's abhorrence of war came through firsthand experience. In 1943 she joined the newly formed Catholic Relief Services. In Mexico, Spain, and Portugal she worked with refugees, recording their stories of suffering and loss. After the war she helped conduct relief efforts in Germany to assuage the hunger and suffering of a devastated population. Her experiences led to the conclusion that war was diabolical — even when waged for a "just" cause. In war each of the works of mercy enjoined by Christ — whether feeding the hungry, clothing the naked, or sheltering the homeless — was systematically reversed. Instead of feeding the hungry warmakers sought to increase starvation; instead of sheltering the homeless they deliberately targeted the homes of civilians. The logic of war, she believed, was diametrically opposed to the message of the gospel.

But for Egan peace was never simply the absence of conflict. She avoided the term "pacifist" because of its connotations of passivity. Instead she spoke of "active nonviolence" — a positive force, an effort to transform relationships on the basis of justice and reconciliation. It was in fact the most practical response to situations of conflict. But she also believed deeply in the spiritual basis of nonviolence. Peace proceeded from an intuition of our common humanity, a willingness to recognize other human beings as sisters and brothers. This spiritual insight was sharpened by Egan's early discovery of Mother Teresa, whom she first visited in her Calcutta home for the dying in 1955. For the rest of her life she remembered the sight of "the outstretched hands waving feebly, using what infinitesimal strength was left in search for human consolation." And she adopted as her own Mother Teresa's explanation of her mission: "Our work calls us to see Jesus in everyone. He has told us that he is the hungry one. He is the thirsty one. He is the naked one. He is the one who is suffering. These are our treasures. They are Jesus. Each one is Jesus in his distressing disguise."

In addition to her friendship with Mother Teresa, Egan's life was marked by her relationship with Dorothy Day. Egan had visited the Catholic Worker in its early days, thinking that she might join the community on the Bowery. Day apparently sensed that this was not Egan's vocation. Yet the two became intimate collaborators and traveling partners over many decades. Egan served as a contributing editor of the *Catholic Worker*, where she published most of her articles on peace. One of her constant efforts, later elaborated in her final book, *Peace Be with You*, was to show that the spirit of nonviolence was an inextricable dimension of the gospel, evident not only in Jesus' words, but in his death on the cross. His entire mission had been to teach us a new commandment: to love one another, *as he had loved us*. And yet within the early centuries of the church, largely through the work of St. Augustine, Christians had replaced this teaching with a new doctrine: the teaching of "just war," or the way of "justified violence." The effect was to *justify* virtually every subsequent war.

Thus we arrived at the present, when even preparations for the violent destruction of all life on earth could be contemplated as reasonable and justified in the name of national defense. In the name of Jesus, Egan pursued her own mission: to vindicate the ancient spirit of nonviolence, to work toward the day when the word "Christian" might once again be synonymous with "peacemaker."

To work with Eileen Egan was to observe firsthand the qualities that made her such a formidable champion of peace. Always patient, courteous, and apparently compliant, she nevertheless kept her eye trained on her goal, and her will was an immovable object. On any subject with which she disagreed she would always begin by replying, "Yes, I see what you mean," only to stick to her own point until all opposition wilted. This quality enabled her to pursue over several decades the frustrating and seemingly fruitless task of lobbying for peace from the margins of the United Nations, the Vatican, and the American Catholic Bishops' Conference — bodies seemingly as fixed as mountains. Yet when, after decades of effort, she rested from her labors, it was evident that the mountains had moved.

In 1969 it was Egan, acting as a representative for Catholic Relief Services, who first introduced a motion to the U.N. Human Rights Commission to recognize the universal right of conscientious objection. For decades this quixotic cause floated through the back halls of the United Nations — barely noticed, and yet ever alive — until in 1987 it was finally adopted. Similarly, Egan's efforts at lobbying the church went back to Vatican II, when she worked behind the scenes — as Dorothy Day and others fasted — to urge the Council Fathers to take a prophetic stand for the cause of peace. She was rewarded in the last session when the bishops declared that any attack on cities using weapons of mass destruction would constitute "a crime against God and man himself that merits unequivocal and unhesitating condemnation." It was, as she liked to point out, the only condemnation issued by the council.

In the 1960s she was one of the founders of the American branch of Pax Christi. She lobbied the U.S. bishops to take a stand against the Vietnam War and to recognize the right of selective conscientious objection. She was a key advisor to the American bishops in preparing their historic pastoral letter of 1983, "The Challenge of Peace," which recognized gospel nonviolence as an authentic Catholic tradition. (At the time of her death over one hundred American bishops were members of Pax Christi USA.)

She personally practiced the values she taught. In 1992, when she was seventy-nine, Egan was mugged on her way to Mass. She suffered a broken hip and fractured ribs. Yet all her concern was for the homeless man who had attacked her. After his arrest, she reached out to him with concern and forgiveness and tried to see that he received the counseling and treatment he required.

Egan proudly stood beside those who risked prison for the cause of peace. But this was not her way. She was, rather, the one who attended the endless, boring meetings, spoke with anyone who would listen, and did the unglamorous and apparently unheroic work behind the scenes, fostering channels of dialogue that might ultimately yield unexpected fruits.

She died on October 7, 2000, at the age of eighty-eight.

See: Eileen Egan, *Peace Be with You: Justified Warfare or the Way of Nonviolence* (Maryknoll, N.Y.: Orbis Books, 1999); *Such a Vision of the Street: Mother Teresa — The Spirit and the Work* (New York: Doubleday, 1986).

Dorothee Soelle
Theologian (1929–2003)

"God, your Spirit renews the face of the earth.
Renew our hearts also
And give us your spirit of lucidity and courage.
For the law of the Spirit
Who makes us alive in Christ
Has set us free from the law of resignation.
Teach us
How to live with the power of the wind and of the sun
And to let other creatures live."

Dorothee Soelle was born in Cologne, Germany, in 1929. As a child she played no personal role in the rise and fall of the Third Reich; she was fifteen when the war ended. But as revelations unfolded about the full extent of the Nazi crimes she was filled with an "ineradicable shame": the shame of "belonging to this people, speaking the language of the concentration camp guards, singing the songs that were also sung in the Hitler Youth." Her young adulthood was spent reflecting on the great question of her generation: How could this have happened? The hollow answer of the older generation, that "we didn't know what was happening," impressed on her the duty to question authority, to rebel, and to remember "the lessons of the dead."

The moral and existential challenge of her times led Soelle to study philosophy and, later, theology. She was one of the principal authors of the so-called "political theology" — an effort to counter the privatized and spiritualized character of "bourgeois" religion through the subversive memory of Jesus and his social message. In light of the Holocaust she was particularly critical of a "superficial understanding of sin" largely confined to personal morality. "Sin," she wrote, "has to do not just with what we do, but with what we allow to happen." Her initial challenge was to develop a "post-Auschwitz theology," an understanding of God who does not float above history and its trauma but who shares intimately in the suffering of the victims. Such an understanding of God defined, in turn, a new meaning for Christian discipleship.

A true prophet, Soelle did not simply denounce the way things were, but looked forward to a "new heaven and a new earth." Her theology was inflected with poetry and drew on her wide reading of literature and her love of music and art. She bore four children from a first marriage. The experience of motherhood strengthened her hope for the future, while reminding her that pain and joy are inextricably combined in the struggle for new life. She met her second husband, at the time a Benedictine monk, when they collaborated as organizers of a "Political Evensong" in Cologne. Beginning in 1968, this ecumenical gathering of Christians joined to worship and reflect on scripture in light of the political challenges of the day — whether the Vietnam War, human rights, or the campaign for social justice. It became a hugely popular event, regularly drawing up to a thousand participants. The gatherings were controversial, however. Their notoriety was among the factors that prevented Soelle — despite her thirty books — from ever receiving a full professorship in a German university.

Nevertheless, from 1975 to 1987 she spent six months each year as a professor of systematic theology at Union Theological Seminary in New York. It was a particularly fruitful time for her, as she broadened her theological perspective in dialogue with feminism, ecological consciousness, and third world liberation theologies. She also continued to translate her theology into political activism — in solidarity with embattled Christians in Central and South America, in the struggle against apartheid in South Africa, and in particular in resisting the nuclear arms race.

The decision of NATO in 1979 to deploy tactical nuclear weapons in Europe made her decide "to spend the rest of my life in the service of peace." She was arrested several times for civil disobedience and was tireless in challenging the churches to take action against what she saw as preparations for a new global holocaust. In an address to the General Assembly of the World Council of Churches in 1983 she began, "Dear sisters and brothers, I speak to you as a woman from one of the richest countries of the earth. A country with a bloody history that reeks of gas, a history some of us Germans have not been able to forget." It was this experience that impelled her to raise a cry of alarm. Never again should a generation of Christians employ the excuse that "we didn't know" about plans and preparations for mass murder.

In her later writings she increasingly spoke of the need to join mysticism and political commitment. She defined mysticism not as a new vision of God, "but a different relationship with the world — one that has borrowed the eyes of God."

Soelle died on April 27, 2003, at the age of seventy-three.

See: Dorothee Soelle, *Against the Wind: Memoir of a Radical Christian* (Minneapolis: Augsburg Fortress, 1999); Sarah K. Pinnock, ed., *The Theology of Dorothee Soelle* (Harrisburg, Pa.: Trinity Press International, 2003).

BLESSED ARE THOSE WHO ARE PERSECUTED FOR RIGHTEOUSNESS' SAKE

A young mother • a "heretic" • a recusant Catholic • a devout Protestant • an obstinate Quaker • a conscientious nun • a "witch" • four who shared "the same fate as the poor"

Christ predicted persecution for his followers, a prophecy fulfilled in the very first generation of the church. In the following years, when Christianity was an outlawed sect, persecution and martyrdom were the consummate signs of faithful discipleship — the defining marks of sanctity. In fact, the veneration of the martyrs was the original basis for the cult of the saints. Among these holy witnesses, women held a special place.

Though Christianity was eventually embraced by the empire, the era of persecution never truly ended, nor can it, so long as the gospel message continues to interfere with the values and powers of this world. In every age the church has been renewed by the witness of those members who remained faithful to the end, regardless of the cost.

That "cost of discipleship" might take different forms, not all of them involving the shedding of blood. Daily life supplies its own smaller arenas: the challenge to stand up for a stranger, to defend an unpopular principle, to confront friends and family members when they are wrong. Each situation asks us to determine where our heart's loyalty ultimately lies. We can never anticipate when we may be called to account for our faith. But to all who shoulder his cross, Christ made this promise: "The Kingdom of Heaven will be theirs."

St. Blandina and Companions
Martyrs of Lyons (177)

*"They asked for life and He gave it them; they shared it with their neigh-
bors, and departed to God in every way victorious. Having always loved
peace and having ever commended peace to us, they went in peace to God,
leaving no sorrow to their Mother [the Church], nor strife nor conflict to
their brethren, but joy and peace and concord and love."*

Roman persecution of Christians in the first three centuries occurred
in sporadic waves. Long periods of benign neglect were punctuated by
fierce storms, often of quite specific location and duration. One notable
storm occurred in 177 in the city of Lyons in the province of Gaul. The
story of this persecution was recorded in great detail in a letter from
the Christians of Lyons. One of the most precious documents of the
early church, it was included in the famous Ecclesiastical History by
Eusebius.

The process started with social ostracism, as Christians were excluded from the public baths and markets. This led to greater indignities — insults, blows, stone-throwing — until finally the state stepped
in, rounding up Christians for public interrogation. When this yielded
no incriminating information, non-Christian slaves were brought in for
questioning. Their damning testimony — regardless of how it was induced — of incest, cannibalism, and other abominations fully confirmed
the prejudices of the court and incited the fury of the attending mob.
Afterward, the Christians were subjected to unspeakable tortures. Still,
they would neither confess to any crime nor renounce their faith, saying
only "We are Christians, and nothing vile is done among us."

The martyrs, who numbered close to fifty, were executed in a variety
of ways. Some were fed to wild beasts in the arena. Others were roasted
alive. According to the contemporary account, "They offered up to the
Father a single wreath, but it was plaited of diverse colors and flowers
of all kinds."

Among the individuals featured in this account were Bishop Pothi-
nus and a slave girl, Blandina, "in whom Christ made manifest that the
things that appear mean and contemptible among men are esteemed of
great glory with God, on account of that love of Him which is shown
in truth and not in appearances." Her companions, who included her
"mistress according to the flesh," feared that Blandina would wilt under
pressure. Instead, "she was endued with so much power that even those

who in relays tortured her from morning until evening grew faint and weary."

When she was hung on a stake, she became for her fellow Christians an image of Christ himself: "The sight of this woman, as it were crucified, praying with a loud voice, put much heart in the combatants. Their sister showed to their fleshly eyes him who was crucified for them, assuring those who believed on him that everyone who suffers for the glory of Christ has fellowship with the living God forever."

The last among her party to die, this slave was likened to "a mother of high degree," who, "after encouraging her children and sending them on before as victors to the King, hastened to join them — rejoicing and triumphing over her departure as if she had been summoned to a marriage feast instead of being cast to the beasts.... The heathen themselves confessed that they had never known a woman to show such endurance."

After their deaths, the bodies of Blandina and her companions were thrown into the Rhone River so as to leave no relics or graves for their friends. As it turned out, however, their story provided a living memorial. News of their witness quickly traveled throughout the empire, thereby — defying the intentions of their enemies — inspiring and strengthening the resolve of the faithful.

See: Eusebius, *Ecclesiastical History* (New York: Fathers of the Church, 1953).

Sts. Perpetua and Felicity
Martyrs (d. 203)

"Stand fast in the faith, and love ye one another;
and be not offended because of our passion."

There are few more poignant documents of the early church than "The Passion of Sts. Perpetua and Felicity." Indeed, the story of these two early martyrs was so popular in the North African church that St. Augustine complained that it was more widely read than the Gospels. Perpetua was a prosperous young woman, married and the mother of a newborn son, who lived in Carthage in the late second century. At the age of twenty-two she was arrested with her servant Felicity and several male companions, apparently for violating a prohibition against conversion to Christianity.

Part of the striking power of this narrative derives from the fact that it purports to represent the voice of Perpetua herself, as she languished in prison under sentence of death. It is thus a uniquely personal document, filled with painfully intimate details and strikingly free of the stereotypical conventions of later hagiography. Perpetua emerges not simply as a "type," but as a fully realized person, subject to hunger, fears, and even — as a nursing mother, separated from her child — the pain of swollen breasts.

The last detail points to the other obvious distinction of the narrative. This is not the disembodied voice of a generic Christian — but a Christian *woman*. The modern reader can hardly ignore the pervasive significance of gender throughout the narrative. While the overall "plot" focuses on Perpetua's approaching passion, she is called throughout to negotiate a series of complications arising from her status as a woman — daughter, mother, and spouse (though interestingly her husband is never mentioned). Throughout we sense the struggle of a woman to claim her own identity and vocation amid the various competing claims imposed by society. Even at her trial the proconsul appeals to her sense of duty toward her aged father and her infant son. Perpetua answers the court with the simple declaration, "I am a Christian." One senses that in Christ she has found the power and freedom to name herself and the courage to accept the consequences.

And yet there is no suggestion that Perpetua scorns motherhood or the bonds of family. The narrative describes in touching detail the sufferings caused by the separation from her infant. But when he is restored to her and she is able to nurse him, "straightway I became well, and was lightened of my labor and care for the child; and suddenly the prison was made a palace for me, so that I would sooner be there than anywhere else." The main torture for Perpetua comes from the pleading of her aged father, who resorts to bullying threats as well as abject tears in an effort to dissuade her from her path. Perpetua looks upon him with genuine pity for his "unhappy old age," but also with sadness at the thought that he, as a non-Christian, cannot rejoice in the prospect of her passion.

Perpetua herself does not relish the prospect of death. But in a series of prophetic visions she finds the conviction that her fate is ordained and that her brief suffering will lead to eternal reward. She is consoled finally to be able to entrust her son to safe hands, and so receives the grace to bear whatever may come. She is undeterred when, at their trial, she and her companions receive the most terrifying sentence — to fight with wild beasts in the amphitheater. For in another dream she perceives that she will be fighting "not with beasts, but against the devil; and I knew that mine was the victory."

Her portion of the narrative ends on a haunting note — the actual words of a prisoner on the eve of her death: "Thus far have I written this, till the day before the games; but the deed of the games themselves let him write who will."

Eyewitnesses did complete her narrative. And so we also learn something about her companion and servant Felicity. Eight months pregnant at the time of her imprisonment, Felicity was fearful that because of her condition she would be separated from the fate of her companions. But after a night of ardent prayer, she went into labor and gave birth to a daughter, whom she was able to entrust to Christian friends.

On their last day of life the prisoners celebrated a "Love Feast," attended by many local Christians. The next morning, "the day of their victory," the prisoners went forth from the darkness of their prison into the glaring amphitheater, "as it were to heaven, cheerful and bright of countenance." Perpetua wore the expression of a "true spouse of Christ," while Felicity, rejoicing that her child was born in safety, "came now from blood to blood, from the midwife to the gladiator, to wash after her travail in a second baptism."

Once more Perpetua was urged to abjure her faith. But she refused. We hear her voice a final time — now with a conviction that resounds through the ages: "For this cause came we willingly unto this, that our liberty might not be obscured. For this cause have we devoted our lives."

Perpetua and Felicity were set in the arena together. At first they were stripped, causing the crowd to shudder "seeing one a tender girl, the other her breasts yet dropping from her late childbearing." And so in a final ironic concession to their womanhood they were permitted to cover themselves. They were then exposed to a savage cow, which tossed them about on its horns. When they had survived this ordeal the executioner was ordered to put them to the sword. But the swordsman was apparently a novice and had trouble striking a true blow. The narrator relates that Perpetua, in the final mark of mastery over her fate, directed the sword to her own neck: "Perhaps so great a woman could not else have been slain had she not herself so willed it."

A final poignant image remains. The narrator notes that before meeting the sword the two young women, formerly mistress and servant, now sisters in Christ, turned to one another before the jeering crowd and exchanged a kiss.

See: "The Passion of SS. Perpetua and Felicity," trans. Walter Shewring, in *Saints Are Not Sad*, ed. F. J. Sheed (New York: Sheed & Ward, 1949).

St. Crispina
Martyr (d. 304)

"A religion that inflicts torture on those who do not adhere to it is not a religion."

Crispina, a Christian noblewoman from North Africa, was the mother of several children. During a period of anti-Christian persecution in 304 she was arrested and brought before Anulinus, the proconsul of Theveste. In the transcript of her trial, our main source of information about her life, she emerges as a woman of exceptional courage and self-possession. Clearly unimpressed by the power of her judge, she confronts his threats with stern patience and uncompromising dignity. Having overcome the fear of death, she has nothing to fear from any mortal adversary. Her attitude brings to mind the words of Julian of Norwich several centuries later: "The worst has already happened and been repaired."

ANULINUS: Crispina, do you know the text of the religious edict?

CRISPINA: Not at all. What does it command?

ANULINUS: To sacrifice to all our gods for the safety of the emperors....

CRISPINA: I have never sacrificed and I will not sacrifice, except to the one true God and to our savior Jesus Christ, his Son, who was born and suffered.

ANULINUS: Renounce your superstition and bow your head to the statues of the Roman gods.

CRISPINA: Each day I invoke my almighty God; I know no others than him.

ANULINUS: You are insolent and out of your mind. You will learn at your cost the rigor of our laws.

274

CRISPINA: No matter what happens, I will readily suffer in the name of the faith that I have embraced.

ANULINUS: Do you have to be so stupid as to persevere obstinately in superstition and not worship our holy deities?

CRISPINA: I worship every day but the one I worship is the true and living God; he is my Lord and I know none other than him...

ANULINUS: But you are obliged to serve these gods whom you disdain, if you wish to remain alive and practice a religion.

CRISPINA: A religion that inflicts torture on those who do not adhere to it is not a religion....I have remained a stranger to your rites, and as long as I live I shall never honor them.

ANULINUS: But you will have to if you want to escape the severity of the law.

CRISPINA: Your threats do not terrify me; they are nothing....I sacrifice to the eternal God who lives forever and ever; he is the true God who is to be feared. He made the sea, the green fields, the sand of the desert. What have I to fear from those who are only his creatures?

ANULINUS: Observe the Roman religion, like our masters, the ever-victorious Caesars, and ourselves.

CRISPINA: I have told you once and I tell you again, I am ready to undergo any torture you may inflict, but I shall never defile my soul through contact with your idols of stone, made by human hands.

At this point Anulinus ordered that her head be shaved, as a sign of degradation, but Crispina remained resolute.

ANULINUS: Do you want to live a long time or die in torment, like so many of your companions?

CRISPINA: If I wanted to die and deliver my soul to the ravages of eternal fire, I would put my faith in your demons.

ANULINUS: I will cut off your head if you refuse to worship our venerable gods.

CRISPINA: I give thanks to God for such an end. With all my heart I accept having my head cut off for my God.

After hearing the sentence, Crispina replied: I bless my God and thank him for the grace that he accords me in thus freeing me from your hands. Thanks be to him.

After marking herself with the sign of the cross, Crispina knelt and offered her neck to the executioner.

See: "The Acts of Crispina," Bruno Chenu et al., *The Book of Christian Martyrs* (New York: Crossroad, 1990).

Marguerite Porete
Beguine Martyr (d. 1310)

"I beg you, those who read these words, try to understand them inwardly, in the innermost depths of your understanding, with all the subtle powers at your command, or else you run the risk of failing to understand them at all."

It is hard to imagine any greater betrayal of the spirit of Christ than the impulse to crucify and burn one's enemies. Sadly, it is an impulse that the church itself, through a good part of its history, has found hard to resist. One such victim was the Beguine mystic and preacher Marguerite Porete.

What little we know of Marguerite Porete is preserved in the proceedings of the Inquisitorial court in Paris that condemned her as a heretic in 1310. The record and her writings suggest that, whatever her errors, she was a holy woman whose heart burned with the love of God. Of the men who condemned her, whatever may be said of their good intentions, it is hard to conclude otherwise than that they loved orthodoxy more than they loved Christ.

Marguerite was identified as a Beguine, that is, a member of a loosely organized religious movement of women popular in the Lowlands of her time. The origin of the term "Beguine" is disputed; among its opponents it served as a term of contempt, like the label of "heretic" itself or, more recently, "communist." Strictly speaking it referred to a network of small communities of Christian laywomen united in a life devoted to prayer and charity. These women sought to live quiet lives of devotion without taking religious vows, thus basically opting out of the economic and ecclesiastical structures of their society.

As religious women attempting to define a spiritual identity in the world without recourse to ecclesiastical approbation, the Beguines were subject to waves of persecution. But they also had their protectors. A number of well-known mystics were associated with the Beguines, including Mechthild of Magdeburg and Hadewijch, whose writings were widely read and admired.

Marguerite Porete was somewhat outside the usual mold in that she was apparently not based in a particular community, but chose to travel and publicly preach her spiritual message. She also wrote a book, *A Mirror for Simple Souls,* that describes her mystical spirituality. It was because of these ideas and her persistence in preaching that she was arrested by the Inquisition in Paris.

A Mirror for Simple Souls is a mystical discourse on divine charity, written in the form of a dialogue between the Soul and Reason. The aim of the book is to encourage the pursuit of spiritual perfection in a state of loving communion with God and one's neighbors. Addressed to "simple souls" it is anything but a simple work. The Inquisitors who examined her writing converted her poetic language into a series of propositions that were deemed heretical. As was often the case with mystics, she was accused of propagating a spirituality that dispensed with the church in favor of direct communion with God.

On April 11, 1310, a team of canon lawyers proclaimed her guilty of heresy. Her writings were publicly burned. On June 1, after being turned over to the secular arm for punishment, she was herself burned at the stake as an unrepentant heretic. Her death began a new wave of official persecution of the Beguines. Two years later the movement was formally suppressed.

See: A Mirror for Simple Souls: The Mystical Work of Marguerite Porete (New York: Crossroad, 1990).

Anne Askew
Protestant Martyr (1521–1546)

"Lord, I heartily desire of Thee, that Thou wilt of Thy merciful goodness forgive them that violence which they do, and have done unto me. So be it, Lord."

For his role in countering the "Lutheran heresy," King Henry VIII was honored by a grateful pope with the title Defender of the Faith. Though he subsequently placed that title in jeopardy by declaring himself supreme head of the Church of England, Henry continued to hold to certain essentials of the Catholic faith, including the doctrine of Christ's real presence in the Eucharist. While he might execute his old friend St. Thomas More for refusing to recognize the king's supremacy over the church, he could be equally merciless in the persecution of Protestants. The stories of these latter witnesses form the final chapter of *Foxe's Book of Martyrs,* an "anti-papist" martyrology that did much to fuel the Reformation movement in England.

Among Foxe's celebrated martyrs was Anne Askew, a young woman of twenty-four who was arrested and executed for her beliefs in 1546. She was born to a noble family in Lincolnshire in 1521. When she was fifteen she was forcibly married to a widower named Thomas Kyme. Though Anne went on to bear two children, it was an unhappy match. Among other things, Kyme apparently objected to his wife's religious zeal. "She was the devoutest woman I've ever known," he commented, by which he intended no compliment. She eventually left him and traveled to London to find a happier community among her fellow Protestants. It was there, where she took up preaching and distributing religious tracts, that she was arrested and brought to trial.

In jail she was subjected to cruel torture on the rack, an effort to force her to reveal the names of her associates. Though she endured all this without yielding, she was left so broken — unable to walk or stand — that she had to be carried into her trial on a chair. Her own account of her interrogation was later smuggled abroad, where it became one of the great inspirational documents of the Reformation.

With her tart replies and frequent citations of scripture, Anne met and parried all her interrogator's questions. When asked directly if she did not believe that the sacrament hanging over the altar was the very body of Christ, she "demanded this question of him: wherefore Saint Stephen was stoned to death. And he said he could not tell. Then I answered that no more would I assoil his vain question." When asked if it was true that she had said she would rather read five lines in the Bible than hear five masses in the temple, she confessed that she had, for "the one did greatly edify me, and the other nothing at all." To the question whether a mouse eating the host received God or no, she gave no answer, but merely smiled.

In the end she was convicted of heresy and sentenced to die. She spent her last hours writing an account of her ordeal that ended with this prayer: "O Lord, I have more enemies now than there be hairs on my head. Yet, Lord, let them never overcome me with vain words but fight Thou, Lord, in my stead: for on Thee cast I my care."

She was carried to the stake on July 16, 1546. After she was doused with gunpowder, a messenger from the king arrived with the promise of pardon if she would recant or name her confederates, but she would not retreat. And so, as John Foxe recorded, "Having passed through so many torments, having now ended the long course of her agonies, being compassed in with flames of fire, as a blessed sacrifice unto God, she slept in the Lord, in anno 1546, leaving behind her a singular example of Christian constancy for all men to follow."

See: John Foxe, *Acts and Monuments* (1563).

St. Margaret Clitherow
English Martyr (d. 1586)

"Jesu, have mercy on me."

Margaret Clitherow was the first woman martyr for the Catholic faith in England during the reign of Queen Elizabeth. The daughter of a wealthy wax merchant of York, she married John Clitherow, a prosperous butcher, at the age of sixteen. Though raised as a Protestant, Margaret converted to the Catholic faith some years after her marriage, apparently inspired by the sufferings of so many Catholics under the repressive penal laws of the time. John Clitherow did not share his wife's new faith, but he placed no obstacles in her way, even when her public reputation as a Catholic incurred fines and other penalties. At one point Margaret was imprisoned for almost two years. She welcomed this as a period of retreat and put her time to good use by learning to read.

Despite the proven risks, Margaret offered a safe haven in her home for fugitive priests, housing them in a specially hidden room where she and other underground Catholics could attend Mass. Her husband turned a blind eye to these goings-on, though she made little secret of her faith. Often she was seen praying at the site of the gallows where many priests had offered their lives. On March 10, 1586, she was arrested. A search of her house uncovered the secret room along with vestments and other vessels and books obviously intended for Mass. Charged with sponsoring illegal religious services, she refused to enter a plea, hoping thus to spare her family and friends the risks of testifying in a trial. She knew, however, that this would automatically incur a judgment against her and the terrible penalty of death by pressing.

In vain the judge urged her to seek the mercy of the court, entreating her to consider her obligations to her husband and children. "I do honor my husband and love my children, according as duty and nature bindeth me," she replied with stalwart conviction, "but I am so far from seeking to help them by yielding unto your desires as that I wish both husband and children might suffer death with me in this good cause." While she was imprisoned she was not permitted to see her children, and only once saw her husband in the presence of the jailer. When he heard of her sentencing, John Clitherow "was like a man distracted, crying out that they would murder the best wife within the kingdom and the best Catholic."

She spent the last night of her life in prayer, accompanied by the jailer's wife, whose company she had requested ("Not that I fear death, for that is comfort; but the flesh is frail"). The next morning, March 25, she was taken to the site of her execution. Aside from her executioners there were a number of persons present, including several women. The sentence required that she be stripped naked for execution. The sheriff refused her request to forego this humiliation, but he and the men agreed to avert their eyes while the women undressed her.

Urged to beg the queen's forgiveness and also that of her husband, she replied, "If ever I have offended him, I do ask him for forgiveness from the bottom of my heart." Then she was placed on a sharp stone with a board laid over her on which steadily increasing weights were applied. She endured this punishment for only fifteen minutes before her ribs were shattered. Her last words were "Jesu, Jesu, Jesu, have mercy on me."

She was canonized in 1970 by Pope Paul VI. Her feast is celebrated on October 25 among the "Forty Martyrs of England and Wales."

See: Father John Mush, "Bl. Margaret Clitherow," in *Martyrs: From St. Stephen to John Tung,* ed. Donald Attwater (New York: Sheed & Ward, 1957).

Mary Dyer
Quaker Martyr (d. 1660)

"In obedience to the will of the Lord I came,
and in His will I abide faithful to the death."

Three hundred years after her death, a bronze statue of Mary Dyer was placed in front of the State House in Boston, near the site where she was hanged. It bears the inscription: "My life not availeth me in comparison to the liberty of the truth."

Mary Dyer first arrived in Boston in 1635. Governor Winthrop of Massachusetts later described her as "the wife of one William Dyer, a milliner in the New Exchange, a very proper and fair woman." At first there was little to distinguish the Dyers from their Puritan neighbors, until, as Winthrop put it, they were "both of them notoriously infected with Mrs. Hutchinson's errors." The source of this "infection" — Anne Hutchinson — was a prophet whose preaching and free spirit scandalized the elders of the Commonwealth, leading to her arrest and expulsion from Boston. The Dyers were among those who followed Hutchinson into exile in Rhode Island. But for Mary this was not the end of her spiritual journey. During a later trip to England she embraced the teachings of George Fox and became a convinced Quaker.

The Quakers rejected external religious authority in favor of the Inner Light dwelling in each soul. Though they matched the Puritans in their plain and simple style, their commitment to freedom of conscience and religious tolerance was anathema to the governors of Massachusetts. In 1656, just before Mary's return from England, the Massachusetts General Court enacted a series of severe laws against "the cursed sect of heretics...commonly called Quakers," which authorized the banishing, whipping, and imprisonment of any Quaker apprehended in the Commonwealth.

Mary was unaware of these new laws when she returned home by way of Boston. Nevertheless, she was arrested on the spot and held in jail for over two months, until her husband found her. He won her release upon his promise that she would return no more to Massachusetts.

In 1658 a further law was passed in Boston imposing the penalty of death on unrepentant Quakers. When Mary learned that several of her Quaker friends were imprisoned there, she ignored the danger and went to visit them. Again she was arrested. And yet again she was released and banished — this time under threat of execution should she return. But when two of her companions returned to Boston, determined "to look the bloody laws in the face," Mary returned once more and was imprisoned again. This time she was sentenced to death.

On October 27 Mary and her two companions were marched through the streets to an elm tree on Boston Common that served as a gallows. Walking hand in hand, they were accompanied by beating drums to prevent them from speaking to the gathering crowd. Their expressions gave no evidence that they were walking toward their deaths. "It is an hour of the greatest joy I can enjoy in this world," Mary said. "No eye can hear, no tongue can speak, no heart can understand, the sweet incomes and refreshings of the spirit of the Lord which now I enjoy." Mary watched as her fellow Quakers were hanged. Then she herself was bound and blindfolded, the noose was placed over her neck, and she readied herself for death, only to be spared by the arrival of a last-minute reprieve.

Back in her cell, stunned and shaken by this cruel charade, Mary addressed a letter to the court: "Once more [to] the General Court, Assembled in Boston, speaks Mary Dyer, even as before: My life is not accepted, neither availeth me, in Comparison of the Lives and Liberty of the Truth and Servants of the Living God, for which in the Bowels of Love and Meekness I sought you; yet nevertheless, with wicked Hands have you put two of them to Death, which makes me to feel, that the Mercies of the Wicked is Cruelty: I rather chose to Dye than to live, as from you, as Guilty of their Innocent Blood."

Again Mary was forcibly removed from the Commonwealth under threat of certain death if she should return. But her conscience would allow her no heed for her own safety. She was determined to defy the authorities, challenging them to annul their unjust laws or, by her death, to awaken popular indignation against them. Six months later, without warning her husband, she returned again to Boston, and for the third time she was arrested.

On May 31, 1660, she appeared in court before Governor Endicott and was sentenced to die the next morning. When she heard the sentence, Mary replied, "I came in obedience to the will of God to the last General Court desiring you to appeal your unrighteous laws of banishment on pain of death, and that same is my work now, and earnest request, although I told you that if you refused to repeal them the Lord would send others of his servants to witness against them."

The next day, June 1, she was led to her death. One of her persecutors was heard to observe, "She hangs there as a flag for others to take example by" — a statement subject to more than one interpretation. In any case, Mary Dyer was the last Quaker executed in Boston.

See: Jessamyn West, *The Quaker Reader* (Harrisburg, Pa.: Morehouse, 1992).

Mary Ward
Founder of the Institute of the
Blessed Virgin Mary (1586–1645)

"I think, dear child, the trouble and the long loneliness you hear me speak of is not far from me, which whensoever it is, happy success will follow.... The pain is great, but very endurable, because He who lays on the burden also carries it."

In the lives of the great founders and reformers of religious orders there is ample record of the obstacles, calumnies, and persecution they endured as the price for charting new waters. Many of these stories end on a seemingly inevitable note of triumph. The story of Mary Ward, however, reminds us of the many others whose lonely struggles failed to surmount the obstacles in their path and whose dreams had to be entrusted to future generations.

Mary Ward's life began against the background of Elizabethan England and the intense persecution of the Catholic religion. Her family was among the landed gentry whose wealth and title allowed some private space to resist the severe anti-Catholic decrees. Her childhood was marked by secret visits from priests — often Jesuits — who had been quickly ordained overseas, smuggled into the country, and secretly passed from house to house to celebrate their forbidden Masses. This illicit practice of the Catholic religion was an act of treason, which could mean death not only for the priest but for the sheltering family.

Mary was beautiful and clever, and her family urged her to accept one of the marriage proposals that were readily available. But Mary would have none of it. She insisted instead that she was called to become a nun. This was a somewhat fantastic ambition, given that at the time there was not a single convent in England. Nevertheless, with the grudging support of a confessor, she won her family's approval and so was smuggled out of the country to Catholic Belgium.

When she presented herself there to a bishop, she was disappointed when he instructed her to accept a position as a lay Sister — essentially a servant — to a community of Poor Clares. Though she found this assignment uncongenial, she nevertheless complied obediently, until a visiting superior of the order recognized her special qualities and set her free to pursue her true vocation.

Unfortunately, Mary had difficulty finding such a vocation among the opportunities at hand. Her search led her through a number of false starts and dead ends. She had come to believe that she was not called to conventional enclosed religious life. Instead, inspired by the example of the Jesuits, she conceived of an institute of women living in a non-enclosed community, free of episcopal authority, who could carry out apostolic work in the world. To say the least, it was an idea ahead of its time.

Nevertheless, Mary was able to convince a number of influential church authorities, including a good Jesuit confessor, of the value of her plan. There followed the first of a number of clandestine visits to England to seek recruits for her community. If she did not have to resort to the subterfuge of the underground priests, she still had to be wary of the constant threat of spies. In the disguise of a traveling gentlewoman she made her rounds of the Catholic households, exhorting the faithful, assisting priests in preparing people for baptism and the other sacraments, visiting and comforting priests in prison, and inspiring a half dozen women to take the leap with her into the unknown.

During one of her visits she was finally discovered and thrust into prison. Sentenced to death, she fully expected to meet her end. But as a result of external political factors of the time, she was spared the ultimate punishment and was instead permitted to accept exile. Back in Europe Mary went about forming her band of followers into a religious community as she simultaneously engaged in the labyrinthine pursuit of official approval for her Institute. She traveled to Rome and won an audience with the pope, who gave her tentative permission to develop her project. The formal recognition she sought, however, was not forthcoming.

As she discovered, her enemies were not only in Protestant England. Her devotion to the spiritual vision of St. Ignatius fed the distrust of secular clergy, who were rivals of the glamorous Society of Jesus. Her Institute was mocked as a house of "Lady Jesuits." But beyond the territorial jealousies of English Catholics, there was the wider resistance, in principle, to the radical program that Mary outlined. While elements of her program were admired — especially her proposal for free schools for Catholic girls — her adamant insistence that the Institute be non-enclosed and that it remain free of episcopal jurisdiction ran head-on against the prescribed place of women in the church. While some bishops offered polite approval for her plans, most ultimately shared the opinion of one priest who, while admiring the Sisters' fervor, noted, "When all is done they are but women!"

After she had established houses in a number of cities and had won wide admiration for her exemplary schools, notification came from Rome in January 1631 that the Institute was to be suppressed. Within days messengers arrived to take Mary into custody on the charge of being a "heretic, schismatic, and rebel to the Holy Church." Though her imprisonment in a convent was brief, the suppression of the Institute continued in effect, and she remained under a cloud of ecclesial disapprobation.

In broken health she returned to England. The penal laws against Catholics were still in effect, and once again she faced surveillance and the possibility of arrest. She died in York at the age of sixty on January 23, 1645. In 1703 the Rule of her Institute was finally confirmed by Pope Clement XI.

See: Mary Oliver, I.B.V.M., *Mary Ward* (New York: Sheed & Ward, 1959).

Rebecca Nurse and Companions
"Witches" of Salem (1692)

"I have nobody to look to but God."

It began in early 1692 in the town of Salem, Massachusetts, with a circle of young girls who liked to meet in the forest and dabble in charms and potions. When some of them began exhibiting strange symptoms of mania, doctors and divines of the town suspected the Devil's handiwork. Their suspicions were confirmed when first one, then another, and finally the whole coterie of these girls began identifying witches and wizards among their neighbors. In lurid detail, they described terrifying visitations by "spectral images" who inflicted various physical and mental torments on their victims and who bid them cast away their souls and sign their names in the Devil's Book.

In Puritan New England, where fear of the Devil was as palpable as the fear of God, such charges were taken with the utmost seriousness. Even those who might stumble over the Ten Commandments could easily recite the fearsome words of scripture, "Thou shalt not suffer a witch to live."

For most of a year the search for and discovery of witches among the denizens of Salem was like a raging storm. Over a hundred men and women were arrested and imprisoned. Twenty in all were put to death, while another eight perished in jail. In virtually all these cases the verdict rested on so-called "spectral evidence," the claim — impossible to verify or disprove — that the Devil had assumed a witch's "shape" in order to haunt some righteous soul. Everyone accepted, as an article of faith, that it was only by a witch's consent that the Devil could assume her appearance.

The trials were conducted in the presence of the "afflicted children," who would cry out and shriek, as if under some phantasmal attack, whenever any doubt was expressed as to their credibility. While most of the defendants protested their innocence, a sufficient number saved their lives by "confessing" their guilt and pointing an accusing finger toward other "unrepentant" confederates. Such confessions helped fuel the flames.

Some of the accused witches were persons of suspect character. It was an especially troubling development, however, when charges were leveled against persons of pious reputation. Notable among these was Rebecca Nurse, a seventy-one-year-old wife and mother of eight, widely known for her faith, her charity toward all, and her simple goodness. It is notable evidence of her character that thirty-nine prominent members of the community, at considerable risk to their own safety and reputation, signed a petition on her behalf.

A deposition by two of her neighbors described how they had gone to visit Rebecca soon after the first accusations were leveled against her. Rebecca reportedly "grieved" for the poor girls and "pitied them with all her heart and went to God for them," though she was troubled by the belief that some of the accused were "as innocent as she was." When she learned that she herself had been named by the girls, she exclaimed, "I am as innocent as the child unborn."

Even the magistrate who first interrogated Rebecca on March 24 seemed skeptical of the charges, repeatedly asking the accusers if they could be certain that it was Goody Nurse who had tormented them. The charges, however, were particularly serious. One of her accusers claimed to have been visited by the spirits of babies whom Rebecca Nurse had supposedly murdered. Whenever the judge wavered in his attitude, the girls would scream and faint. When Nurse, attempting in vain to speak in her own defense, extended her hands, the girls were seemingly compelled to mimic her motions.

In the face of these theatrics, the judge wondered that Rebecca could retain her composure. "You do not know my heart," she whispered.

Rebecca Nurse and Companions

When he urged her to confess and "give glory to God," Rebecca answered, "Would you have me belie myself?"

Astonishingly, the jury hearing Nurse's case on June 30 at first returned a verdict of not guilty. This provoked such an uproar from the audience — both from the "afflicted" girls and the spectators — that the chief justice enjoined the jury to retire and think again. Upon further deliberation, they returned a guilty verdict, and Nurse was sentenced to death.

After being publicly excommunicated from her church, "abandoned to the devil and eternally damned," Rebecca Nurse was hanged on Gallow's Hill with four other women on July 19. Their bodies were cast in a shallow grave. But later, in darkness, Rebecca's children removed her body and buried her in a secret location.

Eventually the fire in Salem ran its course. After some months people grew weary of the drama, with its ever-widening net, and the flimsy evidence that had sent so many people to their deaths. And then, in private shame, they began to confront the horror of what they had done.

Particular discredit fell to the theologians and ministers of the gospel who had proudly, and with so little mercy, arrayed themselves as God's agents in this cosmic battle: How they had hectored and harried their victims, cleaving wives and mothers from their husbands and children; how they had favored the frenzy of disturbed children over the faithful witness of a Rebecca Nurse; how, when George Burroughs, a former minister of the town, was hanged as a wizard, they had urged the crowd to close their ears against his "blasphemous" recitation of the Lord's Prayer.

All this would be remembered. And so would Rebecca Nurse. In 1712 her excommunication was formally lifted. The poet John Greenleaf Whittier later supplied this epitaph for her unmarked grave:

> O Christian Martyr who for truth could die
> When all around thee owned the hideous lie!
> The world redeemed from superstition's sway
> Is breathing freer for thy sake today.

See: Marion L. Starkey, *The Devil in Massachusetts* (New York: Doubleday, 1969).

St. (Mother) Theodore Guerin
Founder of the Sisters of Providence
of St. Mary of the Woods (1798–1856)

"We are not called upon to do all the good possible, but only that which we can do."

In 1840, six Sisters of Providence, clad in their religious habits of heavy black serge, stepped off the sailing ship that had carried them from their motherhouse in France to begin a new mission in America. They were, by their own admission, "strangers to the country, to the manners and customs, to the ways of America," and they knew not one word of English. Nevertheless, they had been selected by their order to answer a call from the bishop of Vincennes, Indiana. Sister St. Theodore, a forty-one-year-old nun, had been selected to lead this mission — to establish a novitiate and schools and to otherwise assist in the work of building the local church.

Their journey was long — a month by sailing ship, followed by a series of trains, steam boats, and wagons, until they arrived late one night at their destination: "St. Mary-in-the-Woods." Instead of being located in a town, as they had expected, they found that their new foundation consisted of a log cabin in the middle of the forest. "It is astonishing that this remote solitude has been chosen for a novitiate and especially for an academy," Sister St. Theodore observed. "All appearances are against it."

The Sisters were unprepared for the primitive conditions and for the extremes of weather — the harsh winter, the heat of summer. They contended with fires, locusts, droughts, and floods. And yet they gradually established roots and prospered, drawing eager students from the widely scattered pioneer families, and even attracting new postulants to their community. But in undertaking this venture the Sisters had failed to clarify the exact nature of their relationship to the motherhouse in France and to the authority of the local bishop of Vincennes: Bishop de la Hailandière. Before long this ambiguity would become a source of bitter strife.

Mother Theodore, as she was now called, at first described the bishop as "an excellent father." Never, she said, had she found "a heart more compassionate under an exterior so cold." But before long she was describing his temperament as "one of those which makes martyrs of their possessors and still more of those who must put up with them." The problem was simply that the bishop regarded the community as his personal possession, and he sought to control and manage its affairs in every detail. "I have the greatest aversion to this kind of administration," Mother Theodore wrote. "It seems to me it would keep our sisters in a species of slavery."

In 1843 Mother Theodore acceded to the bishop's recommendation that she return to France to seek funding. Her trip was a success. After a meeting with Queen Marie-Amélie she received pledges of support from many wealthy Catholic families. On returning home she felt moved to kiss the soil of Indiana. "This land was no longer for me the land of exile," she wrote; "it was the portion of my inheritance." But her joy was diminished when she discovered all that had happened in her absence. The bishop had admitted novices to vows, closed and opened new schools, and called for the election of a new superior — all without consultation with the Sisters or any reference to their Rule. Though the Sisters had, in defiance of his will, unanimously reelected Mother Theodore as their superior, he had made it clear that he considered himself the true authority. When Mother Theodore met with the bishop he subjected her to a long harangue, accusing her of having a disobedient spirit and even of having stolen money from him in Paris. While claiming that he had no wish to interfere with the congregation's Rule, he insisted that neither Mother Guerin nor any other Sister leave the diocese without his written permission. Claiming that the land under their home was his, he announced, "I am the proprietor, spiritual and temporal, of that house."

Tensions continued to rise. Mother Theodore, ill and weary from the constant threats and accusations, offered to resign as superior of the congregation. In writing to Bishop de la Hailandière she said, "My conscience is my witness that I have done all that I could to avoid this misfortune, for I love Indiana with my whole soul. To do good there, to see our Congregation solidly established there before I die, was my whole ambition; the good God has permitted that you did not wish it; may his will be done." She would not, however, accede to his insistence on dispensing with their Rule.

In a subsequent meeting the bishop locked Mother Guerin in his house and said she must remain until she agreed to all his demands. He set her free only when her worried Sisters came searching for her. The next day he declared not only that Mother Guerin was no longer the superior, but that she was now not even a Sister of Providence, for he had released her from her vows. He ordered her to leave the diocese and "go elsewhere to hide her disgrace." He forbade her even to write to any of the Sisters; "they had no need of her letters."

To the Sisters of St. Mary's he sent word that if they yielded to his views, he would "love and protect" them; but if they opposed his views, they ran the risk of sharing their Mother's fate. When they heard this distressing news they all, to a Sister, agreed that they would never submit to these demands: "We will follow our Mother wherever she will go." The bishop countered that he would excommunicate any Sister who left the diocese without his permission. He would permit them to take nothing with them, and he might even have them pursued by the law. But the Sisters would not retreat. "We will no longer have anything," they replied. "We will be considered by Monsignor as the reproach of the world, but we shall have done our duty." They began at once to pack their bags and to make preparations to join Mother Guerin, who had in the meantime fallen seriously ill.

At this point Providence intervened in a most unexpected way. Some time before Bishop de la Hailandière had sent a pro forma letter of resignation to the pope. Suddenly word arrived that his offer had been accepted; a new bishop had already been appointed. When the Sisters received the news of their "deliverance" they went immediately to the chapel "to sing a hymn of thanksgiving in honor of the Blessed Virgin." Unpacking their bags, they eagerly awaited the return of Mother Guerin, whose health had shown a sudden improvement. Upon her arrival, "We all thanked our Lord together and this good day ended with Benediction of the Blessed Sacrament."

Under their new bishop and his successors the Sisters lived happily ever after. The congregation grew and prospered. Mother Guerin died on May 14, 1856. She was canonized in 2006.

See: Penny Blaker Mitchell, *Mother Theodore Guerin: A Woman for Our Time* (St. Mary-of-the-Woods, Ind.: Office of Congregational Advancement, Sisters of Providence, 1998).

Bd. Mary McKillop
Founder of the Sisters of St. Joseph
of the Sacred Heart (1842–1909)

"The Cross is my portion — it is my sweet rest and support."

With her beatification in 1995 Mary McKillop, otherwise known as Mother Mary of the Cross, became the first recognized saint of Australia. She was the founder of a remarkable congregation, the Sisters of St. Joseph, who devoted themselves to providing free education and other services to the poor and needy.

What is most remarkable about Mary McKillop, however, is not so much the charitable work by which she expressed her faith as the utterly uncharitable treatment she received at the hands of many priests and prelates in her time. Indeed Mary McKillop might serve as the patron saint of all who have suffered the petty persecution of narrow-minded religious authorities, convinced they are acting in the place of God. That Mary remained free of bitterness, despite her ordeals, is considerable evidence of her sanctity and sufficient cause for honor.

Mary was born in Melbourne in the colony of South Australia on January 15, 1842. Her parents were poor Scottish immigrants. While working as a governess she met a charismatic young priest, Julian Woods, who inspired her to consider a religious vocation. Together they conceived the idea of a congregation dedicated to the needs of the poor. In 1866 Mary put on a plain black dress as a sign of her dedication to religious life, and the next year she took religious vows. It was the start of a new congregation, the Sisters of St. Joseph.

From the beginning Mary had given much thought to the type of congregation suited to the needs and rugged conditions of Australia. The constitutions she devised for her community had several important features. In the first place, since the congregation was devoted to the poor, she felt it was essential that her Sisters themselves adhere to a strict vow of poverty. Her preference was that the congregation not own any property at all. There were also to be no social distinctions within the community between "choir" and "lay" Sisters. She insisted on radical equality.

Most important of all, however, was her insistence that the congregation be subject to "central government." This meant that instead of allowing each of her far-flung communities to be administered under the authority of a local bishop, they would be governed by an elected mother general who would answer directly to Rome. This provision proved to be the source of extreme tension between the congregation and the Australian bishops.

In almost no time Mary had attracted scores of young women to her congregation, and houses were established in a number of cities and outback missions throughout the territory. At a time when almost no public services were available for the poor, the Sisters of St. Joseph won the admiration and gratitude of Australians of all classes and religious persuasions. Many bishops were initially eager to welcome the Sisters.

But inevitably they tried to interfere in the management and direction of the Sisters' work. To this Mary put up spirited resistance.

When Mary remained adamant in her commitment to central government, the bishops' support gave way to a shameless campaign of harassment and vilification. In one dramatic episode she was actually excommunicated by her local bishop. Though he later, on his deathbed, rescinded the order, she continued to operate under a cloud. Another bishop had her expelled from his diocese and refused to allow the Sisters to do any fund-raising. The bishop of Queensland sent damning letters to Rome claiming that the Sisters were "infected with fanaticism and insubordination to authority" and that Mary's aim was "to subvert the whole system here."

To shore up her position, Mary traveled to Rome and spent two years seeking authorization for her constitutions. Eventually she found an audience with Pope Pius IX. He was personally intrigued by the story of "the nun who was excommunicated." When she returned to Australia she held a papal document formally approving her congregation. Still, the persecution did not cease. A team of bishops and clerics, claiming falsely to be authorized by Rome, subjected her community to a rigorous "visitation," seizing financial records and interviewing the Sisters under a supposed "vow of secrecy" to discover scurrilous information about Mother Mary. Afterward the bishop of Adelaide leaked the slanderous story that Mary was an alcoholic and that she had misappropriated funds belonging to the congregation.

It turned out that the "visitation" had no authority from Rome. An official inquiry by Rome, provoked by this incident, completely exonerated Mother Mary. Still the harassment continued. The Australian bishops voted to overturn the constitutions of the congregation and subject the Sisters once more to diocesan control. Once more, Rome came to the rescue, nullifying the bishops' authority in the matter. The congregation would remain under central government. Mother Mary had won at last.

Although she suffered terribly from the constant attacks on her virtue and her faith, Mary never disdained the occasion to endure injustice or injury. She referred to such ordeals as "presents from God." Innocent suffering, she believed, was an opportunity to shoulder the cross and so to grow closer to God. Those who caused this suffering were thus "instruments in the hands of God"; they were, indeed, her "most powerful benefactors." Nevertheless, she acknowledged that "God's presents were often hard to understand," and that she was "too often cowardly in accepting them."

Bd. Mary McKillop

Mother Mary lived on to see her congregation firmly established throughout Australia and New Zealand. After many years of painful illness, she died on August 5, 1909. Her passing was mourned throughout Australia.

See: Lesley O'Brien, *Mary McKillop Unveiled* (Victoria, Australia: CollinsDove, 1994).

Agneta Chang
Maryknoll Sister and Martyr (d. 1950)

"I have tried innumerable times to write to you but I cannot say how many times I took up my pen to begin a letter only to find that all turned black before me and I could not hold back the tears that blinded me."
— Sister Mary Peter Kang, O.L.P.H.

With these words a Korean nun began her account of the final days of Sister Agneta Chang, a Korean-born Maryknoll Sister who died among her people in 1950.

From the early years of their foundation, the American-based Maryknoll Sisters welcomed foreign vocations. Agneta Chang and a younger cousin were among the first Korean Sisters to join in 1921. In her application to Maryknoll, Sister Agneta, answering a question about her reason for applying to a religious community, wrote, "In order to become holy and then to help my country and people." Agneta came from a prominent and devoutly Catholic family in Korea. One of her brothers would later become the prime minister of the Republic of Korea.

After spending her novitiate in the Maryknoll motherhouse in New York, Agneta was assigned to her own country. There she spent many peaceful years in catechetical and parish work before the outbreak of World War II. When the American Sisters were imprisoned by the Japanese and then repatriated, Sister Agneta stayed behind to help develop the first Korean women's congregation, the Sisters of Our Lady of Perpetual Help (O.L.P.H.). For the duration of the war she and the small community of twenty-nine young Korean women were cut off from the rest of the world.

When the war ended and communication was resumed it was hoped that Sister Agneta would be reunited once again with her Maryknoll community. But it was not to be. Korea was divided at the 38th Parallel, trapping Sister Agneta and the novitiate in the Soviet-occupied North.

By the time Russian troops departed in 1949 leaving Korean communists in control, the situation had became particularly grave. Soon it was no longer possible even to smuggle messages to the outside. Many priests and even bishops were arrested and killed. After the government ordered the disbanding of all religious communities Sister Agneta and a companion, Sister Mary Peter, found refuge in a Catholic village.

For years Agneta had worn a back brace, the result of an old injury. She was in constant pain, and by now virtually bedridden. Nevertheless, she received word to report for mandatory civil defense work. When she could not comply, soldiers came looking for her. They ordered her neighbors to carry her outside and place her in a waiting ox cart. She made no complaint, but only exclaimed, "Lord, have mercy on us." It was October 4, 1950, the last time Sister Agneta was seen alive. As Sister Mary Peter described the scene,

> The time was about eight in the evening. The world was wrapped in dusk. The only sound was that of the ox cart jogging down the quiet mountain trail together with the groaning and sound of her prayers. Oh miserable night! My heart seemed to shatter and break into a thousand pieces and it seemed pitiless to me that the ground did not cleave open.

While Sister Mary Peter and some other O.L.P.H. Sisters eventually made their way to the South, another twelve remained in the North, where their fate was never learned. Word was later received that Sister Agneta Chang and a number of other women had been shot. Their bodies were buried in a nearby ditch.

See: Penny Lernoux (with Arthur Jones and Robert Ellsberg), *Hearts on Fire: The Story of the Maryknoll Sisters* (Maryknoll, N.Y.: Orbis Books, 1993).

Alicia Domon
Martyr (d. 1977)

"I didn't come here [to the shantytown] to tell people what they had to do but in order that we could help each other and share life's joys and sorrows, here where we take each other for what we are. I have probably received more than I have given."

During the period of 1976 to 1983 a military dictatorship in Argentina conducted a "dirty war" against "subversives" and dissidents.

Advocates of human rights and social justice for the poor were among the special victims of the repression. At least four thousand civilians were killed. Another ten thousand were "disappeared" — abducted by the military, never to be seen again. Two French nuns, Sisters Alicia Domon and Léonie Duquet, were among them.

They were both members of the Toulouse Institute of the Sisters of Foreign Mission. Alicia Domon arrived in Argentina in 1967, part of the great wave of foreign religious who flocked to Latin America in the years after Vatican II. At first they engaged in more traditional apostolates. Alicia worked with mentally retarded children, helping them prepare for their first communion. By 1969, however, she and other members of her congregation had moved out of their convent to take up residence in an urban shantytown. Alicia supported herself by working halftime as a household servant while otherwise ministering as a friend and sister to her poor neighbors.

In the following years she spent much time in the countryside, becoming acquainted with the struggles of landless peasants and lending support to their efforts to organize. It was a time of rising hopes in the possibility of peaceful social change. In the 1970s, however, such efforts and hopes were brutally suppressed.

Back in Buenos Aires, Sister Alicia became closely involved with a courageous organization of women, the so-called Mothers of the Disappeared, who gathered in the central plaza each day, dressed in black and bearing photographs of their missing children. This mute but eloquent protest was for many years the only visible sign of dissent in Argentina. The conservative hierarchy of the Catholic Church remained largely silent, when not actually endorsing the military's defense of "law and order."

For Christmas 1977 Alicia had prepared a retreat for the Mothers. On the evening of December 8, however, after leaving a planning meeting of the group, Sister Alicia and twelve other women were seized by armed men in civilian clothing. Two days later, Sister Léonie Duquet was also abducted, apparently because she shared a residence with Alicia Domon. None of them was ever seen again, nor was there ever any official news of their fate.

In subsequent years jokes circulated among the military about the "flying nuns." This was taken to be a reference to rumors that the disappeared were routinely tossed out of airplanes over the Atlantic Ocean. In 1995 these rumors were confirmed by a retired Navy commander, Adolfo Scilingo, who described his own part in two "death flights" in 1977.

According to his account, "At first it didn't bother me that I was dumping these bodies into the ocean because as far as I was concerned they were war prisoners. There were men and women, and I had no idea who they were or what they had done. I was following orders." At some point, however, "It hit me exactly what we were doing. We were killing human beings. But still we continued." Afterward, when he confessed his actions to a military priest, he was told the killings "had to be done to separate the wheat from the chaff."

Asked to describe another mission in December of 1977, Scilingo became distraught and said he could not bear to discuss the details. Despite having received absolution at the time, Scilingo said that in subsequent years, "I have spent many nights sleeping in the plazas of Buenos Aires with a bottle of wine, trying to forget. I have ruined my life. . . . Sometimes I am afraid to be alone with my thoughts."

In her death Sister Alicia attained her most intimate union with the poor and rejected to whom she was drawn. After her disappearance the police who requisitioned her house were surprised to discover that, like the poorest peasant, she did not own so much as a change of clothes. Several months before her disappearance she had written to the archbishop of Toulouse, "I would ask you not to do anything to save me which could endanger others. I have already made the sacrifice of my life."

See: Martin Lange and Reinhold Iblacker, *Witnesses of Hope* (Maryknoll, N.Y.: Orbis Books, 1980); "Argentine Tells of Dumping 'Dirty War' Captives into Sea," *New York Times* (March 13, 1995).

Maura Clarke and Companions
Martyrs of El Salvador (d. 1980)

"One cries out, 'Lord, how long?' And then too what creeps into my mind is the little fear or big, that when it touches me very personally, will I be faithful?" —Maura Clarke

On a December morning in 1980 a small assembly of priests, nuns, and peasants gathered in a cow pasture in El Salvador to witness the exhumation of four North American women. One by one their broken and disheveled bodies were dragged from the shallow grave: Maura Clarke and Ita Ford, both Maryknoll Sisters; Dorothy Kazel, an Ursuline Sister, and Jean Donovan, a lay missioner, both from Cleveland. They had been missing since December 2 when Dorothy and Jean, in their distinctive white minivan, had left for the airport to pick up Maura and Ita on their return from a meeting in Nicaragua. Two days later some peasants alerted church authorities and led them to the site of this hasty burial.

Each woman had followed a different path. Maura and Ita had spent many years in mission in Nicaragua and Chile. Dorothy Kazel was the longest in El Salvador. Jean Donovan, only twenty-seven, had wrestled with the possibility of marriage and the security of a lucrative career before choosing, instead, to remain in El Salvador. But for each one, called by Christ to live out her faith in solidarity with the poor, the path had led to the same cow pasture.

It was a possibility they had all wrestled with and faced up to. After all, they had all to one extent or another been touched by the witness of Archbishop Oscar Romero, assassinated only nine months before. In words that Ita Ford quoted on the night before she died, he had said, "One who is committed to the poor must risk the same fate as the poor. And in El Salvador we know what the fate of the poor signifies: to disappear, to be tortured, to be captive, and to be found dead."

The death of the four women had an enormous effect on the North American church, galvanizing opposition to U.S. funding for the Salvadoran government. But at the same time, the deaths provoked a backlash on the part of apologists for these policies. As one American official noted, "The nuns were not just nuns, the nuns were also political activists...on behalf of the Frente [the guerrillas]." The U.S. secretary of state went so far as to describe a "prominent theory" that the churchwomen may have been killed "in an exchange of fire" after they were believed to be running a roadblock.

This "prominent theory" had little to do with the readily determined facts of the case: that the four women were targeted for assassination by Salvadoran officers; that soldiers, dressed in civilian clothes for a "special assignment," had followed the Sisters on their way home from the airport; that the women were killed many hours later in a different place; that they were shot in the head at close range; and that before being killed two of them were raped.

In fact the four women were anything but "political activists." Their work, in support of the Salvadoran church, involved ministering to the needs of refugees; shepherding priests on the run; delivering supplies;

offering solace to isolated and terrified catechists. These were night-
mare years in El Salvador. The women's work confronted them with
scenes from hell. They saw villages where the security forces had committed massacres and then refused to allow the survivors to bury the
dead. "The other day," wrote Maura, "passing a small lake in the jeep
I saw a buzzard standing on top of a floating body. We did nothing
but pray and feel." They each had identified with the church's "preferential option for the poor," believing that the effective witness to the
gospel was inseparable from the witness to life and solidarity with the
oppressed. In El Salvador this was enough to label one a subversive.

And yet in bearing witness to the cross they were also witnesses to
the resurrection. Among the believing poor of El Salvador there was not
only death, but a faith and a stubborn hope that inspired them to carry
on — or at least, kept them from fleeing. As Ita wrote to her sixteen-
year-old niece:

> This is a terrible time in El Salvador for youth. A lot of idealism
> and commitment are getting snuffed out here now. The reasons
> why so many people are being killed are quite complicated, yet
> there are some clear, simple strands. One is that people have found
> a meaning to live, to sacrifice, struggle, and even die. And whether
> their life spans sixteen years, sixty or ninety, for them their life has
> had a purpose. In many ways, they are fortunate people.
>
> Brooklyn is not passing through the drama of El Salvador, but
> some things hold true wherever one is, and at whatever age. What
> I'm saying is that I hope you can come to find that which gives life
> a deep meaning for you, something that energizes you, enthuses
> you, enables you to keep moving ahead.

Jean Donovan, at twenty-seven, was the youngest of the four, and the
only laywoman among them. From a privileged background, with a degree in business and a promising career, she had been drawn to the
mission in El Salvador and stayed on even when the risks became clear.
Two weeks before her death she wrote, "Several times I have decided
to leave — I almost could except for the children, the poor bruised victims of adult lunacy. Who would care for them? Whose heart would be
so staunch as to favor the reasonable thing in a sea of their tears and
loneliness? Not mine, dear friend, not mine."

The history of the church is written in the blood of martyrs. But these
four women represented a different kind of martyrdom, increasingly

common in our time. Their murderers dared to call themselves Christians, indeed defenders of Christian values. And they died not simply for clinging to the true faith but for clinging, like Jesus, to the poor.

See: Donna Whitson Brett and Edward T. Brett, *Murdered in Central America* (Maryknoll, N.Y.: Orbis Books, 1988); Penny Lernoux (with Arthur Jones and Robert Ellsberg), *Hearts on Fire: The Story of the Maryknoll Sisters* (Maryknoll, N.Y.: Orbis Books, 1993).

Index

Addams, Jane, 245
Agnes, St., 202
Agnes of Bohemia, St., 20
Angela Merici, St., 22
Angela of Foligno, Bd., 49
Anna, 9
Anointer of Bethany, The, 44
Askew, Anne, 277
Aylward, Gladys, 108
Bakhita, St. Josephine, 27
Beatrice of Nazareth, 211
Bernadette Soubirous, St., 219
Bernall, Cassie, 233
Bethune, Ade, 38
Birgitta of Sweden, St., 119
Blandina, St., and Companions, 270
Bossis, Gabrielle, 105
Bowman, Sister Thea, 111
Brigid of Ireland, St., 158
Cabrini, St. Frances Xavier, 178
Catherine of Alexandria, St., 203
Catherine of Genoa, St., 55
Catherine of Siena, St., 240
Chang, Agneta, 293
Christina of Markyate, St., 206
Clare of Assisi, St., 15
Clarke, Maura, and Companions, 296
Connelly, Cornelia, 59
Crispina, St., 274
Day, Dorothy, 252
Delanou, St. Joan, 162
Delbrêl, Madeleine, 31
Dickinson, Emily, 92
Doherty, Catherine de Hueck, 154

Domon, Alicia, 294
Donnelly, Daria, 235
Drexel, St. Katherine, 29
Dyer, Mary, 280
Dymphna, St., 84
Egan, Eileen, 262
Elizabeth Feodorovna, St., 25
Elizabeth of Hungary, St., 18
Elizabeth of Portugal, St., 242
Fell, Margaret, 131
Frank, Anne, 103
Fry, Elizabeth, 167
Gertrude the Great, St., 214
Godiva of Coventry, 118
Goretti, St. Maria, 222
Grimké, Sarah and Angelina, 134
Guerin, St. (Mother) Theodore, 288
Hadewijch of Brabant, 212
Hagar the Egyptian, 42
Hamer, Fannie Lou, 152
Hawthorne, Rose, 180
Heloise, 47
Hilda of Whitby, St., 205
Hildegard of Bingen, St., 208
Hillesum, Etty, 223
Houselander, Caryll, 184
Hutchinson, Anne, 126
Inés de la Cruz, Sor Juana, 129
Javouhey, Bd. Anne-Marie, 169
Jeanne de Chantal, St., 24
Joan of Arc, St., 122
Jones, Mother, 144
Jugan, Bd. Jeanne, 171
Julian of Norwich, Bd., 89

Kempe, Margery, 52
Kitahara, Satoko, 187
Kollwitz, Käthe, 248
Lee, Mother Ann, 217
Lernoux, Penny, 260
Lester, Muriel, 250
Liuzzo, Viola, 149
Louise de Marillac, St., 160
Lydia, St., 82
Lydwina of Schiedam, Bd., 51
Magdeleine of Jesus, Little Sister, 33
Marcella, St., 14
Margaret Clitherow, St., 279
Margaret Ebner, Bd., 87
Maritain, Raïssa, 228
Martha and Mary of Bethany, Sts., 10
Martyrs of Birmingham, 107
Martyrs of El Mozote, 71
Mary, Mother of Jesus, 8, 117
Mary and Elizabeth, 117
Mary Magdalene, St., 12
McKillop, Bd. Mary, 290
Mechthild of Magdeburg, 85
Mechtild of Hackeborn, St., 159
Mirabehn, 257
Monica, St., 45
Mothers of the Disappeared, 69
Mott, Lucretia, 137
Nagle, Nano, 164
Nightingale, Florence, 173
Nurse, Rebecca, and Companions, 285
O'Connor, Flannery, 230
O'Halloran, Maura, 190
Peace Pilgrim, 255

Perpetua and Felicity, Sts., 271
Petre, Maude Dominica, 61
Porete, Marguerite, 276
Powers, Jessica, 73
Puleo, Mev, 36
Quinn, Edel, 101
Rahab, 116
Ramabai, Pandita, 142
Rogers, Mollie, 226
Samaritan Woman, The, 43
Scholastica, St., 83
Scholl, Sophie, and Companions, 246
Seton, St. Elizabeth Ann, 165
Skobtsova, St. Maria, 182
Slessor, Mary, 97
Soelle, Dorothee, 265
Stein, St. Edith, 64
Syrophoenician Woman, The, 80
Tekakwitha, Bd. Kateri, 216
Ten Boom, Corrie, 192
Teresa of Avila, St., 124
Teresa of Calcutta, Bd. (Mother), 195
Thecla of Iconium, St., 200
Therese of Lisieux, St., 94
Truth, Sojourner, 139
Tubman, Harriet, 176
Tucker, Karla Faye, 75
Underhill, Evelyn, 99
von Speyr, Adrienne, 67
Ward, Mary, 283
Weil, Simone, 146
Wells, Ida B., 243
Woman with a Flow of Blood, The, 81
Xenia of St. Petersburg, St., 57

About the Author

Robert Ellsberg was born in 1955 and raised in Los Angeles. He graduated from Harvard College with a degree in religion and literature and later studied theology at Harvard Divinity School. From 1975 to 1980 he was a member of the Catholic Worker community in New York City, serving for two years (1976–78) as managing editor of the *Catholic Worker* newspaper. Since 1987 he has served as editor-in-chief, and now publisher, of Orbis Books. He has written or edited a number of books, including *Dorothy Day: Selected Writings* (Christopher Award), *Fritz Eichenberg: Works of Mercy* (Christopher Award, Catholic Book Award), and *The Saints' Guide to Happiness* (translated into six languages), as well as anthologies of the writings of Flannery O'Connor, Gandhi, Charles de Foucauld, Carlo Carretto, and Thich Nhat Hanh. With Penny Lernoux and Arthur Jones he wrote *Hearts on Fire: The Story of the Maryknoll Sisters* (Catholic Book Award). In 1998 he received a third Christopher Award for his bestselling *All Saints* and the Veritas Medal of Dominican College for service to peace and justice. In 2002, Ellsberg was named a recipient of Harvard Divinity School's First Decade Award. His most recent book, *Blessed Among All Women*, was honored with three Catholic Book Awards. Ellsberg lives in Ossining, New York, with his wife and their three children.

Also by Robert Ellsberg

ALL SAINTS

Daily Reflections on Saints, Prophets,
and Witnesses for Our Time

All Saints is a daily reader that presents short yet comprehensive biographies of 365 official and unofficial "saints" from the Christian tradition. From Therese of Lisieux to Mother Teresa, from Moses to Martin Luther King Jr., this inspiring treasury combines traditional saints with other spiritual masters whose lives speak to the meaning of holiness for our time.

"Quite simply the best contemporary one-volume compendium available. The writing alone ranks it well above others. A rich resource for reference and for daily reading. Individuals, families, preachers, teachers, and any number of parish groups looking for reflection material for prayer services or to start meetings will find this book a treasure for years to come." — *Church* magazine

"A dazzling display of ancient and modern greatness that in many cases approaches godliness. An irresistibly inspiring experience." — *Spirituality*

"This book can change your life. Buy it now, read it every day, and you won't be able to part with it. You will just have to buy more copies for everyone you love." — *National Catholic Reporter*

"This book renews hope. The stories are beautiful witnesses to the fact that people can be fully human, yet so illuminated with concern for others that they serve as true signs of God." — Catholic News Service

"A remarkably rich collection of meditations on men and women from all ages, mostly Christian, one for every day of the year. Most of them are capable of inspiring us to wish to do more with our lives: to dedicate ourselves to serving truth and justice in the way these heroes did. The whole book amounts to a kind of encyclopedia of moral and spiritual greatness." — *The Chesterton Review*

crossroad

Comments on Robert Ellsberg's

ALL SAINTS

"This remarkable book sets a new standard by which all future books on the lives of the saints will be measured."
— *U.S. Catholic*

"By a verbal artist with the heart of a prophet and a scholar's eye for important detail." — *America*

"*All Saints* will become something of a classic. Read as part of a daily schedule, it can keep us mindful that what is most real is immeasurable but nonetheless accessible, and that the community in which we have a part extends far beyond our own space and time." — *Fellowship*

"A wonderfully broad, knowing, and narratively compelling look at human goodness as it has been tested by life. This book will give us the very best kind of moral and spiritual education." — Robert Coles

"In these short, splendidly wrought profiles, Robert Ellsberg gives us a vigorous cloud of witnesses — mystics, martyrs, social activists, artists, writers, composers — who do what all saints do: mediate the many and surprising ways in which grace makes discipleship possible."
— Kenneth L. Woodward, *Newsweek*

0-8245-1679-6, $24.95 paperback

Please support your local bookstore,
or call 1-800-707-0670 for Customer Service.

For a free catalog, write us at

THE CROSSROAD PUBLISHING COMPANY
16 Penn Plaza, 481 Eighth Avenue
New York, NY 10001

Visit our website at
www.crossroadpublishing.com
All prices subject to change.

crossroad